Sex, machines and

CHESTER
UNIVERSITY PRESS

Sex, machines and navels

Fiction, fantasy and history in the future present

FRED BOTTING

Manchester University Press
MANCHESTER AND NEW YORK

distributed exclusively in the USA by St. Martin's Press

Published by Manchester University Press
Oxford Road, Manchester M13 9NR, UK
and Room 400, 175 Fifth Avenue, New York, NY 10010, USA
http://www.man.ac.uk/mup

Distributed exclusively in the USA by
St. Martin's Press, Inc., 175 Fifth Avenue, New York,
NY 10010, USA

Distributed exclusively in Canada by
UBC Press, University of British Columbia, 6344 Memorial Road,
Vancouver, BC, Canada V6T 1Z2

British Library Cataloguing-in-Publication Data
A catalogue record for this book is available from the British Library

Library of Congress Cataloging-in-Publication Data applied for

ISBN 0 7190 5536 9 *hardback*
     0 7190 5625 X *paperback*

First published 1999

05   04   03   02   01   00   99   10   9   8   7   6   5   4   3   2   1

Typeset in Bulmer with Rotis display
by Koinonia, Manchester
Printed in Great Britain
by Bell & Bain Ltd, Glasgow

✧ Contents

Acknowledgements   *page* vii

1   Navels

Navel-gazing   1
The question of the navel   11

2   Lacan's navel

Psychoanalysis through the navel?   19
The navel of the dream   22
Reading navels   30
The navel's return   45

3   Jokes and their relation to postmodernism

The joke that is not one   62
The navel of the joke   64
Jokes and their relation to the Other   71
Postmodernism's navel   80
Paternal metaphors?   86

4   History, holes and things

History's navel   97
Natural history and the navel   104
Holes and things   110
Wombs, texts, hystery   120
Repetition, revolution, drive   130

5   Of meat and the matrix

Future history and the navel   141
Plugging into the One   153
Other matrix, other meat   165
Navel, image, screen   186

6   Romance of the machine

Navels in the machine   210
Going nodal   223

Bibliography   230
Index   237

✧ Acknowledgements

Thanks are due to those friends, colleagues and students who supported, criticised and ridiculed the curious pathology informing this book. Members of SHaH provided many intellectual gifts in the course of writing, Scott Wilson and Jonathan Munby in particular. I am also grateful to the editor at Manchester University Press, Matthew Frost, for his help and encouragement and to the readers who, anonymously or not (Bill Ross and Elisabeth Bronfen), offered numerous insightful contributions on the manuscript. The latter deserves extensive thanks for her constructive involvement in the whole process, from the provision of illuminating material to valuable critical suggestions. Sara Ahmed and Anne Wilbourn made helpful comments on earlier drafts, and Karen Juers-Munby read the manuscript in rigorous detail, making numerous inventive suggestions. Any quirks and mistakes left in the book must be put down to private idiosyncrasy alone.

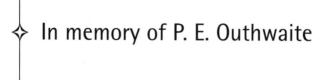 In memory of P. E. Outhwaite

1 ✧ Navels

Navel-gazing

With their cyborgs, clones, androids, robots, replicants and terminators, cultural texts of the late twentieth century replay various versions of the fraught relationship between (sexed) human bodies and machines of awesome super- or post-human power. The strange yet increasingly familiar spectacle of diverse couplings between bodies and technology appears as a symptomatic response to a transitional age characterised by the prefix 'post': from industrialised to postindustrial society, from modernity to postmodernity, from reality to post-reality, a movement of uncertain direction introduces a division in accounts of a present split between nostalgic desires for a return to older structures of value and meaning and technoerotic fantasies precipitating future immersion in new and inhuman codes (computer software, engineered DNA). The object of anxiety and desire appears the same: a horrifying or eroticised technology takes sexual energy beyond sex, beyond corporeality and beyond difference in an ultimate obliteration of every human trace. Sex and machines, then, seem highly appropriate (if overly fashionable) topics for a discussion of representations of organic and artificial systems. But the third term – navels – interrupts the comfortable conjunction or clear dissociation of body and technology.

Navels? In relation to the serious conjunction of sex and machines, navels seem of slight significance, their presence in the title little more than a flippant addition. An idle, useless and all-too academic addition, how can so pointless a physical feature as the navel contribute to knowledge or human understanding? The belly button, far from being a useful organ, does nothing, either biologically or symbolically. Unlike the eyes which become windows of the soul, or the brain where mind and consciousness reside, or the heart beating with the vitality of human passions, the navel simply forms an indentation or protuberance on the human belly. Collecting fluff. In popular usage, the navel's only meaning is reserved, negatively, to describe singularly self-indulgent inactivities: navel-gazing signifies the time wastefully expended in idle cogitation upon unanswerable questions, useless speculation or circular self-reflection.

The very pointlessness of the navel remains, precisely, the point. Instead of grand existential claims concerning human futility by way of the navel that separates the *raison* from the *être*, it is, perhaps, on anthropological grounds that navels possess a certain distinction. Standard classifications describe humanity as *Homo sapiens*, a species distinguished by intellectual capacity. In science fiction futures, when machines have mimicked and supplanted the bodily and mental powers of humans, the defining characteristic shifts from knowledge or reason to feeling: *Homo sentiens* separates organic from biotechnological beings while *Homo datum* refers to those beings whose daily lives are spent in information networks.[1] And then there's Dolly, a sheep in sheep's clothing. When cloning, already separating birth mother from genetic mother, renders the natural, bodily connection of reproduction superfluous, only the umbilical cord's scar will differentiate between otherwise identical beings, so *Homo umbilicus* may become the next species name. It is, however, more than the physical fact of the navel which may be distinctive. If knowledge, consciousness, feeling, language, tool use or laughter are seen as definitive human attributes, then navel-gazing also denotes a distinguishing characteristic. Humans can be marked out from other animals as a species possessed of an ability to gaze at their navels, a feature also separating humans from the intelligent and artificially conscious machines who will, so the stories go, be perfectly rational entities unable to comprehend the irrational quirks of their nearest relatives. Commander Data, the accomplished android in *Star Trek: The Next Generation*, is such a figure, fascinated and perplexed by the senseless elements constitutive of human behaviour. While tin men, like Data, may eventually, by grace of human myth, be rewarded with hearts, the endowment of navels may be less forthcoming.

The navel, merely appended to a discussion of sex and machines, becomes strangely central to their articulation: its lack of function or symbolic status associates value and difference not with use but with uselessness, with something in excess of sensible classification. Indeed, the navel undermines arguments promoting a human essence, spirit or heart over the cold rationality of machines. This opposition, determined by a

Sex, machines and navels

certain Romantic humanism, founders over the navel: a knot of skin on the body's surface, it is a sign of natural reproduction. But it is nonetheless a sign, a mark of separation as well as connection, a scar forming the first mark of culture on the body. And the scar is produced by a tool, a cutting tool that, these days, would hardly be recognised as belonging in the category of technology. A peculiar and ambivalent juncture between sex and technology, the navel opens, literally and figurally, on to questions of difference. A knot between phylogenesis and ontogenesis marking a missing link in a chain of biological being, the navel is a nodal point in an immense matrix of creation.[2] Metaphorically, moreover, its nodal position extends within a network of associations entwining nature, culture, humans and machines, and in which bodies, language, history and futurity intermingle and engender multiple possibilities. Gazing at the navel discloses an intricate tracery of relationships and an immense web of other very suggestive metaphors with the matrix figuring prominently along with cuts, holes, scars and signs.

To gaze at the navel is to find more than an unanswerable object of indulgent speculation: it discovers navels of various shapes and sizes appearing quite regularly in a range of past, contemporary and futural texts. This book will focus on some of those representations: the navel of psychoanalysis; the navel of the joke and postmodernism; the navel of history and natural history; and future navels. There are other instances, detailed briefly below, which raise questions of human origins, meanings and destinations. Whether Adam had a navel, of course, remained a burning question for theologians over centuries. Sir Thomas Browne, in his *Pseudodoxia Epidemica* (1646) takes issue with pictorial representations of Adam and Eve which furnish them with navels: 'another mistake there may be in the Picture of our first Parents, who after the manner of their posterity are both delineated with a navel. And this is observable not only in ordinary and stained pieces, but in the Authentick draughts of Urbin, Angelo and others.' It should not be allowed, Browne asserts, that 'the Creator affected superfluities, or ordained parts without use or office'.[3] While the 'seminality of his fabrick' contains the capacity to produce subsequent umbilical marks, Adam's non-physical connection to God retains a 'conjunctive part', a metaphorical umbilicus: Browne supposes that some connection exists, 'a monumental Navel with his Maker', 'an umbicality even with God himself' that forms the 'one link and common connexion, one general ligament, and necessary obligation of all what ever unto God' (Browne, 1964, 2: 347). The absence of a bodily mark or physical connection significantly gives rise to a metaphorical link. In contrast, in the mid-nineteenth century, the presence of the navel forms the crux of a pro-Creation argument against the emerging weight of geological and evolutionary facts. In *Omphalos*, Philip Henry Gosse makes a case for Adam's navel: 'The Man would not have been a Man without a Navel' (1857: 349). The navel maketh man, it seems. Where the superfluity or uselessness of the navel is reason enough for Browne to reject the idea that God would have included it in his design of the first human, the useless and deceptive scar is crucial to Gosse's defence of a divinely created world, a theory of origins then being powerfully challenged by the research of Charles Lyell and Charles Darwin. Evolutionists and geologists overlook the 'Law of Prochronism in Creation' which states that the great cycle of life on Earth is created at an instant and with 'indubitable evidences of a previous history' (Gosse, 1857: 335). Fossils, and Adam's navel, have their explanation in this law. Gosse's reconciliation of scripture and natural history met with scorn and indifference. In the twentieth century, Gosse's theory has served as an object lesson in scientific practice (Gould, 1995). In contrast, Jorge Luis Borges has admired its 'monstrous elegance' and noted 'its involuntary reduction of a *creation ex nihilo* to absurdity' (Borges, 1973: 24–5). Jean Baudrillard praises the 'prophetic air' of Gosse's theory as it turns God into 'an evil genius of simulation': 'his hypothesis is coming true: the whole of our past is sliding into a fossilized simulacrum, but it is man that has inherited the evil genius and artifice which was God's' (1996: 21). The question of the navel, as an umbilical link to both the world and to woman, no longer concerns Baudrillard since the advent of in-vitro fertilisation marks a return to the 'anomphalos' condition of Adam. Perhaps the 'Tele-tubbies', alien/baby creatures in a BBC children's television programme of the same name, are examples of anomphalic existence: these pre-linguistic babblers in bright, rotund romper suits have no navels. Instead, with appropriate hyperrealism, TV screens cover their bellies.

If the navel is to be eclipsed in the future, its disappearance will bear upon the past as well as sexual identity. Navels have a long cultural history, as long, of course, as human civilisation. In Greek myth the navel (*omphalos*) has a prominent place in the story of Apollo's supercession of the female-centred cult of Gaia (Bronfen, 1994: 79–80). In literary terms, the absence of a navel brings issues of gender to the fore. Nancy Huston compares two literary characters who are without navels, Kazik in David Grossman's *See Under: Love* and Pilate in Toni Morrison's *Song of Solomon*.

Sex, machines and navels

A male character in a novel by a man, the anomphalic Kazik's growth rate is accelerated so that his entire life unfolds in twenty-four hours, the time it takes to read the book: 'a child without a navel ... can only be a novel' (Huston, 1995: 718). In the case of a female character in a novel by a woman the issue of novels and navels is more complicated. No reason, in the *Song of Solomon*, is offered to explain the complete healing of Pilate's navel, though its absence, for others in the novel, signifies a magically dangerous and curative feminine power. The ambivalence of the navel is telling: 'If Grossman's navelless son is the emblem of the novel, Morrison's navelless daughter is perhaps the emblem of the novelist mother: "living proof", so to speak, that certain entities hitherto thought to be logical monstrosities actually can and do exist' (Huston, 1995: 721). In excess of logic, a point confounding the relationship between representation and reality, the navel is not only a gendered limit, but a site of monstrous possibilities.

In the nineteenth century the navel was also the cause of a joke. What happens when you unscrew your navel? Your arse falls off! In Herman Melville's *Moby Dick* the joke is extended. Captain Ahab's ship, the *Pequod*, has its own navel: 'Here's the ship's navel, this doubloon here, and they are all on fire to unscrew it. But, unscrew your navel, and what's the consequence?' The gold coin, riveted to the mainmast, serves no real purpose. Nonetheless, it exerts a peculiar hold over the crew, a talismanic object which imaginarily binds sailors and ship together. Often taken for granted by the Captain in his daily rounds, the doubloon arrests his attention and becomes a site of longing, hope, and curious interpretation:

> But one morning, turning to pass the doubloon, he seemed to be newly attracted by the strange figures and inscriptions on it, as though for the first time beginning to interpret for himself in some monomaniac way whatever significance might link in them. And some certain significance links in all things, else all things are little worth, and the round world itself but an empty cipher, except to sell by the cartload, as they do hills about Boston, to fill up some morass in the Milky Way. (Melville, 1994: 409)

The insignificant object nailed to the mast is covered with mysterious inscriptions that do not immediately offer themselves up to understanding. Itself an empty cipher, the ship's navel is covered in empty ciphers. But the absence of meaning requires that the emptiness be filled with a significance at once monomaniacal (thus exhibiting a self-consuming reflection of a gaze upon the navel) and cosmic in that it bears upon the production of meaning and value. The empty cipher announces the necessity of finding meaning and value in the face of the horrifying alternative of utterly meaningless existence. Meaning and meaninglessness are articulated in the object that, withdrawn from circulation, holds a different value, a value hesitatingly posited as lying beyond the world of commercial exchange. The doubloon is 'set apart and sanctified to one awe-striking end' and revered by the sailors as the 'White Whale's talisman'. The ship's navel, useless and overlooked on a daily basis, is, when examined from another angle, invested with sacred value.

The navel forms a detail which, between sense and nonsense, is both redundant and central, a pointless point requiring the work of interpretation. In an extensive analysis of Rembrandt's paintings, the navel assumes a significance greater than the bodily mark so evident in numerous nudes: in the Dutch master's *Danae*, for instance, though an actual navel is fully visible, it is the figure's genital area that, by arresting the gaze, metaphorically suggests the navel. In another nude painting, *The Toilet of Bathsheba*, the navel of the pictorial text 'is the left-hand corner of the letter the naked woman is holding' (Bal, 1991: 22). The navel forms a suggestive interpretative crux for other images. Elisabeth Bronfen, in a discussion of Jeffrey Silverthorne's photograph *Listen ... The Woman Who Died in Her Sleep*, identifies 'the navel of the image' as the uncanny presence of death within representation: it is linked to Barthes's photographic *punctum*, an arresting detail in the picture to which the viewer is emotionally and umbilically tied (Bronfen, 1994). As a theoretical or conceptual figure the navel can be found, both by name and in the form of a 'nodal point', in numerous psychoanalytic texts: in *The Interpretation of Dreams*, Sigmund Freud describes a particularly entangled conjunction of dream thoughts as a 'navel'; Jacques Lacan takes Freud's metaphor further so that jokes, speech and logic also have navels. In Lacan's topological theory the navel becomes a particularly suggestive metaphor linked to knots, cuts, scars, holes and networks of language and the unconscious.

In *Ecce Homo*, Friedrich Nietzsche employs the metaphor in the context of a discussion of the role of the university in relation to the state: the *umbilicus* forms a site for the reproduction of law; its openness resembles 'both an ear and a mouth' (Derrida, 1985: 36). As it extends in significance, the navel discloses a series of associations connecting deconstruction and psychoanalysis. Bal (1991) underscores the metaphoric navel's disseminative and anti-phallic potential in the work of interpretation.

In a reading of the connection between Freudian dream analysis and the 'discourse of flowers', the navel again appears. Flowers are seen as navel-like points inaugurating the disseminative movement which leaves texts open to the play of difference:

> Thus, while it appears that the emergence of flowers in texts points to an obscure 'nodal' point in the text which resists hermeneutic analysis, their appearance also seems motivated by the writer's desire to repair the Cartesian division of body and mind, subject and object, inside and outside. As a result this model of signification appeals to those modernist or postmodernist writers who, either thematically or conceptually, oppose the mimetic, logocentric, & patriarchal order of the world. As the issue and agent of dissemination, flowers point, on the one hand, to the disseminative – rather than the centered – nature of linguistic production, and on the other, to our own scattering by the forces of language. (Sartillot, 1993: 42)

Flowers, evincing the ambivalent and deconstructive articulation of navels, undermine the oppositions that structure the relations of everyday life. What appears at first glance to be no more than a flowery and rhetorical figure entangles the fundamental distinctions of rational philosophy and realistic representation.

An element of fear, perhaps, emerges as what seemed to be an innocuous and insignificant object turns into an unknown disruptive element undoing the binding between language and the rationalised world. Oppositions do not remain at a secure distance, but intermingle and confound each other: a nodal and diversely suggestive position within a network of metaphors manifests a disarming ambivalence. And the absence of a navel can be as telling as its presence. The double significance of the navel is exploited by Patrick McGrath in his contemporary gothic short story, 'The Angel'. Set in 1980s New York during a heatwave, the story describes a young man's encounter with an eccentric and shabby old man, Harry Tallboys, who tells stories about an angel he once knew, an angel with the unlikely name of Anson Havershaw. According to Harry, he recognised Anson was not human when, after becoming friends, he saw him naked and his eye fell upon 'a belly punctuated by the merest suggestion of a navel': '"There was a slight flap of skin midway between his hipbones, and believe me, Bernard, a flap is all it was; there was no knot to it. It was" – Harry grasped for words – "vestigial! It was ... decorative."' (McGrath, 1989: 9). The listener, however, remains unconvinced by this vivid description of an encounter with a non-human being and speculates on Harry's tacit confession of a homosexual relationship.

The denouement is queerer still. The young man, prompted by his theory that the angel is only an imagined *alter ego*, a displaced projection of Harry's homosexual identity, confronts the storyteller with the assertion that Anson Havershaw never existed. Harry replies with the declaration that Harry Tallboys, not Anson Havershaw, is the person who never existed. To prove his point, Harry/Anson removes his clothes and the discoloured plastic surgical corset encasing his torso from chest to lower belly:

> Harry's flesh had rotted off his lower ribs and belly, and the clotted skin still clinging to the ribs and hipbones that bordered the hole was in a state of gelatinous putrescence. In the hole I caught the faint gleam of his spine, and amid an indistinct bundle of piping the forms of shadowy organs. I saw sutures on his intestines, and the marks of neat stitching, and a cluster of discolored organic vessels bound with a thin strip of translucent plastic. He should have been dead, and I suppose I must have whispered as much, for I heard him say that he could not die. (McGrath, 1989: 17)

More than a sign of difference or absence denoting non-human and non-natural origins, the navel's vestigial and decorative mockery undoes the differences around which identity is knotted, separating body and soul, life and death: the angel's quasi-navel is no longer the knot articulating body and mind or spirit, or natural being and cultural identity; it marks the point, the decomposing hole, where vital distinctions fall apart. A locus of death, of foul physical corruption rather than the severed link to the womb of life, the angel's 'navel' confounds fundamental distinctions to a horrifyingly degree. Death, in the story, is presented as a blessing as much as a curse since without its work, life collapses into the putrescence of unthinkable horror. The navel, scar of birth, also announces the work of separation and death as integral to the life of all mortal beings.

'The Angel' separates life or spirit from the body that is represented as the vilest example of religion's sinful and corrupt flesh. The repulsive image of the body, however, reappears in current accounts of the technologically determined near future: in cyberspace mind is presented as transcending the physical, spatial and temporal limitations of the body, the latter made redundant, along with reality, by the vast powers of digital computer processing. Michel Serres (1993) associates the mercurial attributes of communications technologies with the disembodied figures of angels. The angels that fly rapidly, lightly and virtually in the machines of the future have a derogatory name for the all-too corporeal thing that they contemptuously leave behind: it is called 'the meat', the rotten lump of flesh which machines make redundant. The future, it seems, transforms humanity at the navel: 'future "humans" will have no navels' (Baudrillard, 1996: 23).

The significance of the navel becomes stranger still in fictions imagining the life of beings who are constructed rather than born of woman. Rudy Rucker's cyberpunk novel, *Wetware*, includes an unexpected speculation on the question of the navel. The speculation is provoked not by the existence of a navel but by its significant absence: one female character in the fiction, an intelligent robot, chooses an artificial body in the shape of a curvaceous woman and deliberately leaves the navel out of her design. In a novel concerned with the origins of and relationships between organic and inorganic life, this small detail assumes a greater importance: more than an omission in keeping with a future in which life has evolved beyond organic patterns, the absent navel highlights the question of origins on which the fiction turns. If the absence of navels in representations of future life accords with contemporary projections of human extinction or subservience to hyperintelligent, self-replicating machines, then the presence of navels, whether literal or metaphorical, constitutes a remarkable corporeal residue in futures that imagine the supersession of organic limitations. The near future distopia of *Blade Runner* includes 'replicants', genetically engineered beings who, grown rather than born, ought not to have navels. Strangely enough, however, a navel is visible on the body of a replicant, testimony to the residual humanity that shadows artificial and yet mortal existence. In another cyberpunk fiction, William Gibson's *Idoru*, the navel is employed as a metaphor: associated not with bodies but with machines, it is a figure for the complex nodal patterns of a world lived largely in an immense digital matrix.

The navel, the juncture of individual beings with the mother who pre-exists her child, remains as a striking metaphor of historical process along a chain of being, a mark of life's movement across time. Appearing in the future, albeit in contemporary fictions, the movement in which the navel forms a significant nodal point is also prospective. Between a past from which one is separated and a future upon which one can only speculate, the navel marks a point of continuity and discontinuity, an interruption causing retrospection and projection, a black hole consuming difference and identity. In this light, the navel forms a suggestive image for an uncertain present positioned between a grand and progressive human history to which it cannot return and a future imagined in utopian and distopian colours. Between modernity and postmodernity, the present can only speculate anxiously or wishfully on the inhuman formations of a future dominated by machines. Maybe contemporary fashion, with a fondness for sporting navels on Paris catwalks, chic clubs and city streets, tacitly acknowledges the precariousness of the present in its open display of the feature that, in its uselessness, signals a human difference most inimical to the incursions of biotechnological futures. To follow the injunctions of fashion further and pierce the navel may send a different signal. Although an assertion of individuality in the defiance of the machinery of conformity and normalcy, the pain of piercing is enjoyed as a particularly human feeling at the same time as the body is submitted to a ritual in which a new knot or ring cuts and joins nature with a cultural machine. The union of metal and flesh provides a striking image of the technical prostheses and biotechnological possibilities already so promiscuously advanced.

The visibility of the navel, whether displayed on the naked bellies of the fashion-conscious or adorned with the exotic charm of shiny metal, endows a previously inconsequential anatomical site with a curious and obscure erotic charge. There seems no obvious reason for an eroticisation of so historically covered-over a site other than its visible centrality to the body that itself has become central to cultural identity. The late twentieth-century culture of the body makes the human form into another garment to be worn, shed and transformed, a locus of identity and self-image connected to surfaces rather than subjective or essential depths. In this respect, the 'sexualisation of the navel' undertaken by pop icon Madonna is significant:

> The most erogenous part of my body is my belly button. I have the most perfect belly button – an inny, and there's no fluff in it. When I stick a finger in my belly button I feel a nerve in the centre of my body shoot up my spine. If 100 belly buttons were lined up against a wall I would definitely pick out which one was mine. (Fiske, 1989: 100)

Madonna's identification of her most erotic zone privileges a sexual pleasure outside masculine jurisdiction: 'in choosing the navel upon which to center it, she is choosing a part of the female body that patriarchy has not conventionally sexualized for the benefit of the male' (Fiske, 1989: 100). Central to her bodily pleasure, Madonna's navel is also a site, so it seems, of immense autoerotic gratification, a zone that needs no one other than herself to satisfy. Self, indeed, is centred on the navel in ways other than the gratifications of physical pleasure: cleaned of fluff, an idealised rather than concealed site, the navel becomes a distinguishing mark rather than an ubiquitous scar, a sign of oneself so special it will stand out in any identity parade. A central point of the body and its pleasures, the navel becomes a centre of being on the body's surface charged with the autoerotic articulation of one's unique self-image.

The question of the navel

The diverse and suggestive appearances of navels in numerous cultural texts pose questions of the present's distance from and proximity to a past which is rewritten but not reclaimed, a history elusively inscribed in narratives whose linearity enables speculative but ungraspable futures to be imagined, anticipated and planned. The present, perhaps now more than ever, refuses the security of a fixed point in space or time to anchor being and its narratives. Writing of being and time, Derrida notes how philosophically the *nun* (the now) is 'given simultaneously as that which is *no longer* and that which is *not yet*':

> The *nun*, the element of time, in this sense is not in itself temporal. It is temporal only in becoming temporal, that is, in ceasing to be, in passing over to no-thingness in the form of being-past or being-future. Even if it is envisaged as (past or future) nonbeing, the now is determined as the intemporal kernel of time, the nonmodifiable nucleus of temporal modification, the inalterable form of temporalization. Time is what overtakes this nucleus, in affecting it with no-thing. But in order to be, in order to be a being, it must not be affected by time, it must not become (past or future). (Derrida, 1982: 40)

An 'intemporal kernel', the now places being at odds with time, an in-temporality causing time and the narratives inscribing its becoming while remaining alien to inscription. Con-temporary accounts of the present, situating the now between irrecuperable histories and projected futures manifest this in-temporality in the production of so many narratives of becoming inimical to the place of being. Between an irrecuperable past and a deferred future, the now is marked by the absent connectedness of the navel, locus of unknown and yet endlessly imaginable relations.

The present, along with the future that furnishes its narratives of becoming, appears 'fabulously textual' in the sense of Derrida's (1984) discussion of the nuclear apocalypse as an event, endlessly imagined and deferred in texts, presenting the possibility of a last word obliterating every word, every relation, every human trace. At the in-temporal point of the present the incursions of futures vividly projected in so many scientific, cinematic and novelistic fictions fill the 'no-thingness' of con-temporaneity with an all-too inhuman becoming. Where postmodernity simultaneously sustained a temporal distance and historical link to modernity's narratives through the future anterior, the assurance of the 'will have been' has ceded to the 'no longer' which signifies an irreversible rupture in time and narrative. The end of history is marked by the advent of a 'posthuman' condition (Bukatman, 1991). The arrival of the future present marks the severance from history and the effacement of the present in a prospective loop of time in which empty no-thingness is overwritten by the rapid encroachments of ever-nearer futures as, in Zoe Sofia's words, a 'collapse of the future on the present' (Csicsery-Ronay, 1991: 186). At the same time, these terminating futures emerge from the no-thingness of the now. William Gibson's influential fictions are concerned with the present, not with 'an imagined future' (Rosenthal, 1991: 85). The near future is con-temporary. For Gibson temporality is a matter of 'total ambivalence' since his fictions are concerned with how technology 'has *already* affected our lives' rather than standard science fiction extrapolations involving rational prediction (McCaffrey, 1991: 274).

The in-temporal loop moves in two directions at once, forwards–backwards and backwards–forwards around the no-thingness of the now. Chris Hables Gray notes 'the long-standing co-operation between some sf writers and the military has deepened considerably' (1994: 315). Science fiction, as much as futurism and futurology, predicts what will happen, also providing the narratives in which the future is inscribed as it will be lived: in 1985, at Wright Patterson Air Force Base, a conference including science fiction writers among futurists and military personnel prompted Joe Haldeman to comment that 'we saw the future there' (Gray, 1994: 321). In the future present fiction and truth become indistinguishable. When he was a Vice-presidential candidate Dan Quayle cited Tom Clancy's *Red Storm Rising* in a political speech. One commentator glossed the reason: 'the point isn't that Quayle necessarily wanted to fight World War III, but rather that he saw *Red Storm Rising* as an authoritative text about military policy ...' (Hables Gray, 1994: 322). Unanchored and ungrounded, the future present remains open to inscription to the extent that narratives do not simply imagine fictional futures but enable their rapid technological realisation: idle speculation becomes wish fulfilment and future becomes fact.

Navel-gazing may not, after all, prove so idle or pointless an exercise as it is popularly assumed to be. Examining an object simultaneously so visible and so overlooked reveals not only the variety of navel appearances on the textual bodies of culture but also diverse networks of significance in which the navel emerges as a crucial node. In theory, too, the navel has shifted from an entirely insignificant and inconsequential knot, overlooked by interpretation, to a site central to the work of analysis. A metaphorically ambivalent point at the intersection of diverse and multiple meanings, the navel is a fruitful figure for deconstruction, tracing the play of difference, aporia and dissemination. Avowing a specifically gendered relationship affecting all humans, the point of lost connection to maternal pre-existence, the navel, in feminism, announces the priority of sexual difference. In psychoanalysis, the navel also possesses extensive significance as a condensation of unconscious processes. Moreover, its significance, as cut and hole, alludes to the sexually determined relations dominated by castration and to the indeterminable nature of feminine sexuality so problematic in psychoanalytic theory. An ambivalent nodal point, the navel operates as a 'boundary figure': like the human body it exists on the borders of organic and technological significance. Moreover, 'gender, like the body, is a boundary concept' (Balsamo, 1995: 215–16). The navel, then, is more than a figure for the eruption of the body within the network of cultural metaphors: it also irrupts within the language inscribed upon the body and the unknown. Hence, for Lacan, whose version of Freudian psychoanalysis stresses the function of signification in subjective, social and unconscious formations, the navel is linked to the operations of the signifier.

The 'question of the navel', as addressed in feminist and psycho-analytical terms by Shoshana Felman, remains irreducible to either language or body. Her reading of Freud's dream interpretation foregrounds the resistance of sexual and figural difference to analysis. 'The dream of Irma's injection', in which Freud introduces the concept of the navel, is not solved by analysis but requires that psychoanalysis transform itself in the face of female difference (Felman, 1993). Remaining open to difference depends on the resistance of the navel in the work of interpretation. It implies an ethical relation to otherness rather than an imperative of exclusion and mastery based on assumptions of male priority. The question of the navel leaves the matter of sexual difference open, reformulating psychoanalysis as a discourse not possessing the truth of sexuality but addressing sexuality as a question. Thus, the reformulation places psychoanalysis in close proximity to ethics, with sexual difference as an ethical crux, a stumbling-block to moral and interpretative imposition: 'Freud placed in the forefront of ethical enquiry the simple relationship between man and woman. Strangely enough, things haven't been able move beyond that point' (Lacan, 1992: 84). Ethical questions also affect the understanding of psychoanalysis' primary locus of enquiry, the unconscious: 'the status of the unconscious, which, as I have shown, is so fragile on the ontic plane, is ethical.' (Lacan, 1977b: 33) And this ethical and unconscious point is also the locus where the navel appears.

The ethical question of sexual difference appearing at the point of the navel further problematises the way in which the difference between bodies and machines is currently understood: a gap inhibits the reduction of one to other, forming an obstacle and excess to the technological replacement of humans. Discussing artificial intelligence, Lyotard comments that 'thinking machines will have to be nourished not just on radiation but on irremediable gender difference'. This observation is quoted and underscored by Claudia Springer: 'the force that propels thought is the desire induced by gender difference' (1993: 727). Bodies and machines are not diametrically opposed, as popular representations rather automatically suggest, but involve an irreducible difference, neither cultural nor natural. In accounts of the relationship between sex and technology, gender is not considered to be an exclusively natural entity, but a cultural construction: 'like sexuality, gender is not a property of bodies or something originally existent in human beings, but "the set of effects produced in bodies, behaviors, and social relations," in Foucault's words, by the deployment of "a complex political technology"'. This elaboration of the 'technologies of gender' revises Foucault's approach: 'to think of gender as the product and the process of a number of social technologies, of techno-social or bio-medical apparati, is to have already gone beyond Foucault, for his critical understanding of the technology of sex did not take into account its differential solicitation of male and female subjects' (de Lauretis, 1987: 3). Though sex figures very differently in these accounts of technology it nonetheless remains prominent in a the problematisation of the oddly opposed relationship between bodies and machines. Describing the development of the disciplines which reshaped bodies, nature and social life from the seventeenth century, Foucault observes that 'the human body was entering a machinery of power that explores it, breaks it down, rearranges it' (1979: 138). As natural, social and individual life is transformed by scientific and economic modes of managing life two strategies of discipline are manifested: one centres on 'the body as a machine'; the other regulates populations as a whole. Together they represent a 'great bipolar technology – anatomical and biological' (Foucault, 1981: 139). In the face

Sex, machines and navels

of such an immense technological effort inserting bodies in machines and reconstructing them as machines the realm of an unregulated nature is almost completely eclipsed.

Navels remain alien to technology at the same time as they are the result of a technological cut, a slight but inaugural transformation of the body: they are a feature of the body and a mark of the separation of bodies, never of the body alone. The remainder is neither the property of nature nor the possession of cultural machines. Difference escapes determination. Sexuality, like the navel, inhabits the gap identifiable as neither nature nor culture, neither body nor machine. Joan Copjec interrogates the notion of sexual identity as a performative effect to argue that Judith Butler

> proceeds as though she believes that the deconstruction of the fiction of innate or essential sex is also, or must lead to, a rejection of the notion that there is anything constant or invariable about sexual difference, that sex is anything other than a construct of historically variable discursive practices into which we may intervene to sow 'subversive confusion'. (Copjec, 1994: 202)

Questioning 'the very *twoness* of sex' assumed by Butler, Copjec contends that the binarism need not necessarily be so and continues with the question, 'what is sex?': 'echoing Freud's contention that sexual difference is not unambiguously marked either anatomically, chromosomally, or hormonally, that is, questioning the prediscursive existence of sex, Butler automatically assumes… that sex must be discursively or culturally constructed' (1994: 203). The question, however, refuses any reduction to an either/or proposition, since sex is never fully explained by anatomy or cultural convention but occurs as the excess interior to discourse:

> While sex is, for psychoanalysis, never simply a natural fact, it is also never reducible to any discursive construction, to sense, finally. For what such a reduction would remain oblivious to is *the radical antagonism between sex and sense*. As Lacan puts it, 'Everything implied by the analytic engagement with human behaviour indicates not that meaning reflects the sexual, but that it makes up for it.' Sex is the stumbling block of sense. This is not to say that sex is prediscursive; we have no intention of denying that human sexuality is a product of signification, but we intend, rather, to refine this position by arguing that sex is produced by the internal limit, the failure of signification. It is only where discursive practices falter – and not at all where they succeed – that sex comes to be. (1994: 204)

Sex is grounded neither in cultural construction nor in an idealised and essential notion of nature: bound up with signification, it emerges where words fail, in the form of an excess that is both interior to and outside the parameters of discourse. This position establishes the point from which psychoanalysis proceeds to address questions of sexuality, a point, as it were, forming the navel of Lacanian theory. In the published and edited transcript of Lacan's seminar delivered in 1954–55, not only does the question of sexuality and analysis receive considerable attention in the reinterpretation of Freud's specimen dream where the navel makes its first psychoanalytic appearance: the volume also employs insights from cybernetics and repeatedly returns to questions of the difference between humans and machines (Lacan, 1988b).

Psychoanalysis, rather than deconstruction or feminism, forms the nodal theory in this book-length gaze upon navels. Although psychoanalysis has been an object for the theoretical interventions and criticisms of both deconstruction and feminism, it has remained curiously central to the development of the theories loosely grouped under the name of poststructuralism, the major figures of which having all critiqued psychoanalysis in general and Lacan in particular. Psychoanalysis evokes anything but indifference and, more often, has provided the counterpoint for diverse theoretical departures. Opposition can imply a kind of respect, and criticisms of psychoanalysis often rework its propositions. Also, given that Lacan's career spans a significant episode of French intellectual history, it is hardly surprising that his work addresses that era's prevalent issues, if not setting many of the terms of debate. Language, subjectivity, difference, desire and otherness, though never the exclusive domain of psychoanalysis, are topics that have come to be seen, refracted or diffracted, through the prism of psychoanalysis so that, even after the sustained critiques from deconstructive and feminist positions, psychoanalysis remains significantly nodal in the vast matrix of contemporary theory.[5]

Psychoanalysis not only informs the reading of a diversity of navels undertaken in the following pages, it is read at the level of the navel. The first section introduces psychoanalysis through the navel, not only in the way the metaphor is explicitly employed but in terms of its general implications for psychoanalytic interpretation and Lacan's famous 'return to Freud'. The navel mutates throughout Lacan's texts but remains recognisable as a figure that connects his work to Freud's while inaugurating a movement in an irrevocably different direction. Appearing insistently, the navel also furnishes a point from which the tenets of Lacanian psychoanalysis can be carefully unravelled. Symbolic law, and the phallus so central to it, is not, in this reading, the be-all and end-all of the account:

Sex, machines and navels

the navel implies something in excess of metaphor, a point that, while making metaphor possible, offers no final or authoritative guarantees for interpretation. There is, of course, a contemporary, sceptically 'postmodern', inflection to such an argument: how can psychoanalysis proceed in a world incredulous to any claim to truth, authority or metalanguage?

In this light, the second section interrogates postmodernist fiction and theories of postmodernity from the position of the navel of the joke, that is, in terms of the play of language and difference. In the array of images and ironies associated with postmodernist practices, the present finds itself psychotically adrift in a sea of simulations empty of meaning and content. The third section looks back on history from the knotty position afforded by contemporary theory and fiction. The navel offers a vantage point for reflections on and consumptions of history, a particular knot in the diverse threads linking grand narratives and little stories: something, a knot or hole, works in excess of historicism both to cause historical enquiry and leave it hysterically unfinished, a point lying beyond empirical origins while marking a space in which cultural change can be envisaged. Such change may be different from the upheavals which, in the present period of digital revolution, are advertised with abandon.

The last section addresses navels of the future through the fictions and theories promoting or denigrating the technological phenomenon of cyberspace. Strangely, navels are still in evidence in several cyberpunk fictions, despite numerous projections concerning the end of humanity. Here, the navel prompts serious questions about the status of living machines and the fantasies and anxieties by which the future presses upon the present. Sex and bodies, ostensibly discarded by intelligent machines, are not fully erased but are significantly transformed: the question of the navel suggests that, in excess of a choice between meat or machine, something else remains at work confounding apocalyptic oppositions and demanding an extensive theoretical reappraisal of the narrative structures shaping the future. If machines have navels, and some, so it seems, do, then the question of the navel concerns the future as much as the past.

Notes

1 *Homo datum*, as it appears in Pat Cadigan's *Synners*, is discussed by Balsamo (1993: 684).
2 The navel, of course, is not literally a knot, but the site where a knot – a ligature – has been tied around a cord so that it can be cut. The operation allows the skin to wither and heal to form a scar of superficial depth indenting or protruding from the body, a hole or button.
3 Browne (1964, 2: 345). He also discusses the corruption of the flesh and observes 'the man without a Navell yet lives in me' (Browne, 1964, 1: 86). Browne's 'Observations on Anatomy' notes the relative conspicuousness of the navel which distinguishes humans from animals, and implies that culture, rather than hairlessness alone, is involved: the navel 'may happen to bee so discernible in man not only from the bareness of the skinne, butt from the ligation wch is made upon it before it bee cutt off, & a thick skinne wch after covereth it. For in quadruped beasts the *funiculus* being bitt of, gradually rotteth away till cometh to the skinne & so maketh no *umbo* or readily visible bunch as in man' (Browne, 1964, 3: 335). The human navel does not naturally wither away, but exists as a scar, the result of cultural or technological intervention.
4 Melville (1994: 414). Seltzer (1992: 113) finds echoes of the nineteenth-century navel joke in Stephen Crane's *Red Badge of Courage* and Thomas Pynchon's *V*.
5 In unravelling and retying the complicated threads of postwar French theory, this book encounters a navel suggested by the title and author of another book: Laurence Bataille's *L'Ombilic du rêve* (1987). To pursue its significance here would take the discussion far afield.

2 ✧ Lacan's navel

Psychoanalysis through the navel?

Lacan's navel, not Freud's, affords the focus for an examination of the role of metaphor in psychoanalysis. Freud, of course, introduced the figure, somewhat hesitatingly, in his *Interpretation of Dreams* to negotiate a problem encountered in his first dream analysis. The navel appears twice: once in a footnote as a point of interpretative closure and then, much later in the text, as a concept central to the psychoanalysis of dreams, the point where the dream-wish is glimpsed among a tangle of dream-thoughts. In the second instance the navel is linked to a related figure, a mushroom. The displacement veils a correspondence between terms: despite their different semantic associations navel (belly *button*) and mushroom both have the shape of the bump that rises through the tangle of unconscious dream-thoughts.

While undergoing a series of displacements the figure of the navel permeates Lacan's writings. Adopted and reiterated by Lacan, the navel of Freudian psychoanalysis becomes a point of umbilical connection between Freud's texts and Lacan's theory, a point at which the latter is bound to and differentiated from the work of the father of psychoanalysis. The navel of the dream is taken further and applied to the analysis of jokes, speech and logic. It also appears in a variety of other guises retaining the same distinctive shape: as quilting point, darning egg and as knot, the navel manifests its importance in Lacanian theory. The shape is recognisable, too, in the figure of the hoop net and in the diagrams of the drive and the dialectic of desire, the latter, in its completed stage, taking the form of two darning mushrooms traversed by the threads of psychoanalytic conceptual relations. Beyond the navel as an isolated figure lies a web of metaphors: in Freud's account the navel describes 'a tangle of dream-thoughts' situated within the 'intricate network of our world of thought', a 'meshwork'. The navel, as knot, as unconscious nodal point, opens on to a topographical system. And Lacan's texts never cease to argue in topological terms. The navel of psychoanalysis is tied up with a development of Freudian metaphor, a development which distinguishes something different in Lacanian psychoanalysis, something new, a discovery which, though it arises from Freudian texts, remains fundamentally Lacanian, linked to the discovery that Lacan saw as his major innovation and which he finally named, after broaching it by way of the quilting point and *das Ding*, the *objet petit a*.

The navel, overlooked in Lacanian psychoanalysis, is related to the notion of the gaze which has received much more attention: both manifest the function of the *objet petit a* that escapes the symbolically ordered world of representations and perceptions. In-visible, rather than open to sight, the gaze manifests a 'strange contingency' as a darkness or stain within vision: while it constitutes the possibility of perception, it eludes direct visibility (Lacan, 1977b: 72–3). It forms a point of lack inaugurating desire, a space for fantasy and signification outside the grasp of symbols, a locus articulating the known and visible world with an impenetrable and unconscious realm. Gaze and navel conjoin effectively at the heart of psychoanalysis. But it is a little misleading to propose an examination of psychoanalysis *through* the navel: the metaphor provides space for the reflection of something alien to the light of the everyday world, not a reflection of a ready-made and symbolised object that can be seen, grasped and defined. The navel does not allow a mirror to be held up which renders the obscure discourse of psychoanalysis transparent; it does not suddenly make everything plain and allow the curious eye to penetrate directly into the mysterious and uncharted realms of the human unconscious. As a strange point of reflection on psychoanalysis, the navel draws attention to surfaces rather than depths, a metaphor linked to metaphorical relationships and connections as well as to the absence of metaphor. In the topological dimension of mushrooms, mycelium, nodal points and matrices, the densely woven fabric of signifying knots is bound together by nothing other than holes and threads of connection: the spaces in the fabric remain as significant as the knots.

The impossibility of conceiving of a network without gaps remains integral to Lacanian thinking. The gaze, for example, connotes a hole in vision, neither seeing nor seen but an in-visible cause around which perception turns. While Freud's navel has been discussed by Lacan and others, Lacan's navel has generally escaped critical observation. The navel, excluded from and central to psychoanalysis, is a strange figure not immediately glimpsed as the representative of something but denoting a dark space that has remained overlooked, a blind spot in interpretation. As the term for a problem in Freudian dream analysis that, only belatedly, is endowed with conceptual significance as a mark of the end of interpretation, the navel, for Lacan, establishes a point of repeated return at the same time as it inaugurates a series of conceptual departures, a site of reiteration and new interpretation. Connecting Lacan to Freud even as it fundamentally distinguishes their positions, the appearance of the navel in the still partially published *corpus* of the former assumes an important role in Lacan's return to Freud, a return, he emphasises, to the meaning of Freud. Given that meaning and metaphor, for Lacan, are closely related, the return to the meaning of Freud also constitutes a return to Freudian metaphor, to metaphor as it is inscribed on the body of Freud's texts and as it inscribes something of the body in Freud's texts. As a mark of corporeality, a scar that no longer serves any purpose except as a reminder of bodily dis/continuity, the navel constitutes a remainder and an incorporation of excess into metaphor: it ties a crucial knot that remains both literal and metaphorical, the end and the excess of metaphor.

The metaphor of the navel is not simply a conceptual tool to demonstrate the masterful authority of psychoanalytical interpretation. Its significance at the limit of metaphorical clarity does not reveal one term in which the whole is condensed, but discloses the point at which understanding hesitates and conceptualisation falters before the unknown. In her reading of Freud's dream, Shoshana Felman notes that 'the doctor is no longer *master* – of the cure or of the patient, of the illness or of the "solution" to the illness. The analytical fecundity proceeds, precisely, from the doctor's destitution from his mastery (this is what the Irma dream is all about) – from the *destitution*, in effect, *of mastery as such*' (Felman, 1993: 111). The metaphor does not signal the achievement of mastery but underscores its limits, thereby enabling an important revision of both the practice of analysis and the notion of the return to Freud performed by Lacan: it is not a return through the navel, through the metaphor of the father of psychoanalysis to the authority of his truth as the author of a discourse establishing definitive knowledge of sexuality. On the contrary, it returns to the question of metaphor in Freud, to the role of signification and the unconscious, to something beyond the possession of anyone, even Freud. Here, the navel opens on to a dimension in excess of analytical understanding, a matrix irreducible to metaphor. The return, it seems, transforms Freud: his texts become a matrix that, in excess of writer and interpretation, make analysis possible. The movement reopens the gap between text and reading, the space between paternity and metaphor, while retaining the metaphors of connection and difference.

The navel of the dream

Freud had a dream about a female patient who was not particularly responsive to his analysis. Nonetheless, he immortalised both the dream and its analysis by offering it as the specimen example in *The Interpretation of Dreams*. In a footnote to the analysis of 'the dream of Irma's injection', the notion of the navel makes its first appearance. Here, the navel is introduced to mark a stumbling-block for analysis, the limit beyond which it cannot proceed:

> I had a feeling that the interpretation of this part of the dream was not carried far enough to make it possible to follow the whole of its concealed meaning. If I had pursued my comparison between the three women, it would have taken me far afield. – There is at least one spot in every dream at which it is unplumbable – a navel, as it were, that is its point of contact with the unknown (Freud, 1976a: 186n.)

Hesitatingly introduced, 'as it were', the metaphor over which interpretation falters also serves to draw the analysis to a close despite the detours of condensation and displacement. Incomplete and yet finished, interpretation falls short of the whole meaning, encountering the point where the dream opens on to the 'unplumbable' and unknown depths of the unconscious.

The navel, first invoked to account for a limit to psychoanalytic dream interpretation, finds itself reintroduced at a much later stage in Freud's text: its general significance as the unplumbable spot in 'every dream' establishes its theoretical importance for the work of dream analysis. The navel's conceptual citation offers a brief glimpse of the unknown, a view beyond the navel that constitutes a figurative plumbing of the unplumbable. Freud writes:

> There is often a passage even in the most thoroughly interpreted dream which has to be left obscure; this is because we become aware during the work of interpretation that at that point there is a tangle of dream-thoughts which cannot be unravelled and which moreover adds nothing to our knowledge of the content of the dream. This is the dream's navel, the spot where it reaches down into the unknown. The dream-thoughts to which we

Sex, machines and navels

are led by interpretation cannot, from the nature of things, have any definite endings; they are bound to branch out in every direction into the intricate network of our world of thought. It is at some point where this meshwork is particularly close that the dream-wish grows up, like a mushroom out of its mycelium. (1976a: 671–2)

Changing its name and becoming a mushroom in the course of this glimpse into the unknown, the navel retains its button-like shape, a knot of the meshwork or mycelium describing the intricate tangle that Freud associates with the unconscious. The topological outline Freud sketches, moreover, imagines an unconscious that, in contrast to the nether region suggested by the term 'depth psychology', appears curiously depthless: it is both 'unplumbable' and, like the superficial density of fabric, a texture woven around nothing. The navel, Freud observes, 'adds nothing' to interpretation in a strangely supplementary manner: nothing is the remainder of interpretation, an assurance of its completion while acknowledging that the discovery of the whole meaning of the dream has been deferred. And what Freud adds in his second account of the navel is precisely nothing: an image of the unknown is projected on to an unplumbable locus and traced out as a meshwork, an indeterminate dimension itself constituted as much by spaces as by tangles, connections and knots.

As a knot, a locus of the condensation integral to the work of dreams, the navel emerges as a nodal point from which metaphors blossom in every direction: beyond the nodal point they reach into the unknown space of the unconscious world of dream-thoughts. On the other side, as it were, they branch into the theory of psychoanalysis itself. Unravelling this web of metaphoricity threatens the very integrity of interpretation by opening on to a space that has no 'definite endings'. However, the navel is identified by Freud, not so much with meaninglessness or multiple meanings, but as the point from which meaning emerges: compared to the mushroom that grows from an entangled root structure, the dream-wish is distinguished from the meshwork of dream-thoughts. The former provides the analyst with the meaning of a patient's dream, the very basis of a dream's meaning. As the point around which interpretation turns, its cause and object, the navel is doubled in respect of analysis: both the end and the start of interpretation, it also signifies the absence of 'definite endings' and the uncertainty of beginnings.

The rhizomatic tangle of metaphors inaugurated by the navel branch out in every direction, while meaning, the dream-wish, is produced through deracination from the mycelium. The metaphoric tangle engenders associations central to psychoanalysis, involving, as Freud briefly notes, sexuality. A woman patient, Irma, constitutes the 'principal figure' of the dream, around whom meaning is condensed: her features and her symptoms form the point of configuration for a series of associations made in the dream between her, a female friend, Freud's wife and his elder daughter (1976a: 399). The significance of these women seems to lie in their resistance to the process and cure of psychoanalysis: The 'recalcitrance' of Irma's symptoms, her 'pains in the throat, stomach and abdomen', a 'big white patch' of 'whitish grey scabs' and 'curly structures' embody resistance as a hysterical reaction to psychoanalytical authority. Resistance occurs at the level of female sexuality. Just as the navel describes a knot of meaning that resists full interpretation, so Irma's symptoms signal knots that silently refuse psychoanalytical treatment. Feminine sexual difference, furthermore, marks the limit of psychoanalysis's knowledge, the point and object at which interpretation falters. The navel embodies this difference: a scar of one's lost connection to another body, a body that is always female, whose otherness is traced on the body of the child. A mark of separation from this Other body, the navel anatomically signifies a point of disconnection from a lost origin. The cut also allows individual existence to emerge: its metaphorical incarnation within a tangled interconnectivity is severed in order to deliver meaning. What remains is the trace of resistant otherness.

In Freud's analysis of his dream of Irma's injection, it is not only female figures who condense his anxieties: a cluster of medical men appear and underline the sense of criticism and self-doubt governing the dream. Otto, and his relative Leopold, along with Dr M., Freud's elder brother and his friend Wilhelm Fliess, are the main protagonists. These men are condensed in the figures of Otto, who gives Irma an injection of trimethylamin, and Dr M., who arrives to examine her. Both doctors have at one time or other expressed disagreements with the techniques of psychoanalysis. Indeed, the disorders of the dream, with its emphasis on conventional medical practice and physical illness, are positioned between organic and psychological causes. For Freud the psychoanalyst, the meaning of the dream lies in the wish it announces: to be absolved of guilt and responsibility for the continuance of Irma's illness. She has rejected the solution provided by the conclusion of analysis so, Freud dreams, the answer lies elsewhere, literally in the 'solution' of trimethylamin injected by Otto with a dirty syringe: 'I was not responsible for the persistence of Irma's pains, but that Otto was. Otto had in fact annoyed me by his

Sex, machines and navels

remarks about Irma's incomplete cure, and the dream gave me my revenge by throwing the reproach back on to him' (1976a: 196). All the factors in the dream, Freud states, are explained as the fulfilment of his wish to be exculpated of Irma's illness.[1]

The dream's details revolve around personal and professional health. As a professional concern for Freud, the question of health also includes the well-being of psychoanalysis threatened both by a perceived failure to cure Irma and the criticisms directed at it by conventional medicine. A series of anxieties about health and psychoanalysis are condensed in Irma's symptoms: a complaint of his wife's during pregnancy; an illness suffered by his elder daughter, Mathilde; a patient of the same name who nearly died; a male friend of Freud's who died through excessive use of cocaine; and a male patient who had been, wrongly, Freud suspected, diagnosed as suffering from dysentery. Irma's symptoms also betray Freud's concerns about his own health. Coming close to home, actual ill-health coincides with symbolic dis-ease. Anxieties about psychoanalysis are evinced in the criticisms of Otto, Irma, and Dr M., the last two disagreeing with the solution Freud proposes. Irma's incurable symptoms reiterate resistance on a symbolic level: her unwillingness to accept Freud's solution aligns her with the reproaches of Otto and Dr M. Throughout the dream, a cluster of figures are identified in opposition to Freud and psychoanalysis. Another group, later called the 'Fliess group', are situated antithetically to the 'Otto group' (1976a: 401). Some of Irma's symptoms suggest both the nasal problem suffered by Freud and his friend, Wilhelm Fliess, a nose and throat specialist. Freud had also discussed trimethylamin with Fliess, the latter being 'a person whose agreement I recalled with satisfaction whenever I felt isolated in my opinions' (1976a: 194). The second group includes Leopold, a relative of Otto's in the same branch of medicine but in competition with him. Irma's friend, too, compares favourably as a person Freud would like to have in analysis, a person whom he imagines would be more responsive to treatment: 'she would have yielded sooner. She would have *opened her mouth properly*, and have told me more than Irma' (1976a: 186).

The specimen dream of psychoanalytical interpretation becomes a dream with the question of psychoanalysis at its core. Freud is caught between Otto's group of critical figures, resisting Freudian analysis, and Fliess's group of sympathetic personae. In the course of the analysis, criticised or supported, Freud proceeds from uncertainty and doubt to confident interpretation: blame for Irma's illness is shifted to Otto, a movement accompanied by shift in focus from physiological to psychological causes and treatments. Literal or bodily causes vie with metaphorical questions. Freud is divided and multiplied – doubled – in the process: resisted by Irma who also embodies his own symptoms and his own anxiety, he remains, as a physician, concerned by organic illness while, as a psychoanalyst, his interest lies in psychological causes. An 'either/or' structure dominates dreams. Freud states later: '"an either–or" is mostly used to describe a dream-element that has a quality of vagueness – which however, is capable of being resolved' (1976a: 428). The dream of Irma's injection announces the question of either psychoanalysis or medicine, either Otto's or Fliess's group. The medical reproach directed at him by Otto is resolved and the general reproach of psychoanalysis, too, is dealt with in the dream. Part of the dream is interpreted as Freud's hostile response to medicine's lack of knowledge, an expression of 'derision at physicians who are ignorant of hysteria' (1976a: 191). Ironically, psychoanalysis manages to avoid culpability in the dream by shifting the blame for Irma's illness on to Otto and organic infection, that is, by invoking medical explanation. It recovers its own meaning, however, at the level of interpretation: the two levels are joined in the 'solution' to the dream. The solution of trimethylamin that Otto injects with an unclean syringe is established as the cause of illness while this same solution, with its formula written large in the dream itself, delivers the psychoanalytical answer: a byproduct of sexual metabolism (a result of the decomposition of sperm), trimethylamin brings the issue of sexuality to the fore. And the focus on sexuality in the development of illness is precisely what differentiates psychoanalysis from conventional medicine.

In the dream sexuality is identified in terms of a contrast within as well as between gender roles. Irma and her friend are both widows. The lack of a husband is seen as the source of the hysterical symptoms:

> Irma's pains could be satisfactorily explained by her widowhood (cf. the trimethylamin) which *I* had no means of altering. Irma's pains had been caused by Otto giving her an incautious injection of an unsuitable drug – a thing which *I* should never have done. Irma's pains were the result of an injection with a dirty needle, like my old lady's phlebitis – whereas *I* never did any harm with my injections. (1976a: 197)

The condensations of these inconsistent but exculpatory explanations return to sexual causes under the thinly veiled symbolism of injection. For Irma the absence of sexual satisfaction contrasts not only with the

Sex, machines and navels

'satisfactory explanation' of analysis but with Freud's wife, pregnant at the time. The latter appears in the dream in connection with the old lady with phlebitis:

> I had at once thought it must be an infiltration caused by a dirty needle. I was proud of the fact that in two years I had not caused a single infiltration; I took constant pains to be sure that the syringe was clean. In short, I was conscientious. The phlebitis brought me back once more to my wife, who had suffered from thrombosis during one of her pregnancies; and now three similar situations came to my recollection involving my wife, Irma and the dead Mathilde. (1976a: 195)

There are different levels of satisfaction connected with the injection: sexual (Irma), personal (his wife) and professional (Mathilde and his conscientiousness). The death of Mathilde constitutes 'a tragic event' in Freud's practice and involves a different chemical: Mathilde suffers a 'severe toxic state' as a result of Freud's prescription of sulphonal, 'at that time regarded as a harmless remedy'. A few lines later it is described as a 'poison'. Sulphonal is not the only remedy that becomes a poison: in the previous paragraph Freud mentions how the prescription of cocaine (for which he had been seriously reproached) 'hastened the death of a dear friend' (1976a: 187). Further, the dead Mathilde is connected by name to Freud's daughter who suffered a serious illness with symptoms resembling Irma's. The associations imply a terrible reproach on Freud himself: 'it struck me now almost like an act of retribution on the part of destiny'. The substitutions of dream-figures raise the question of his conscientiousness and the spectre of Old Testament law: 'Mathilde for Mathilde, an eye for an eye and a tooth for a tooth. It seemed as if I had been collecting all the occasions which I could bring up against myself as evidence of lack of medical conscientiousness' (1976a: 188).

The anxiety associated with the administering of drugs as poison and/or remedy further involves Otto. The latter, Freud comments, had 'a habit of making presents on every possible occasion' and made a gift of a liqueur to the Freuds. The gift had gone bad, so that Freud countermanded his wife's idea of passing it on to the servants, arguing 'that there was no need for *them* to be poisoned either'. The gift that turns into poison is again connected with sexuality in that, Freud hopes, 'some day he [Otto] would find himself a wife to cure himself of the habit' (1976a: 192). Underlining the issue of sexuality and the poison/cure, it is Otto who injects Irma with a dirty needle. The administration of cures, then, remains a site of ambivalence, an issue of either/or affecting the position of Freud personally and professionally, medically and psychoanalytically. The ambivalence implicates sexuality and conscientiousness, binding Freud within a knot of associations in which desire appears on two levels that the analyst tries to keep separate. On one level there is no desire, on the other, too much: recounting how Irma, in the dream, is examined through her dress (a practice carried out by a medical colleague), Freud insists that he had 'no desire to penetrate more deeply' (1976a: 194). Which is to say that his syringe is clean, unlike that of Otto. However, there remains a desire to penetrate more deeply into interpretation, a desire constituted precisely by the limit that brings interpretation to an end. In the conclusion to the analysis of a specimen dream Freud states:

> I will not pretend that I have completely uncovered the meaning of this dream or that its interpretation is without a gap. I could spend much more time over it, derive further information from it and discuss fresh problems raised by it. I myself know the points from which further trains of thought could be followed. But considerations which arise in the case of every dream of my own restrain me from pursuing my interpretative work. If anyone should feel tempted to express a hasty condemnation of my reticence, I would advise him to make the experiment of being franker than I am. (1976a: 198)

Given time, further interpretative work could be undertaken: so much Freud knows. But the knowledge claimed remains shadowed by a desire to pursue interpretation, a desire that has to be restrained. Noting others' condemnation of his reticence, Freud performs desire in withholding information, a coy gesture that both maintains and refuses a position of knowledge, marking the latter with a residue that leaves the reader, apparently unlike Freud himself, unsatisfied.

The distance Freud inscribes between what he knows and what he offers in writing is precisely the distance that the analysis throughout attempts to negotiate, threatened by the very fact of offering one of his own dreams as a specimen of psychoanalytic interpretation. The distance, or lack of it, is announced at the start of the preamble: Irma was not only a patient, but 'a young lady who was on very friendly terms with me and my family'. Such a relationship 'may be the source', Freud continues, 'of many disturbed feelings in a physician and particularly in a psychotherapist': 'while the physician's personal interest is greater, his authority is less; a failure would bring a threat to the old-established friendship with the patient's family' (1976a: 181). Professional authority falters in the face of personal interest. The indeterminable line between the two constitutes a significant anxiety of the dream in that both poles are rendered unstable. Personal interest threatens ethical codes, as the concerns with conscientiousness attest. Throughout, the desire articulated in the dream involves Freud's authority, an authority that is contested at both a personal and a professional level: a configuration of women resist psychoanalysis and a cluster of physicians question its soundness. In between, the dreamer seeks out sympathetic figures to identify a secure position but cannot fully extract itself from the ambivalence, the tangle of the dream itself. Distinguished from Irma professionally, Freud's personal interest reappears in her symptoms, some of which are his own. The 'solution' is similarly ambivalent: the chemical which causes medical harm and infection and signals sexuality and desire also satisfies the desire of psychoanalysis to be free of blame, exculpated from causing infection or failing to cure: it remains both poison and remedy.

The dream rests on an 'either–or' structure, turning on the very ambivalence represented by the navel. An 'either–or' structure, like the interpretation itself, is never fully resolved. Indeed, far from being a matter of either professional authority or personal interest, the dream entangles both; family, friendship and work are repeatedly interwoven. Rather than being a question of either female resistance or male medical criticism, it is matter of both at once, with Dr M. and Irma allied in their disagreement with Freud's solution. And the 'solution' is precisely the point at which the knot of female resistance is tied up with the cluster of medical criticism. At the same time, the point at which the answer is distinguished remains, for Freud the psychoanalyst and the conscientious doctor as well, both the separation and conjoining of medical practice and psychoanalytical cure. It marks a conjunction, crucial to psychoanalysis, of body and speech, sexuality and knowledge, a conjunction that also discloses the gap from which desire emerges in a double movement. In relation to the knot of resistance and reproach, Freud's dream distinguishes another knot, a point that articulates the various personal and professional positions that are entangled in the dream: what emerges forms a knot of paternity binding the father of the family to the father of psychoanalysis, a figure defining paternal law. Initially law appears in the dream as a purely negative force, as the retributive destiny that substitutes one person for another, an eye for an eye, a tooth for a tooth. For Freud it discloses a professional doubt, a 'lack of medical conscientiousness' (1976a: 188). But it also reveals a law crucial to dream analysis: the law of condensation, of substituting one figure for another. By means of this law Freud finds both the solution to the dream, its meaning, and elaborates the process of dream interpretation: he discovers a metaphor, hesitatingly introduced and then conceptually elaborated, that discloses the ambivalence of meaning and the process of interpretation.

The doubleness of the metaphor of the navel inscribes the possibility of the paternal metaphor. It is ironic that a term associated with a maternal act should deliver such a contrary figure but the navel is not only a knot separating infant from its maternal origin with a difference that is also a residue of a connection: as a scar, it forms the trace of a cut, an act of differentiation dividing one into two distinct identities while acknowledging the bond that has been lost. The figure of the navel, as it emerges in the tangle of Freud's dream-thoughts, operates in the same way in interpretation: it is the point at which meaning, Freud's meaning, can be separated out from a meshwork that remains excessively meaningful and beyond meaning at the same time. A double knot, meaningful and meaningless, separated by a cut, a knot that, but for the cut of differentiation and the gap it introduces, would remain entangled in a multiplicity of knots, the navel retains a trace of the knottiness of the Other from which it is separated. As limit and figure of endless interpretation, as connection and separation between meaningful element and entangled structure, indeterminable origin and incomplete end, the navel is the point of ambivalence, the hyphen in Freud's 'either–or' formulation that binds personal and professional, medical and psychoanalytic, male and female in relations that are also non-relations, differences that are also points of articulation.

Reading navels

In accounts of Freud's dream of Irma's injection, critical positions continue to be affected by the doubleness of the navel as both knot and cut: it signifies a difference pointing two ways at once. Jeffrey Mehlman's reading of repetition and displacement in the interpretation of Freud's Irma dream focuses on the significance of trimethylamin:

> the formula for the chemical – spaced out in heavy type – serves as a point of maximum intersection of the various associative paths along which affect is displaced. In Chapter VII, it will figure as the example par excellence of what Freud calls a nodal point, a hidden centre in the dream, which is itself

| Sex, machines and navels

manifest, but whose odd centrality or structuring function remains latent. (Mehlman, 1981: 184)

Trimethylamin is, though the word is not used, the navel of the dream. Its significance remains biological and figural, articulating their functions in psychoanalysis through an 'infinitesimal difference'. The difference concerns the move between the origin of Irma's symptoms and the formula or node of the dream: 'such a deviation of the biological into the fantasmatic occupies an important (though insufficiently perceived) place in Freud's metapsychology, and bears the name "Anlehnung" (anaclisis, étayage).' The drive leans on a biological element to enable the move from the real to the object of fantasy in the same way that the formula for trimethylamin tends to

> 'lean on' the substance in order to achieve its independence as a node structuring, in Lacan's formula, 'a signifying flux, the mystery of which consists in the fact that the subject does not even know where to pretend to be its organiser' (*Écrits*, p. 623). Ultimately the wish interpreted by Freud is, through repression, to be free of the threat to the integrity of one's ego posed by that 'flux'. (Mehlman, 1981: 185)

The process of leaning on has two meanings: it charts the move from biology to fantasy crucial to psychoanalysis and Freud's attempt to reconstitute mastery in the face of the dream's unconscious flux. Freud leans on Irma 'in the Mafioso sense, this time – making her cough up (his) truth' (Mehlman, 1981: 186).

The question of mastery surrounds the navel and its interpretations. It remains a question attended by issues of the relation between biological sex and gendered fantasy, a matter of sexual and textual difference. In Shoshana Felman's reading of Freud's Irma dream the doubleness of the navel foregrounds a gendered resistance that lies in the difference between body and text. Signalling both a new psychoanalytical concept and the physical body, the navel constitutes a 'pregnant image' around which questions of corporeality and knowledge cohere: 'it marks... at once the *disconnection* and the *connection* between a maternal body giving birth and a newborn child' as well as, in Freud's dream, marking a point that is 'all at once *tied up* with the unknown and *disconnected* from its knowledge, disconnected from the knowledge of its own begetting' (Felman, 1985: 63). The navel, as knot, signifies a mystery bound up with the figure of the mother and, in the dream, constitutes '*the very knot of female figures*' resisting Freudian analysis. Associated with biological difference, the navel also operates theoretically as 'a *structured female knot* which cannot be untied',

> a knot of female differentiality with respect to any given definitions; a knot, in other words, which points not to the identifiability of any given feminine identity, but to the inexhaustibility, the unaccountability of *female difference*; difference which Freud – as man, as doctor, as interpreter – stumbles on, experiences first as purely negative resistance, but which he then insightfully associates with the inexhaustibility, the unaccountability of the very *nodal point* – the very navel – of the dream (Felman, 1985: 64)

The female knot establishes the point of difference against which the knot of Freud's identity ('as man, as doctor, as interpreter') is constituted in masculine and paternal terms. The differentiation is made possible by the very resistance of the navel which does more than 'explain away' female resistance but also writes, inscribes, the difference it erases: it writes '*the pregnancy of the difference* which its wish fulfilment narcissistically erases' (Felman, 1985: 64). Paternal identity, sublating or sublimating a difference it inscribes and erases, is constituted on another level to that of the navel and its resistance.

The pregnancy of difference to which the navel alludes remains productive, even in its resistance to mastery and knowledge: 'the radical unknown of sexuality and difference *fecundates*' both the dream and psychoanalytical theory. By way of the navel psychoanalysis '*makes contact here with something new*, something which it does not know or under-stand or master, but with which it nonetheless somehow communicates' (Felman, 1985: 65). The newness is the horrifying, gaping cavity of female resistance embodied by Irma's symptoms and the unspeakable pain that they announce: a 'painful knot' prefigures the female knot which, though 'recalcitrant to, and in excess of' Freud's mastery, becomes a 'pregnant concept' a 'textual knot' that offers Freud, beyond his knowledge and understanding, 'some *textual access into the unknown*'. The navel's doubleness, as connection and disconnection, articulates and separates body and speech in respect of what Felman's calls the 'differentiality of pain' and the 'unspeakability of difference': it opens a hole in speech, 'an irreducible *bodily gap in language*' (Felman, 1985: 66–7).

Felman's reading emphasises the productive nature of female resistance and the way the navel confronts psychoanalysis with its own limitations and a network it can neither know nor master. It also discloses its own navel, a knot of pain. Her essay concerns Paul de Man as much as

Sex, machines and navels

psychoanalysis. Written after his death, the essay testifies to the influence of a respected teacher, a brilliant reader, a considerate colleague and a friend. De Man's comments on Felman's account of the navel also redirect her interpretation: 'my only question arises, if I dare say, at the level of the navel. What should we do with the manifest bisexuality of that mark, which separates as much as it unites, and which escapes the difference between the genders? The navel is a knot that's cut, and as such, more philosophical than analytical' (Felman, 1985: 68). De Man's reading of the draft essay presents a question which is received by Felman 'at the level of the body: of the body as the blind spot of an existential knot of pain which makes one write only to speak its own unspeakability; the gut level of a knot of pain which knots at once its gift of comprehension and its residue of incomprehensibility' (1985: 68). 'To ask a question at the level of the navel', Felman continues, 'is to ask a question at the level of a certain birth and of a certain scar: the question is posed out of a certain wound, a certain severance, a certain impossibility of asking' (1985: 69). De Man's question discloses a blind spot in her reading of the navel as a female knot and leads Felman to reconsider the 'manifest bisexuality of that mark' as the deconstructive introduction of 'a self-subversive (sexual) difference' into her text, a difference that concerns self-difference, 'a difference from ourselves' (1985: 70). De Man's reading offers an exemplary lesson in reading for Felman, raising questions about her reading and her relationship with de Man, questions, again, lying at the level of the navel. In opening up the question of differences internal to subjectivity and between subjects, it is precisely at the level of the navel that de Man and Felman relate: in their differences a proximity persists. In spite of those differences of theoretical and political position they maintain a relationship of listening and hearing, an ethics of reading in which identity and difference are not opposed or mutually exclusive terms.

There are many resonances in Felman's reading that open on to the other at the level of the navel. A knot has been cut at a non-textual level: the knot of difference and proximity connecting Felman and de Man has been severed by his death, leaving her with an 'existential knot of pain', 'the gut level of a knot of pain'. The navel thus speaks of loss, 'a certain wound', 'a certain severance', 'a certain scar' and a certain death, marking the irreducibility of a bodily gap and the absoluteness of a certain difference. De Man's death reverses the power of his response that touches 'the gut level of a knot of pain which knots at once the gift of comprehension and its residue of incomprehensibility'. Instead, the unavowable gift of incomprehensibility leaves but a residue of comprehension: the knot that's cut is fundamentally a cut that has been knotted, a severance that leaves the subject in knots. A point of comprehension and incomprehensibility, a point of difference in which difference is also missed, a blind spot for Felman and de Man, the navel signifies self-difference and also, as Felman writes and in what her essay does not utter, an other difference. Pain, loss and difference return to the female knot and open the subject on to an otherness that exceeds comprehension: the navel, scar of birth and (dis)connection from a difference that is resolutely female, also testifies to a self-difference, a mortality, to which all bodies are subject.

Symbolically femininity and death are historically conjoined, as Elisabeth Bronfen (1992) has persuasively argued. In her reading of the navel mortality remains entwined with feminine sexuality. Using the Greek *omphalos* to denote the navel as both an anatomical and a mythopoetic figure, Bronfen addresses corporeal and cult objects: the latter, in Apollo's temple at Delphi, is a legacy of the conflict between the male god and the matrilineal order of Gaia. The navel thus tells another story: it is a 'gravestone' marking 'our lost umbilical cord that once connected us to the maternal body of our prehistory'; it serves 'as a pivotal term for a discussion of how mortality is always inscribed in representations' and 'admonishes us to remember that this maternal signature signifies the legacy of our debt to death'. Connected both to death and sexuality and 'the dark interior realms of the feminine body', the navel is also bound up with representation by means of prosopopeia, the trope, according to Felman and de Man, by which the dead are given facial and vocal features and then apostrophised. This exactly characterises Freud's use of the term: anxious about death himself, he apostrophises 'the lost maternal body, by turning the vanishing point into a figure of the unfathomable' (Bronfen, 1994: 83). The 'double navel' mediating between symbolic and real registers occupies the position of the Lacanian *objet petit a*, the point where 'the lack of a signifier' is transformed into 'a signifier of lack', a move from the object *a* to the phallus. Through this 'double gesture' of inscription and erasure mortality and representation are bound together, simultaneously situating the subject of representation in relation to birth and death: 'the navel is an index for the way mortality inscribes birth in marking the singularity of each mortal existence' (Bronfen, 1994: 85).

The readings which examine the significance of Freud's navel also make explicit reference to Lacanian psychoanalysis. None, however, cite either his sporadic mentions of the navel itself or his extended reading of

Sex, machines and navels

Freud's dream of Irma's injection. Published in 1978 in France in the transcription of his Seminar of 1954–55, and ten years later in English translation, Lacan's reading of the Irma dream is sensitive to the questions of birth, death, language and the body. He notes the significance of sexualised resistance and the symptoms that draw the dreamer/analyst into a web which resonates with his own mortality. But the sites of utter anxiety for Freud are examined within a framework that is distinctly Lacanian. Comparing the dream of Irma's injection to the Wolfman's dream, Lacan writes:

> In the two dreams in question, we find ourselves confronted by a sort of ultimate experience, confronted by the apprehension of an ultimate real. What is most anxiety-provoking in Freud's life, his relations with women, his relations with death, are telescoped in the central vision of his dream and could certainly be extracted from it by an associative analysis. Enigmatic image appropos of which Freud evokes the navel of the dream, this abyssal relation to that which is most unknown, which is the hallmark of an exceptional, privileged experience, in which the real is apprehended beyond all mediation, be it imaginary or symbolic. (1988b: 176–7)

The navel, the limit of mediation, the point beyond which imaginary and symbolic registers fail, opens on to the unsymbolisable real, glimpsed only in its unknown, 'abyssal relation' to analysis. As a knot, the navel articulates the three principal registers of Lacanian psychoanalysis.

The triadic structure of the imaginary, symbolic and real finds its counterpart in the ternary configurations identified in Freud's Irma dream and its interpretation. The opposed triangular clusters point in two directions. In one direction, that announced by the feminine resistance centred on Irma, there is mystery, 'a profusion of intercalations … are knotted together and one ends up confronted with some unknown mystery'. The navel condensing the association of three women is described as a 'mystic trio': ultimately it means one thing, death (1988b: 157). Presented most forcefully in Irma's symptoms, mortality is identified with the mouth that gapes with scabs and a whitish membrane:

> This mouth has all the equivalencies in terms of significations, all the condensations you want. Everything blends in and becomes associated in this image, from the mouth to the female sexual organ, by way of the nose – just before or just after this, Freud has his turbinate bones operated on, by Fliess or someone else. There's a horrendous discovery here, that of the flesh one never sees, the foundation of things, the other side of the head, of the face, the secretory glands *par excellence*, the flesh from which everything

exudes, at the very heart of the mystery, the flesh as much as it is suffering, is formless, in as much as its form in itself is something which provokes anxiety. Spectre of anxiety, identification of anxiety, the final revelation of *you are this – You are this, which is so far from you, this which is the ultimate formlessness*. (1988b: 154–7)

The open mouth figurally consumes meaning, masticating significance into the very formlessness which it presents. The image confronts the subject with what is least palatable, the very fleshliness out of which it is constituted, the corporeality of the real that can neither be mastered nor apprehended, an unimaginable and fragmented body alien to the subject of the signifier. Rather than constituting, as a point of recognition and self-apprehension, subjective integrity, the image of the mouth cum female sexual organ confronts the subject with dissolution, fragmentation, decomposition.

At the limit of imaginary apprehension, the formlessness of the real that appears in the knotted symptoms at the back of the female throat also exceeds symbolisation. Lacan returns to the horrifying image condensing sexuality and mortality as he closes his interpretation of the first direction taken in the analysis of the Irma dream:

> The first leads to the apparition of the terrifying anxiety-provoking image, to this real Medusa's head, to the revelation of this something which properly speaking is unnameable, the back of this throat, the complex, unlocatable form, which also makes it into the primitive object *par excellence*, the abyss of the feminine organ from which all life emerges, this gulf of the mouth, in which everything is swallowed up, and no less the image of death in which everything comes to its end, since in relation to the illness of his daughter, which could have been fatal, there's the death of the patient whom he had lost at a time adjacent to that of the illness of his daughter, which he considered to be some mysterious sort of divine retribution for his professional negligence – *this Mathilde for Mathilde*, he writes. Hence there's an anxiety-provoking apparition of an image which summarises what we can call the revelation of that which is least penetrable in the real, of the real lacking any possible mediation, of the ultimate real, of the essential object which isn't an object any longer, but this something faced with which all words cease and all categories fail, the object of anxiety *par excellence*. (1988b: 164)

The point where words cease and categories fail, the real remains unsymbolisable, the absolute limit of language's symbolic register: as apparition and spectre it is ungraspable, ghostly reminder of the fragility of symbolised reality. The horrifying image is linked to the navel as the 'abyssal relation to that which is most unknown', a relation 'in which the real is apprehended beyond all mediation, be it imaginary or symbolic' (1988b: 176–7) The horrifying encounter with the real induces imaginary decomposition.

The image also involves difference on a symbolic level. The association between the knotted throat and female sexuality articulates the unspeakability of otherness. Beyond castration or the imposition of symbolic differences between sexed subjects, the real is bound up with the entry of subjects into language: it remains inseparable from the symbolic precisely as the site of severance, the point of loss, the locus of the cut of differentiation by which subjects are inscribed in language through a separation of body and language. In this respect the navel marks what may be called the primal cut physically separating the bodies of infant and mother and delivering their distinct identities.

A mark of birth, the navel also announces the presence of death, loss and separation, a point distinguishing an existence supported by another from the breath of an autonomous corporeal rhythm. Life and death, crucial to the being of the newly individuated infant, remain, like the real, ultimately beyond the scope of cultural systems. The navel constitutes the first signifier, the point of separation blocking access to an undifferentiated, formless real: the cut of loss is knotted, rendering the topic of life or death incomprehensible to the subject of language: ·

> The symbolic provides a form into which the subject is inserted at the level of his being. It's on the basis of the signifier that the subject recognises himself as being this or that. The chain of signifiers has a fundamental explanatory value, and the very notion of causality is nothing else.
>
> There is nonetheless one thing that evades the symbolic tapestry, it's procreation in its essential root – that one being is born from another. In the symbolic order procreation is covered by the order instituted by this succession between beings. But nothing in the symbolic explains the fact of their individuation, the fact that beings come from other beings. The entire symbolism declares that creatures don't engender creatures, that a creature is unthinkable without a fundamental creation. In the symbolic nothing explains creation … There is in effect something radically unassimilable to the signifier. It's quite simply the subject's singular existence. Why is he here? Where has he come from? What is he doing here? Why is he going to disappear? The signifier is incapable of providing him with the answer, for the good reason that it places him beyond death. The signifier already considers him dead, by nature it immortalises him. (Lacan, 1993: 179–80)

The fundamental difference between the symbolic and the real means that something, some knot or some body, remains 'radically unassimilable to the signifier'. The 'symbolic *tapestry*', acknowledging Freud's intricate meshwork or mycelium, never obliterates the thing that constitutes subjectivity: bodily difference and biological creation are never fully supplanted in a myth of origins or with an original word. For the subject, given a sense of self and meaning in the fabric of the symbolic, that is, brought into being by the signifier and its cut of symbolic identity, the apprehension of both bodily birth and death remains incomprehensible. Ultimately death, one's own death as with one's own birth, cannot be known at a subjective level, remaining outside the grasp of knowledge and symbols. The navel's knot manifests the impenetrability of questions of life and death. But as knot and cut difference reasserts itself in repeated and unanswered questions of being and existence. They falter precisely at the level of the navel, at the subject's 'own' navel: the point of his/her 'own' life/death remains elusive, leaving the subject between origins and ends, a subject of uncertainty. In this way the dream's meaning disturbs the dreamer/analyst: 'it plays with speech, with decisive and adjudicating speech, with the law, with what torments Freud under the form – *Am I right or wrong? Where is the truth? What is the outcome of the problem? Where am I placed?'* (Lacan, 1988b: 156–7).

In Lacan's analysis of Freud's Irma dream the object of anxiety concludes the first line of interpretation, a conclusion in imaginary decom-
, position. Here the omphalic point leaves the subject uncertainly situated between life and death, between origins and ends, unstably positioned between desire and a meaning that is fatally out of reach. But the knot discloses a direction other than the one that concludes with an object of utter anxiety: dissolution is countered by a symbolic solution. In the triad of men and the triadic structure of the formula that provides the solution for Freud and Lacan alike, another knot appears in which the dream images 'belong more and more in the symbolic knot of resemblance, of identity and of difference': it opens on to another level of significance in a move that can be described in Lacanian terms as a shift from the knot of the real to the knot of the imaginary and symbolic, a knot of resistance, an object *a*, that, inverted, establishes the phallus.

For Freud, the ego is defined as the 'sum of the identifications of the subject'. This implies the 'radical contingency of the ego' is 'like the superimposition of various coats borrowed from what I would call the bric-à-brac of its props department' (Lacan, 1988b: 155). Having

Sex, machines and navels

discussed the way that female figures in the dream present an object of anxiety that threatens imaginary integrity, Lacan examines the function of the dream's male figures in terms of the ego identifications and the meaning of the dream. Dr M (associated with Freud's half-brother, Philippe) is identified as the 'ideal character constituted by the paternal pseudo-image, the imaginary father', while Otto and Leopold, respectively, take on the supporting functions of close friend turned enemy and beloved enemy, mirror figures in Freud's battle for symbolic authority. The dream moves from an imaginary series of identifications to symbolic figures and the function of the paternal metaphor:

> In the midst of all his colleagues, of this consensus of the republic of those who know – for if no one is right, every one is right, a law which is simultaneously paradoxical and reassuring – in the midst of this chaos, in this original moment when his doctrine is born into the world, the meaning of the dream is revealed to Freud – that there is no other word of the dream than the very nature of the symbolic. (Lacan, 1988b: 160)

The stress on symbolic functions leads away from biological associations to do with birth, reproduction and death, while continuing to resound with their metaphorical significance. The birth with which the dream is concerned is, metaphorically, that of psychoanalysis itself, its subject rather than an individual being or ego. This birth brings forth the world of language, metaphors and symbols, all anxiously circulated by the question of Freud's symbolic authority.

The question of psychoanalysis proceeds, in the dream, from female resistance, from the bodily differences that the navel announces, and leads to questions of Freud's symbolic status. At stake is his professional position within, and beyond, medicine: the male figures in the dream 'play a ridiculous game of passing the buck with regard to these fundamental questions for Freud – *What is the meaning of the neurosis? What is the meaning of the cure? How well-founded is my therapy for neurosis?*' (Lacan, 1988b: 157). Questions of meaning testify to an uneasy relationship between medicine, which addresses biochemistry, and psychoanalysis which uses speech. The issue, fundamentally, is a symbolic one: the status of psychoanalysis depends on language. And this is why the 'solution' is so important: 'this explains everything, *trimethylamine*' (1988b: 158). The formula is written down in the dream, printed in heavy type. Though signifying the chemical substance which results from the decomposition of sperm, and thus a male function, it is not the biochemistry but the symbolic significance that is most important. Stressing the formula, rather than the substance, Lacan comments 'there is no other word, no other solution to your problem, than the word' (1988b: 158). The chemical solution becomes the solution to the problem precisely, as the wordplay suggests, at the level of signification (Figure 1).

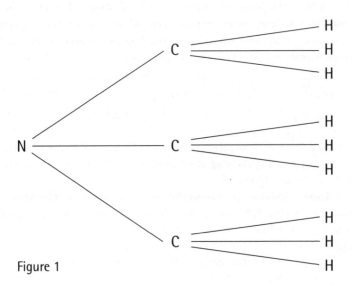

Figure 1

NCH3 is the signifier which provides structure and solution to the dream, displaying the topography of relations going beyond ego and its narcissistic identifications. The chemical formula maps the various ego identifications of the dream to display the subordination of the ego to the signifier. For Lacan, the dream demonstrates

> that analytic symptoms are produced in the flow of the word that tries to get through. It always encounters the double resistance of what we will call just for today, because it is late, the *ego* of the subject and its image. So long as these two interpositions offer a sufficient resistance, they clarify each other, if I may put it like that, within this flow, they are phosphorescent, they flash. (1988b: 159)

The imaginary relation between ego and image is, however, sustained by the symbolic register. The phosphorescence remains fleeting, a flash. In the imaginary, the ego is situated in relation to objects and images, initially,

Sex, machines and navels

the mirror image of body itself: 'whatever in man is loosened up, fragmented, anarchic, establishes its relation to his perceptions on a plane with a completely original tension. The image of the body is the principle of every unity he perceives in objects.' The imaginary subject, in a 'double relation' with itself, only discovers a unity that is elusive, fleeting, unfixed, a position of 'unsatisfied desire' in which 'the diversified images of his ego' serve as 'so many points of anchorage, of stabilisation, of inertia'. These points of imaginary unity remain haunted by 'something originally, inaugurally, profoundly wounded in the human relation to the world' (Lacan, 1988b: 166-7). The relation with one's body-image which founds the subsequent imaginary unity with the object-world is riven with uncertainty since 'objects only ever appear to man within relations which fade. He recognises his unity in them, but uniquely from without. And in as much as he recognises his unity in an object, he feels himself to be in disarray in relation to the latter' (Lacan, 1988b: 169). It leaves the subject as a mirage, wounded, lacking, open to displacement in a search for a final object, that is, a subject of desire.

Desire, however, is an effect of symbolic relations. The subject's relation to image and object calls for the structure provided by the symbolic register:

> The power of naming objects structures the perception itself. The *percipi* of man can only be sustained within a zone of nomination. It is through nomination that man makes objects subsist with a certain consistence. If objects had only a narcissistic relationship with the subject, they would only ever be perceived in a momentary fashion. (Lacan, 1988b: 169)

Signifiers endow subjects and objects with a degree of temporal permanence. As a pact binding subjects in relation to objects, naming constitutes a fundamental symbolic act: 'if the subjects do not come to an agreement over this recognition, no world, not even a perception, could be sustained for more than one instant. That is the joint, the emergence of the dimension of the symbolic in relation to the imaginary' (1988b: 170). The structure of the symbolic gives the consistency and permanence necessary to the ego at the same time as it decentres the ego with the movement of desire and signification.

The multiple points of ego identification are suggested in the chemical formula: different clusters provide the points at which particular egoic centres emerge. In Freud's Irma dream and in the diagram the different identifications occur in relation to three others, grouped in threes: 'these threes which we keep encountering, again and again, that's where, in the dream, the unconscious is – what is outside all of the subjects' (1988b: 159). While the groups of three might sustain different ego identifications, there is, Lacan contends, no one central point dominated by the ego since the unconscious extends as a network, a symbolic fabric that lies beyond any one particular subject. In the dream, as the solution is reached and written, 'another voice is heard', one that is not that of the dreamer's ego. It is the voice of no one, a voice emanating from signification itself, from the letter N of the formula: 'we could give the name *Nemo* to this subject outside the subject who designates the whole structure of the dream'. No one, no one ego or subject, is dominant; instead, the subject of signification and the unconscious appears: 'what is at stake in the function of the dream', Lacan goes on, 'is beyond the *ego*, what in the subject is of the subject and not of the subject, that is the unconscious' (1988b: 159). Beyond the ego identifications in the dream, identifications which take the form of a 'structured crowd', there is an 'inmixing of subjects' which pertains to the unconscious in its symbolic dimension. For Lacan, Freud's Irma dream discloses the importance of discourse, of a speech and a subject which speaks beyond the ego:

> In this dream there's the recognition of the fundamentally acephalic character of the subject, beyond a given point. This point is designated by the n of the trimethylamine formula. That's where the *I* of the subject is at the moment. And my suggestion to you that you see in the dream's last word wasn't said without humour, nor without hesitation, since that is almost a *Witz*. Just when the hydra has lost its heads, a voice which is nothing more than *the voice of no one* causes the trimethylamine formula to emerge, as the last word on the matter, the word for everything. And the word means nothing except that it is a word. (1988b: 170)

The word with no meaning is the primary signifier, the paternal metaphor that brings signification to a close. The voice of no one is the 'discourse of the Other', the unconscious, 'the acephalic subject', the voice 'of a subject who no longer has an *ego*, who doesn't belong to the *ego*. And yet he is the subject who speaks, for that's who gives all the characters in the dream their nonsensical lines – which precisely derive their meaning from their nonsensical character.' As this discourse makes itself heard in the form of a 'great cacophony' of multiple egos, the object of the dream, Irma's objection and Freud's guilt is heard. At this point, too, 'the object is destroyed... and his guilt, which is what is in question, is destroyed with it' (1988b: 167–8). It is not only, Lacan argues, the dream's object which is destroyed:

| Sex, machines and navels

in effacing Freud's guilt by bringing the symbolic to the fore Freud, the dreamer, is eclipsed, substituted by the symbolic function. Doubled in the process of having and interpreting the dream, Freud emerges as a dreamer who worries about his relations with others, his paternal and symbolic authority and his mortality, and someone who allows something else to be heard, a voice that is and is not his own, over which he has no control but which, nonetheless, he lets speak in the course of the dream and its analysis.

The subject of desire which appears in Lacan's analysis of the dream of Irma's injection is and is not Freud. As in the bi-directionality of the dream interpretation which glimpses, beyond the navel, the horrifying spectre of the real and reconstitutes a subject in relation to the imaginary and the symbolic, there are at least two Freuds. On the one hand there's Freud as one of three, a Freud who, despite the horrifying figures of sexuality and death, wants to go beyond the navel, to plunge inside the feminised network of the unconscious. This oedipal Freud is sustained in rivalrous relation to male figures fighting over resisting female bodies, the one who would fill the speechless female mouths with his own meaning, supplanting female resistance with male mastery in the re-enactment of a sexualised binary opposition that assimilates or overcomes difference. Lacan is aware of this one; he is the figure who appears in the first phase of the dream of Irma's injection:

> we see Freud in his chase after Irma, reproaching her for not understanding what he wants her to understand. He was carrying on his relationships in exactly the same style as he did in real life, in the style of the passionate quest, too passionate we would say, and it is indeed one of the meanings of the dream to say that formally, since at the end that is what it comes down to – the syringe was dirty, the passion of the analyst, the ambition to succeed, were here too pressing, the counter-transference was itself the obstacle. (1988b: 164)

Male sexuality and analysis are equated with clinical precision in the dirty syringe. Carnal and analytical knowledge remain one and the same, an effect of a desire that wants to master the resistant object, wants to make her speak in accordance with his desires, a silent automata to be manipulated by the puppeteer. The fulfilment of ambition, as a fantasy, demands possession, conquest.

As the culmination of one reading of the Irma dream, the very male and patriarchal Freud that appears is bound up with the imaginary function. The ego is possessed by the image reflected from its objects, a specular relation dominated by the grand vision of psychoanalysis's birth and haunted by the uncanny, horrifying image of anxiety and dissolution beyond the navel. Analysis involves too much passion on the part of the analyst rather than the analysand. Freud's passion depends on the alien image of femininity and the competing mirrors of the male medical establishment. His identifications lead to dislocation: 'the subject passes beyond this glass in which he always sees, entangled, his own image. All interposition between the subject and the world ceases. One gets the feeling that a passage into a kind of a-logic occurs, and that's where the problem in fact begins, for we see that we are not in it' (Lacan, 1988b: 177). The passion for the unknown, the mystery beyond the unplumbable navel taking the subject beyond disparate ego images and objects, also encounters the horrifying real, the object of anxiety and imaginary decomposition. Beyond the navel, the subject disappears. But at this point Freud moves in another direction, the direction that absolves him of guilt, the direction of the symbolic.

In the second direction there is the Other one, the one who is no longer Freud, the one for whom the object is no longer to decipher the dream fully, but who instead delivers the speech that, in the dream, remains unconscious, acephalic. In what Lacan describes as the 'second phase' of the dream 'the relations of the subject change completely. He becomes something totally different, there's no Freud any longer, there is no longer anyone who can say *I*.' It is the moment, also, in which Freud calls to the Other, the community of his peers, of doctors and analysts (Lacan, 1988b: 164). The call of no one speaks, emanating from the position of N, *nemo* and navel. No longer Freud, nor an ego within the dream nor, even, a particular unconscious wish plucked like a mushroom from a mycelium. What speaks is the notion, the very subject, of the unconscious in its nascent and to-be-recognised state. It is, Lacan observes, 'Freud's speech' – *Freudian discourse* – that emerges in the dream, in the sense that the dream's anxieties concern a dangerous discovery, the discovery of the psychoanalytical unconscious (1988b: 162). The discourse of the Other, in him more than him, appears in the course of the dream and, more importantly, in the work of dream analysis. The dream speaks, and not just to Freud. It makes Freudian discourse heard: 'he is already dreaming for the community of psychologists, of anthropologists. When he interprets this dream, it is us he is addressing.' The dream opens on to the Other, the community of psychologists, by way of analysis. Something in and more

Sex, machines and navels

than Freud addresses the Other, speaks from the position of the Other: 'by means of this dream it's him who speaks, and who realises that he is telling us – without having wanted to, without having recognised it at first, and only recognising it in his analysis of the dream, that is to say while speaking to us – something in him and no longer him' (Lacan, 1988b: 170).

It speaks, the unconscious, from the position of the navel, from the point of the unknown. Lacan ventriloquises:

> *Instead of me, there are all the others. Here I am only the representative of this vast, vague movement,| the quest for truth, in which I efface myself. I am no longer anything. My ambition was greater than I. No doubt the syringe was dirty. And precisely to the extent that I desired it too much, that I partook in this action, that I wanted to be, myself, the creator, I am not the creator. The creator is someone greater than I. It is my unconscious, it is this voice which speaks in me, beyond me.*
>
> That is the meaning of the dream. (1988b: 170–1)

Freud's meaning is plucked from the mycelium of the unconscious to mean the unconscious itself, the discovery that effaces Freud in a vast, vague movement of something else, in him, beyond him. His desire, his wish, is taken through the work of interpretation, beyond individual, egocentric creation, proceeding from the navel and towards the Other. The dream of Irma's injection thus has a double momentum: towards the beyond of language, the dream turns in relation to a real object, an object of unavowable desire that becomes the figure which establishes the possibility of meaning and metaphor. In Freud the navel marks the ambivalent point in the dream's interpretation. In Lacan's account, the navel becomes a double knot. Two navels, two knots and two cuts, of the body and of language, signifying a movement from biology to speech in which a new discourse and a very different subject emerges.

The navel's return

Lacan's double reading of the dream of Irma's injection forms an exemplary case of the return to Freud that he inaugurates. In a lecture entitled 'The Freudian thing, or the meaning of the return to Freud in psychoanalysis' and given in 1955, the same year as the seminar presenting his analysis of Freud's dream, Lacan states how this return involves both meaning and truth:

The meaning of a return to Freud is a return to the meaning of Freud. And the meaning of what Freud said may be conveyed to anyone, because, addressed as it is to all, it concerns each individual: to make this clear, one has only to remember that Freud's discovery puts truth into question, and there is no one who is not personally concerned by the truth. (1977a: 117–18)

Lacan's return seems to call upon a truth of Freud, Freud the author, the one invested quite literally as speaker of truth and possessor of an inherent, transparent meaning: the father of psychoanalysis serves as the closure, the origin and termination of his meaning. But Lacan's rather elliptical statement refuses to equate meaning and truth: Freud's discovery 'puts truth in question'. Truth, the point where questions end and meaning is finalised, remains at stake in Lacan's invocation of Freud's meaning.

Truth lies in the Other, exhausting, as Freud's discovery of the unconscious displays, the possibility of its singular possession. Lacan's analysis of Freud's specimen dream emphasises how the Other, the unconscious, remains both in and beyond the dreamer whose anxieties are addressed to the community of doctors and psychologists. For Lacan, Freud's address constitutes a dream for all and an address to what will become the institution of psychoanalysis: it reiterates Freud's concern with the meaning and institution of his discovery. The meaning of psycho-analysis concerns its institution, as both the creation attributed to Freud's genius and the perpetuation of psychoanalytical practice after his death. Throughout his career Lacan remained concerned with the institution of psychoanalysis in both senses: the meaning of Freud remains tied up with the institutional practice of his discovery, a practice that Lacan vigorously and variously contested (Roudinesco, 1990). Indeed, Lacan's challenge to the institution of psychoanalysis, a challenge posed in his declaration of the return to Freud's meaning, impeaches the authority of traditional psychoanalysis in the name of its founder, an appeal to Freud's meaning that puts its institutionalised truth in question. The return to Freud takes the form of a provocative act of interrogation, a return in which the institutional authority invested in the meaning and the name of Freud is turned against itself, played against the very institution that sacralises Freud's name. Little wonder, then, that Lacan's challenging return was construed as an 'excommunication' (1977b: 1–13).

Lacan's return, moreover, causes an ex-communication different from the expulsion beyond the pale of the sacred word. His reading of Freud receives a message outside direct communication, hearing a speech, an address both in and beyond Freud, a discourse no longer simply that of

Sex, machines and navels

Freud's unconscious but of the unconscious, a discourse that emerges in the two phases of the specimen dream. Its emergence turns on the shift made possible by the navel as it announces a limit to interpretation: an impossible tracery of origins and endings is converted into a conceptual figure for the unassimilable object of interpretation. For Felman, discussing the return in terms of its 'originality of repetition' and the 'irreducibly uncanny question' it poses, 'what returns in the Lacanian "return" is precisely what is unassimilable in Freud, the return to Freud is not unlike the return of the repressed ...' (Felman, 1987: 53–4). The hesitation which equates Lacan's return with Freud's repressed is queried in Jane Gallop's elaboration of a transitive return to Freud that draws on the analytical situation itself, a giving back of something by the analyst to the subject:

> Not a return to Freud's presence but a return by Lacan to Freud's text of what Freud was saying that never got recognized. If, as Felman, suggests, Lacan's return is a return of the repressed, but a return of the repressed in a psychoanalytic context where the repressed can be recognized and returned by the interlocutor to the subject for whom it was inaccessible, then it would be a truly psychoanalytical return to Freud. Lacan, by hearing the thing that spoke in Freud, by hearing the Freudian Thing, could recognize it and return it to Freud's text.
>
> Only then, once the Freudian Thing were recognized, could Father Freud really be laid to rest. Only then could Father Freud, having found his own path, die. (Gallop, 1985: 109–10)

Gallop's reading of Lacan's return highlights the death drive in contrast to the return of the repressed and its imaginary preservation of a living father that sustains an egoic rivalry over the meaning of Freud. Gallop, arguing that Lacan's criticisms of ego psychology in 'The Freudian thing' repeat ego psychology, nonetheless finds in Lacan's text a different paternal relation: she invokes the dead father of Freud's *Totem and Taboo*, the father, killed by the sons so his women might be enjoyed and who returns powerfully in their guilt and the renunciation of satisfaction that establishes a social pact based on symbolic law. Death allows desire to find its own trajectory and, in the case of the return to Freud, allows the father to die so that the paternal function can live on symbolically as a discourse. Freud's imaginary presence gives way to his text.

The shift Gallop proposes in her reading of the return follows the pattern established in the analysis of Freud's dream of Irma's injection where Lacan's account turns from the imaginary direction of the dream, centred on the ego and its identifications and dissolution, to the symbolic formation of the unconscious. After declaring the unconscious to be the meaning of the Irma dream, Lacan concludes with a consideration of the death drive. In *Beyond the Pleasure Principle*, the pleasure principle 'governs the measure of the ego and installs consciousness in its relation with a world in which it finds itself'. Beyond this homeostatic, self-preserving mechanism, the death drive manifests itself in the compulsion to repeat: 'if the ego as such rediscovers and recognises itself, it is because there is a beyond to the *ego*, an unconscious, a subject which speaks, unknown to the subject' (Lacan, 1988b: 171). This subject, in and beyond egoic identification, is the Freudian Thing speaking in Freud's text to be recognised and returned by Lacan. In the analysis of the dream of Irma's injection, this Thing is the navel, the point of inaccessible meaning, figure of birth and death, locus of metaphor and interpretation. The scar, the remainder beyond which analysis cannot proceed even as it wants to, the point of imaginary decomposition and narcissistic wound, is also the knot from which meaning is differentiated from the entangled, unconscious matrix. This Thing, the navel, has a double momentum, introducing two births, two deaths, two Freuds: it is encountered at the juncture of imaginary and symbolic registers to divide analysis between two subjects and two objects, the 'game for four players' that Lacan comments on in 'The Freudian thing' and schematises elsewhere as the relation between ego and other, Subject and Other (1977a: 139, 193).

Beyond the pleasure principle, in excess of the ego, desire is articulated in relation to the death drive and the Other, in the gap between the subject and the Other as locus of signifiers structured in an associative, metonymic chain. Lacan discusses desire and interpretation in terms of 'the two extremes of analytical experience'. At the synchronic extreme the primal repressed takes the form of a signifier on which symptoms are structured as 'a scaffolding'. At the other, diachronic, extreme metonymy moves desire in a direction identical to interpretation (1977b: 176). Like the navel, motivating and inhibiting dream interpretation, desire is articulated metonymically in relation to a blockage which redirects it towards the Other whose desire 'is apprehended by the subject in that which does not work, in the lacks of the discourse of the Other ...' (1977b: 214). In between these extremes, Lacan notes, 'there is sexuality' (1977b: 276). Through a 'nodal point' the unconscious is linked to sexual reality:

> This nodal point is called desire, and the theoretical elaboration that I have pursued in recent years will show you, through each stage of clinical experience, how desire is situated in dependence on demand – which, by

being articulated in signifiers, leaves a metonymic remainder that runs under it, an element that is not indeterminate, which is a condition both absolute and unapprehensible, an element necessarily lacking, unsatisfied, impossible, misconstrued (*méconnu*), an element that is called desire. (Lacan, 1977b: 154)

Desire is articulated at the juncture of the unknown and the institution of metaphor. Its lack drives an unsatisfiable demand for wholeness, a fullness of being thwarted by the movements of signification around a hole of unplumbable depth. In the hollow demanding full interpretation, the gap appearing between the wish to fully understand the dream and the unconscious wish to be recognised by the symbolic community, desire lies in excess of the demand, at the precise point, the nodal point, designated by the navel.

Meaning forms the excessive object of Lacan's return, the inapprehensible remainder: the meaning of Freud's thing, the unconscious, orientates desire in interpretation. Indeed, interpretation occurs, not when meaning is recognisable, obvious or apparently self-evident (that is, when it can be easily and pleasurably assimilated in an already-existing structure) but when its object remains difficult to make sense of, hard to perceive, when it is unassimilable, unapprehensible, lacking. Lacan's return thus glimpses what in Freud is seen and not seen. Interpretation cannot be simply equated with perception: the nodal point of desire and interpretation is situated on an axis of (not)seeing, non-sense, (mis)recognition. The navel around which Freud's interpretation and desire turns eludes capture, an object marking the place of something else, an Other desire and forming a stain that arrests movement and calls for understanding. Lacan describes this function as the gaze, 'not a seen gaze, but a gaze imagined by me in the field of the Other' (1977b: 84). The empty place, the screen for the desire of the Other, remains outside perception itself. It is associated with the object *a*, an object, Lacan notes, 'which, in the final resort, can serve no function' (1977b: 242). External to the parameters of usefulness and perception, it remains a 'privileged object'. Both eccentric and at the core, a blind spot of perception, *a* is an extimate point (Miller, 1988). In interpretation it functions like the navel: anatomically superfluous and, at the same time, a point central to the meaning of the dream. The object *a* takes the form of a navel: 'it is a question of this privileged object, discovered by analysis, of that object whose very reality is purely topological, of that object around which the drive moves, of that object that rises in a bump, like the wooden darning egg in the material which in analysis, you are darning – the *objet a'* (Lacan, 1977b: 257). As the navel, in Freud, assumes the shape of a mushroom that arises in the unconscious network, so the darning egg, a topological object, emerges in the gap around which analysis reties the threads, the tapestry of the symbolic.

The figure of the navel appears again when Lacan discusses the function of the object *a* in the primary analytic activity of transference. Again, it suggests the point around which the symbolic network is woven, the gap between ego-ideal and lack:

> The *petit a* never crosses this gap. Recollect what we learned about the gaze, the most characteristic term for apprehending the proper function of the *objet a*. This *a* is presented precisely, in the field of the mirage of the narcissistic function of desire, as the object that cannot be swallowed, as it were, which remains stuck in the gullet of the signifier. It is at this point of lack that the subject has to recognize himself. (1977b: 270)

At the limit of the imaginary register, redirecting desire from the ego to the symbolic Other, the object *a* fills the gap that divides the real from the subject of signification. 'Stuck in the gullet of the signifier', at a point resisting egoic speech, the object is associated with Irma's recalcitrant symptoms in Freud's dream. Lacan's allusion to Irma's symptoms, moreover, also replicates Freud's hesitant introduction of the term, 'a navel, as it were …'. Lacan reads Freud from the position of the navel, from the position structured by the object that does not work, from a point of absence, a lack in perception and understanding calling forth signification and interpretation. Lacan looks at Freud, not to identify an imaginary version of the latter's meaning, but symbolically, from the position of the relation between *a* and Other, the position of the analyst: 'the transference is the means by which the communication of the unconscious is interrupted, by which the unconscious closes up again.' The function of transference in its relation to the closing and opening of the unconscious depends on the identification of a 'knot' (1977b: 130–31). This knot forms the kernel of interpretation's attempt to bring out 'an irreducible signifier', allowing the subject to see 'to what irreducible, traumatic, non-meaning – he is, as a subject, subjected' (1977b: 250–1). The kernel, for Lacan, it seems, is Freud's navel itself.

Knots and gaps, buttons and holes, Freud's navel and its meshwork reappear, explicitly and tacitly, throughout the Lacanian system. The major registers (imaginary, real and symbolic) dominating Lacanian psychoanalysis are interlinked, their juncture taking the form of a Borromean knot. The graph that links the demand of the subject to the desire of the Other – the graph of desire – appears in the shape of two bumps, traversed by the threads of speech and signification. The point around which these theoretical registers are articulated is the object *a*: filling the hole in the real, it establishes the point around which signification and desire are woven (the symbolic) and the kernel which positions the individual being in relation to the image of his/her identity (the imaginary). The object *a* ties the crucial knot, manifesting itself as the decisive theoretical elaboration of the navel, its function borne out by the insistence of the navel in Lacan's texts. The entire Lacanian system turns on the point linking and separating registers. Beyond and in between the system of knots, 'structured like a language', there lies a locus that remains outside symbolisation, unrepresent-able. The lack, the gap testifying to that realm which cannot be represented is, nonetheless, filled by an object that points to the unplumbable unknown:

> For what the unconscious does is shows us the gap through which neurosis recreates a harmony with a real that may well not be determined.
>
> In this gap, something happens. Once this gap has been filled, is the neurosis cured? After all, the question remains open. But the neurosis becomes something else, sometimes a mere illness, a *scar*, as Freud said – the scar not of the neurosis, but of the unconscious ... Observe the point from which he sets out – *The Aetiology of the Neuroses* – and what does he find in the hole, in the split, in the gap so characteristic of cause. Something of the order of the *non-realized*. (1977b: 22)

This gap, this scar of the unconscious, Lacan makes explicit, is the navel:

> It is not without effect that, even in a public speech, one directs one's attention at subjects, touching them at the what Freud calls the navel – *the navel of dreams*, he writes, to designate their ultimately unknown centre – which is simply, like the same anatomical navel that represents it, that gap of which I have already spoken. (1977b: 23)

A trace of the neurotic symptom produced by the Other, the navel's scar thus becomes a signifier, a point from which analytical meaning is organised. For Lacan, symptoms are signifiers of the Other, unconscious speech that analysis attempts to cure: 'the symptom is here the signifier of a signified repressed from the consciousness of the subject' (1977a: 69). But the navel is also a 'non-realized' object emerging in the gap as a remainder or leftover of the real. It is 'of the order of the non-realized' precisely because the real cannot be realised, its very definition being its inassimilability to the reality that, for Lacan, is always structured by the signifier as symbolic reality

(1977b: 55). In and in excess of the field of language, the navel functions as a point of (dis)connection between the symbolic and the real.

Discussing the unconscious as lack, split and rupture, Lacan again alludes to Freud's inaugural dream:

> in an interjection, in an imperative, in an invocation, even in a hesitation, it is always the unconscious that presents you with its enigma, and speaks – in short, at the level at which everything blossoms in the unconscious, spreads like a mycelium, as Freud says about the dream, around a central point. It is always a question of the subject *qua* indeterminate. (1977b: 26)

The unconscious speaks from the navel. Returning again to Freud's navel, Lacan performs the very relation that the navel establishes. Indeed, as the central point at which everything blossoms and spreads like a mycelium, the navel displays its centrality in Lacanian thinking, that knot, which, in respect of the unconscious network, constitutes a veritable 'knot of being': 'the unconscious, this knot of our being – the word "knot", rather than the word "being" is the one that matters – the being of this knot which is driven by the unconscious alone' (1982: 171n.). The navel, however, is never simply a juncture between registers, a knot between being and language. It is also a scar, wound or a cut that has been knotted. The point at which something has been severed, it functions as a signifying lack and calls up the phenomenon of castration, a matter, for Lacan, of cutting and knotting: 'the unconscious castration complex has the function of a knot' (1977a: 28). The navel is the residue of an inaugural act of cutting and knotting, a cut that, like the object *a*, comes 'from some primal separation, from some self-mutilation induced by the very approach of the real' (1977b: 83). Castration describes the process of separation through which individuals become subjects of language. Again the object *a* is central 'in so far as the gaze, *qua objet a*, may come to symbolize this central lack expressed in the phenomenon of castration' (1977b: 77). A symbol of lack, of incompletion, of the loss of real being, the objet *a* is situated in relation to the primary signifier, the phallus, in that it constitutes the point where the real being becomes a subject subordinated to the signifier's 'passion' appearing in the speech of the unconscious so 'that his nature is woven by effects in which is to be found the structure of language' (1977a: 284). Metaphors of a network emerge, woven into Lacan's discussions of the subject and language. Within the web of signification, the subject's relation to language and the world is reformulated: no longer the centre of a world of ideas, no longer the originating ego, but a subject of the signifier (1977b: 206).

Sex, machines and navels

In its earlier incarnation, the in-visible object which occupies the lack in being and establishes the condition for the subject of language is called *das Ding*. In *The Ethics of Psychoanalysis*, the Thing prefigures many of the operations later ascribed to the *objet petit a*. Describing the Thing as a numinous phenomenon outside normal, rational perception and at the limit of moral frameworks, Lacan relates it to the *numen* of pagan religions: 'the *numen* rises up at every step ... it weaves human experience together, and we can still see the traces of it in a great many fields' (1992: 172). Topographically, the Thing becomes the crucial knot connecting and distinguishing the three registers by which subjective and social development are knotted together: 'it is around *das Ding* that the whole adaptive development revolves, a development that is so specific to man insofar as the symbolic process reveals itself to be inextricably woven into it' (1992: 57). *Das Ding*, Lacan translates, is both thing and cause, cause of law and the point that enables the assembly of the symbolic (1992: 43). But, Lacan argues, the Thing is not of the order of experience or symbolised reality: 'the Thing only presents itself to the extent that it becomes word' (1992: 55). It exists at the point of (non)relation between the real and the symbolic register, the gap and knot that establishes their connection and separation.

The Thing, like *a*, functions as a screen in two senses: it veils the real and provides a place for the projection that establishes signification. It can thus be thought of as the gap that appears in the intervals of the signifying network: 'this field onto which is projected something beyond, something at the point of origin of the signifying chain, this place in which doubt is cast on all that is the place of being ...' (1992: 214). What lies beyond and at the centre of signification, however, is a hole: 'the question of *das Ding* is still attached to whatever is open, lacking, or gaping at the center of our desire.' A 'vacuole', the Thing occupies a strange centrality:

> Simply by writing it on the board and putting *das Ding* at the center, with the subjective world of the unconscious organized in a series of signifying relations around it, you can see the difficulty of topographical representation. The reason is that *das Ding* is at the center only in the sense that it is excluded. That is to say, in reality *das Ding* has to be posited as exterior, as the prehistoric Other that it is impossible to forget – the Other whose primacy of position Freud affirms in the form of something *entfremdet*, something strange to me, although it is at the heart of me, something that on the level of the unconscious only a representation can represent. (1992: 71)

Central and excluded, the Thing possesses the extimacy of the object *a*: it is both inside and outside, in and more than the subject, strange and uncanny.

Situated between the real and the symbolic, the Thing also functions in accordance with another key Lacanian register, the imaginary (1992: 99). Before taking its bearings in language, the subject must (mis)recognise him/herself as a unified being. The imaginary serves as the register through which the real being, as fragmented body, anticipates its psychological and motor co-ordination by identifying with the unity presented by its mirror image. This identification in which identity returns from the place and in the shape of an other, that is, the image in the mirror, establishes the condition for its subjection to the Other. The 'mirror stage' is understood '*as an identification*':

> This jubilant assumption of his specular image by the child, still sunk in his motor incapacity and nurseling dependence, would seem to exhibit in an exemplary situation the symbolic matrix in which the *I* is precipitated in primordial form, before it is objectified in the dialectic of identification with the other, and before language restores it, in the universal, its function as subject. (Lacan, 1977a: 2)

Through an identification with the image, an identification that is itself an anticipation and misrecognition of unity, the subject can take its place in the 'symbolic matrix', assuming the identity associated with being able to say 'I'. The jubilant specular assumption of the image, however, only provides a sense of completeness or wholeness through misrecognition: the gap remains between other and ego, between the image of the body and the I that sees 'itself'.

A process of knotting the fragmented body, identification also involves a separation, a splitting of the subject. The 'jubilation' attendant on specular identification retains only a portion of the *jouissance* associated with the real body: the imaginary masks the loss of being's plenitude with an image. *Jouissance*, moreover, is barred with the precipitation of the signifier: specular jubilation translates the fullness of intense bodily pleasure into the pleasure principle organised by metaphor. *Jouis-sens* signifies 'enjoy-meant'. The move from specular, imaginary identity to the 'I' located in the symbolic matrix turns on a knot of identification, recognition and meaning associated with metaphor. The gap around which identity is constituted requires the recognition of a signifier as well as an image: 'the signification of the phallus, I have said, must be evoked in the subject's imaginary by the

Sex, machines and navels

paternal metaphor' (1977a: 199). The phallus, the primary signifier, must be recognised and internalised by the subject, for it is only in the structures of language, in the co-ordinates established by naming and differentiation, that the subject can recognise him/herself as a person who says 'I'. The intensity of fullness, *joussance*, is thus prohibited, barred from the subject of the signifier's law:

> It is the only indication of that *jouissance* of its infintiude that brings with it the mark of its prohibition, and, in order to constitute that mark, involves a sacrifice: that which is made in one and the same act with the choice of symbol, the phallus.
>
> This choice is allowed because the phallus, that is, the image of the penis, is negativity in its place in the specular image. It is what predestines the phallus to embody *jouissance* in the dialectic of desire. (1977a: 319)

The separation of the real and the introduction of the signifier are identical in the constitution of subjectivity, cutting and knotting forming parts of the same act of sacrifice and identification in which the fullness of *jouissance* shifts from the real to the symbolic, from maternal otherness to desire that finds its orientation in the Other of signification. Separated by the sacrificial cut of the umbilical cord from a *jouissance* represented by the fullness of a maternal body, the subject remains wounded, scarred at the navel. From this knot of separation meaningful identity emerges. For Freud, too, the metaphor of the navel signifies a completeness of interpretation so full that it must be prohibited in order that analysis and the dream may mean anything at all: it is a point at which *jouissance* is embodied and rendered metaphorical in an act of separation (the plucking of mushroom from mycelium) thereby prohibiting an albeit impossible entry into a matrix beyond signification and sense.

At this point metaphor assumes its central function. Where the mirror stage works through identification, meaning depends on both identification and metaphor: 'the dimension of metaphor must be less difficult for us to enter than for anyone else, provided that we recognize that what we usually call it is identification' (Lacan, 1993: 218). Identification does not lead to the recognition of meaning as content, but indicates a structural relationship: the subject is located within a matrix governed by the topological role of metaphor, 'sustained by its positional articulation' (1993: 226). Lacan's reformulation of the Saussurean sign provides a crucial turn in the theory of meaning: rejecting the idea that signifier and signified are inextricably linked in the sign, like the two sides of a sheet of paper, he argues that they form distinct planes. Equating Freud's notions of condensation and displacement from the *Interpretation of Dreams*, with Roman Jakobson's distinction between metaphor and metonymy, Lacan establishes the difference between signifier and signified: metonymy, or displacement, is found on 'one side of the effective field constituted by the signifier', while the other side is linked to metaphor or condensation (1977a: 156). The signifier operates associatively, displaced along a chain of signifiers into which the signified emerges to arrest the flow: '... it is in the chain of the signifier that the meaning "insists" but none of its elements "consists" in the signification ...' (1977a: 153). As a result, meanings change, an effect of the 'sliding of the signified under the signifier' in which the latter predominates. Ultimately, there is nothing distinguishing the two principal components of language except 'a condition imposed upon the signifying material' by the means of representation (1977a: 160). Their different functioning is an effect of topological, structural relations rather than the expression of a certain positive semantic content.

Metaphor, the point of condensation that serves to arrest the signifying chain and allow the subject to identify meaning, operates in an imaginary fashion. In Freud's first dream the metaphor of the navel signifies the knotting of dream-thoughts, the condensation designated as the dream-wish: it is the point of meaning and has a metaphorical function. Where, metonymically, the navel could trail off in a tangle of unconscious associations, the point of condensation metaphorically arrests displacement, allowing meaning to appear. The metaphor of the navel displays, in Lacanian terms, the function of metaphor itself. It establishes the point of knotting between signifier and object *a*. To describe the relationship Lacan again invokes the figure introduced in Freud's dream analysis: 'this point around which all concrete analysis of discourse must operate I shall call a quilting point' (1993: 156). The quilting point [*point de capiton*] or upholstery button is Lacan's metaphor for metaphor. It is, he argues, 'essential in human experience', a 'minimal schema' which, in respect of the Oedipus complex, appears insistently in Freud, 'a knot that seems so essential to him that he is unable to abandon it in the slightest particular observation' (1993: 268). The same can be said of the insistence of the omphalic figure of the upholstery button in Lacan: 'everything radiates out from and is organized around this signifier, similar to these little lines of force that an upholstery button forms on the surface of material. It's the point of convergence that enables everything that happens in this discourse to be situated retroactively and prospectively' (1993: 268). In

Sex, machines and navels

the form of metaphor, one signifier arrests the metonymic movement of signifiers, allowing meaning to appear. The upholstery button stands in for another button that condenses a tangled meshwork of unconscious associations: the belly button. Beneath the metaphor for metaphor (the quilting point) lies the metaphor of the navel.

In an account of the way that the quilting point articulates two planes, Lacan again invokes the navel. The scansion of a sentence works at the level of the signifier and metonymy. The plane of the signified, in contrast, presents sense 'as something which flees'

> but by which at the same time presents itself as an extremely full sense, the fleeing of which draws the subject in towards what would be the core of the delusional phenomenon, its navel. You know that Freud uses this term *navel* to designate the point at which the sense of the dream appears to culminate in a hole, a knot, beyond which it is to the core of being that the dream appears to be attached. (1993: 259)

The navel lies at the point where meaning both threatens to evaporate, to unravel beyond the knot that covers a hole, and emerges, particularly condensed, in the fullness of sense. Beyond the knot, in the locus marked by a hole, there is the real, the core of being. Unsymbolisable, unassimilable, impenetrable to sense and signification, the real lies beyond meaning.

The core of being, designated by the navel, is thus simultaneously delusional, a site where the fullness of meaning explodes into meaninglessness, and the hole over which the knot of metaphor is established: 'metaphor occurs at the precise point at which sense emerges from nonsense' (1977a: 158). This is why jokes have navels: 'in the dream, there is an extremely confused navel. Inversely, the navel of the joke is perfectly sharp – the *Witz*. And what expresses its most radical essence is non-sense' (1988a: 280). At this point, too, subjectivity and meaning are knotted together in the manner outlined in Lacan's analysis of the trimethylamin formula. Meaning, an effect of the recognition of metaphorical quilting, constitutes a moment of arrest comparable to the way that the imaginary ego is produced in moments of identificatory inertia. Like meaning, which flees, the imaginary ego is a temporary and fleeting phenomenon. A crucial metaphor, however, remains, the navel articulating the subject in relation to a gap and the unconscious. Hence, in analytical interpretation, the task is to 'isolate in the subject a kernel ... of *non-sense*':

> Interpretation is a signification that is not just any signification. It comes here in the place of the *s* and reverses the relation by which the signifier has

the effect, in language, of the signified. It has the effect of bringing out an irreducible signifier. One must interpret at the level of the *s*, which is not open to all meanings, which cannot be just anything, which is a signification, though no doubt only an approximate one. What is there is rich and complex, when it is a question of the unconscious of the subject, and intended to bring out irreducible, *non-sensical* – composed of non-meanings – signifying elements (1977b: 250)

This irreducible, non-sensical point at which the signifier produces the effect of meaning is the subject's navel: beyond it subjectivity unravels in a hole; at its knot the subject is situated in the symbolic matrix.

The navel is not a final and fixed point in the sense that severs the subject from the real and institutes the dominance of metaphor. It remains a knot of connection which has effects on signification as a topographical system. Language is polyphonic: 'all discourse is aligned along the several staves of a score', and thus, for Lacan, 'there is in effect no signifying chain that does not have, as if attached to the punctuation of each of its units, a whole articulation of relevant contexts suspended "vertically", as it were, from that point' (1977a: 154). Metaphor, a crucial point of articulation, is not, as Lacan makes clear, simply a matter of the substitution of one signifier for another or 'the term by term correspondence of a symbol with something': 'on the contrary, in a given dream, the whole of the dream-thoughts, that is to say the whole of those things signified, the meanings of the dream, is taken as a network, and is represented, not at all term by term, but through a set of interlacings' (1988a: 266). While metaphor, in specific instances, serves as the temporary quilting allowing meaning to emerge, it does so only as an element of an immense network, a tracery of differences and relations in which subjects are positioned at particular points of interconnection. An excess remains, however: metaphor is established in the gap, the site of loss and lack, which leaves something of the subject inassimilable to signification.

Metaphor never exists in isolation even though, in respect of particular subjects, it identifies something in them and more than them, a kernel of being and a site of loss. As an object *a*, this site has a bearing on the entirety of the subject's symbolic life while remaining irreducible, inexplicable, irrational, alien to any sense imposed from without. Metaphor, then, does not simply describe the imposition of a system on a resistant body but sketches the manner in which, through identification and internalisation, bodies become speaking subjects. A metaphor, paternal or otherwise, must be recognised for it to mean, that is, to have effects. But

Sex, machines and navels

due to the gap and the nature of the topographical system these effects are neither singular nor stable. To describe the navel, as Lacan does, as a 'delusional phenomenon' alludes to the mobility produced by the sliding of signification: in psychosis a delusional metaphor supplants the paternal one in an act of repudiation or foreclosure in which any metaphor assumes its organising force. All signifiers, detached from the system that frames sense and arrests meaning, can ultimately have this effect, suggesting that the paternal metaphor is neither absolute nor universal in itself. What makes a paternal metaphor the signifier of law is precisely the modes of identification that recognise it, the locus of convention and community that, in practice, internalise, abide by and enforce its rules.

Without the identification of subjects, the paternal metaphor ceases to function. And it is as a function, a structure and not a substance, that it operates. Here, of course, lies the gap which prevents its institution being absolute. There is never just the father, it seems, secure in his knowledge or enjoyment; no ultimate authority lies outside the Other. The truth of the law operates in relation to imposture:

> Let us set out from the conception of the Other as the locus of the signifier. Any statement of authority has no other guarantee than its very enunciation, and it is pointless for it to seek it in another signifier, which could not appear outside this locus in any way. Which is what I mean when I say that no metalanguage can be spoken, or, more aphoristically, that there is no Other of the Other. And when the Legislator (he who claims to lay down the Law) presents himself to fill the gap, he does so as an impostor.
>
> But there is nothing false about the Law itself, or about him who assumes its authority.
>
> The fact that the Father may be regarded as the original representative of this authority of the Law requires us to specify by what privileged mode of his presence he is sustained beyond the subject who is actually led to occupy the place of the Other, namely, the Mother. The question, therefore, is pushed still further back. (Lacan, 1977a: 310–11)

The gap, all that remains of the place of the mother, impeaches all claims to authority, leaving no solid foundations or external guarantees, no outside-text or determinable origins, no paternal figure without a maternal matrix. The locus of non-return, the place of the (m)Other is a gap to be filled, though never fully, with the institution of law. As a gap, however, it introduces a fundamental otherness into signification, a navel marking the otherness of sex and body, a signifier of self-difference within signification itself. A knot or scar in place of a real connection, the navel emerges as a metaphor prior to the inaugural 'Name-of-the-Father', a juncture between a maternal matrix to which there can be no return except in fantasy and a symbolic matrix which assumes the place of the Other.

The navel, in various ways, offers a better model for the work of metaphor in Lacan than the name at the apex of law and not only, as Bal (1991) suggests, in the mode of a non-phallic figure for disseminative movement. Fulfilling the same function as the paternal metaphor, the omphalic figure retains an ambivalence which discloses the excess of the phallus, the otherness or negativity inherent in it and the pregnancy of difference which cannot, finally, be mastered. The doubleness of the navel manifests a strange performance of the mysterious relation between sexed body and symbolic language and causes an ambivalent twist in the positioning of father and mother. As the point of their interimplication, the navel confounds their separation and forestalls the exclusion of one or other. In a discussion of the metaphorical 'sub-text' to the working of metonymy and desire in Lacan's *Television*, Malcolm Bowie identifies the unnamed signifier as that of 'father' and offers a thoroughly gendered account of metonymy:

> There is a male pregnancy fantasy here somewhere: metonymy is a process of continual parturition for which fathers, not mothers, and fathers to the exclusion of mothers have sole responsibility. Within the phonemic substance of this passage, certainly, the divisive legacies of the father – the first destructive *Autre* – are everywhere re-enacted. (Bowie, 1993: 44)

Opening on to the unconscious by way of a strange paternal and yet pregnant metaphor, the navel, in contrast, gives birth to a fruitful metaphoricity, to figures, relationships and associations blossoming out in an entangled network. The navel's return describes a return with a difference and a locus of no return, a figure which only traces a place to which one cannot return. Governed as it is by a strange metaphor, the significant displacement of figures retain a doubleness, an identity and difference in which connection and disconnection are bound up with metaphor itself. Pointing to an origin which can never be assimilated, to a link that is also a cut, the navel's ambivalence shadows the movement between (textual) bodies and (signifying) subjects. Sexuality, too, is scarred by this ambivalence for, as the trace of an Other and the internal knot of self-difference, the navel remains on and beyond bodies. As a knotted cut, the navel is never fully differentiated, nor completely the same, leaving sex marked by something ambivalently signifying and in excess of signification.

Sex, machines and navels

The navel's metaphorical ambivalence makes it Lacan's metaphor *par excellence*, the metaphor of metaphor, the unavowed and immanent metaknot in the system of the topographer of the unconscious. The navel's return opens up Lacan's texts rather than closing them with the institution of a transcendent paternal metaphor. Returning insistently throughout his writings, the navel, in the manner that Freud's navel metaphor is employed and extended by Lacan, appears to be Lacan's irreducible signifier, the kernel around which his system unravels and the metaphor of his special relation to Freud. Lacan's navel. The name of the father cedes, strangely, to the metaphor of the navel marking the connection and disconnection between Lacan's reading and Freud's corpus, the juncture of Lacan and the Freudian matrix. And 'Freud', his texts and discourse, for Lacan, signifies a matrix:

> One never goes beyond Descartes, Kant, Marx, Hegel and a few others because they mark a line of inquiry, a true orientation. One never goes beyond Freud either. Nor does one attempt to measure his contributions quantitatively, draw up a balance sheet – what's the point of that? One uses him. One moves around within him. One takes one's bearings from the direction he points in (1992: 206)

A locus of movement and a limit one never passes beyond, Freudian discourse is presented as a matrix of possibility to which Lacan is joined and from which he is distinguished, as it were, at the level of the navel. Used, elaborated, unravelled and reiterated, the navel which returns in Lacan's texts is also the crucial knot articulating his position within an Other matrix identifying psychoanalysis as a predominantly nodal theory.

Note

1 Appignanesi and Forrester (1993: 117–45) discuss the theme of exculpation in respect of the identities of the women featured in the dream.

3 ✧ Jokes and their relation to postmodernism

The joke that is not one

'When is a joke not a joke?'
'I don't know. When is a joke not a joke?'
'When it hasn't got a punchline.'

No self-respecting comedian would tell such a joke; no self-respecting audience would laugh at it. Only the most hardened of formalists might brave a smile, a token of enjoyment and recognition at the crude defamiliarisation of technique entailed in a joke about joke form. While formally perfect, the joke fails: it has no effects; it produces no laughter and folds silently back on itself. The lack of laughter signals the absence of an identifiable Other or 'locus of signifying convention' articulating joke teller and audience, or an object over and against which they can bond (Lacan, 1997a: 173). The socially unsanctionable anxiety or hostility that underlies joke-telling is not released in a burst of expenditure which simultaneously unites speaker and addressee in a mutual antipathy towards the butt of the joke. In the joke that turns on itself, the subject of the joke becomes its butt. In the failed joke, the subject's misapprehension of his/her position is marked by the non-recognition of the addressee, the absence of laughter announcing the distance between teller and receiver. Where the successful joke binds imaginary beings in a symbolic economy sustained in relation to the excluded object, the failed joke exposes gaps and differences: one might say, after Lacan, that there is no joke of the joke.

Jokes, successful or not, evince a capacity to link or separate subjects on the level of a cultural or symbolic order, the Other. That there is no joke of the joke, no metajoke, suggests that 'there is no Other of the Other', that is, 'no metalanguage can be spoken' (Lacan, 1977a: 311). The impossibility of a metajoke thus corresponds with Lyotard's (1984a) most basic proposition concerning postmodernity: the prevalent contemporary 'incredulity towards metanarratives' discredits any illusion of transcendent authority and any legitimate guarantees beyond the circulation of discourses or little stories. Given that jokes tend to be culturally specific in form and effect they amply demonstrate the untenability of any global or totalising imperative to institute a universal order of meaning. Jokes, marking the boundaries between different cultural and linguistic formations, depend on an element that is untranslatable, that resists the very processes of symbolisation determining the structure and character of joking. In highlighting the role of language, jokes disclose something in excess of linguistic or cultural sense: the wordplay depends on some relation to nonsense; meaning appears in the 'ab-sense' of meaning. If jokes display the work of the signifier and its daily determinations of intersubjective relationships they also reveal a certain feature of the signifier: the signifier is not grounded in reference to reality; it is not fixed in respect of meaning, but operates through effects, in the very relationships it constitutes. The Other, 'the locus of the signifier', is not held together as a system or language that exists outside its use or users: 'any statement of authority has no other guarantee than its very enunciation, and it is pointless for it to seek in it another signifier, which could not appear outside this locus in any way' (Lacan, 1977a: 310). Where certain signifiers have what appears as a transcendent status – words like truth, god, reason – their authority is guaranteed nowhere other than in the very relations which sustain their authority, relations in which they themselves play a part.

Jokes, so central since Freud to psychoanalytical thinking about unconscious processes, resist any universalisation and thereby impede any attempt to place psychoanalysis on a metadiscursive pedestal. Asking whether psychoanalysis has 'got beyond a joke', Robert Young pokes fun at the easy readings of Freudian criticism which too readily recognise the very obvious patterns of psychoanalysis in any text to assume the righteousness due to a masterful body of knowledge. More seriously, however, the 'reinvention' of the relationship between psychoanalysis and literature in the light of Lacan's work 'had the effect not just of superseding the standing joke of vulgar psychoanalytic criticism but of superseding any notion of a psychoanalytic criticism at all' (Young, 1984: 90). Psychoanalysis, from its early incarnation in the dream of Irma's injection, has been no more than a bad joke or, worse, little better than a dirty joke. Duped by the dream, the psychoanalyst becomes the butt of the joke. With the introduction of the signifier, moreover, castration becomes a joke taken too far, to the extent that all subjects are duped by its effects. In the same way that postmodern practices release a play of meanings that cannot be mastered, the theories of psychoanalysis remain entangled in the very relations they set out to unravel. Jokes mock the work of analysis: exuding the movements of signification, they also impeach any authority in the release of a nonsensical cascade of associations and a rebellious, subversive laughter. Like postmodernism, which eschews all authority, identity and systemic fixity in its playful, plural and fragmented outbursts, jokes manifest an uncontainable energy at the heart of the linguistic structures that would assimilate them. Indeed, as they announce the effects of metaphorical condensation and metonymic displacement, they seem to exceed the primary signifier, the paternal metaphor supposed to determine the symbolic structures of language and culture. Despite the incursions of postmodern theories and practices, despite the jokes that tear holes in its fabric, psychoanalysis remains, strangely, at home in a world which has seemingly superseded it. Not able, perhaps, to identify, let alone identify with, a paternal metaphor, psychoanalysis looks elsewhere, to the point where the metaphor, once knotted, becomes unravelled, to the navel, the navel of the joke, the navel of the joke of postmodernism.

The navel of the joke

'Like the act of theorizing, the act of joking is rhetorically addressed to a *male* accomplice' (Felman, 1993: 95). Women, to judge by the weight of evidence offered by Sigmund Freud in *Jokes and their Relation to the Unconscious*, rarely tell jokes but remain all too often the butt of obscene or smutty jokes between men, objects of sexual excitement, aggression or hostility in displays of male virility and mastery. In the analysis of dreams, however, the reverse may be true. Irma's analysis, for instance, discloses a cluster of female figures that resist the authority of psychoanalytical interpretation, refusing its demand of speech, entangling its interpretative powers and blocking its metaphorical mastery. The ambivalence of femininity within psychoanalysis is situated at a particular point, a point that conjoins the work of jokes and the work of dreams in relation to the theory of the unconscious. Dreams and jokes evince the condensations and displacements of unconscious processes. Jokes, unsanctioned sexual or aggressive energies, circumvent the social taboos regarding obscene or shameful topics. In refined society, Freud notes, smut is only tolerated in the form of jokes, allowing the satisfaction of lustful or hostile instincts in a

Sex, machines and navels

setting which otherwise forbids manifestations of instinctual behaviour. Instinct is negated and conserved at a symbolic level, in the play of words: 'brutal hostility, forbidden by law, has been replaced by verbal invective' (Freud, 1976b: 146). The condensations and substitutions performed in the joke enact, on another level, the baser instincts. Mastery becomes a prime source of pleasure: in innocent jokes the motive force is a display of cleverness (Freud, 1976b: 194). In hostile jokes a displaced form of aggression comes out: 'by making our enemy small, inferior, despicable or comic, we achieve in a roundabout way the enjoyment of overcoming him – to which the third person, who has made no efforts, bears witness by his laughter' (1976b: 147). Where a bad joke turns on a 'point' of connection between terms, a word uniting 'two disparate ideas', the 'good' joke has a stronger instinctual charge. It involves a unification of terms through reference to a 'common third element', the object or butt of the joke. The third person's laughter recognises the hostility or anxiety regarding the butt: the laughter signals precisely that teller and receiver share the same attitudes. The meaning of the joke comes later: at the point of recognition and exclusion, through laughter, of the joke's object.

The intersubjective structure of the joke remains fragile. The joke only works when the third person 'gets' it, showing an identification with the position of the teller and against the butt, only after the joke has been told. There are thus no prior guarantees that the joke will be a joke: the response of the receiver decides it status. The unity or shared position that is retroactively determined depends, moreover, on the point of the joke in both senses: the point connecting the play on words and the object of exclusion over which the shared position is established. There remains a dirty complicity in obscene jokes which, even as it tries to master or exclude the third term, acknowledges the need for that object of hostility and resistance: 'in the case of obscene jokes, which are derived from smut, it turns the third person who originally interfered with the sexual situation into an ally, before whom the woman must feel shame, by bribing him with the gift of its yield of pleasure' (Freud, 1976b: 183). The third man, at first interrupting the smutty relation of joke teller to his object of sexual excitement, moves from being a rival to a co-conspirator in the shaming of the woman as joke object. Placated by the bribe of jocular pleasure, the gift received by the third man betokens his privileged role in the triangle: he, rather than the woman who is sacrificed as an object of a male exchange, is imagined as the one who legitimates the position of the teller. Nonetheless, the relation between men cannot occur without the excluded object of the joke. As the point articulating the uneasy alliance between men, the woman is not only passive, but functions as both an excluded and yet absolutely necessary condition of their possibility. As such, the woman occupies a position in excess of an uneasy and imagined alliance between men, a figure of resistance retaining a charge of energy greater than the momentary expenditure enjoyed in the laugh. In this respect, as in Freud's concept of the navel, femininity is a crucial point of otherness, an ambivalent, double figure (Freud, 1976b: 208). A 'nodal point' in the articulation of dream and dream-thoughts, the excluded and resistant object remains 'overdetermined', a *Knotenpunkt* in an unconscious reservoir which returns jokes to the anxiety which produced them.[1]

Jokes, like dreams, have navels, knotty (dis)connections to an Other in excess of the subjects positioned in the joke. In Lacan's return to Freud the 'navel of the joke' occupies a crucial position in the articulation of subjects, language and the unconscious. For Lacan, the questions of signification that arise in Freud's works on dreams, slips and jokes, though generally overlooked, form the basis of his investigations into the way that, through symptom-signifiers, the unconscious is structured like a language:

> For, however little interest has been taken in it – and with good reason – *Jokes and their relation to the Unconscious* remains the most unchallengeable of his works because it is the most transparent, a work in which the effect of the unconscious is demonstrated to us to its most subtle confines; and the face it reveals to us is that of the spirit in the ambiguity conferred on it by language, where the side of its regalian power is the witticism or 'conceit' (*'pointe'*), by which the whole of its order is annihilated in an instant – the 'conceit', in fact, where its domination over the real is expressed in the challenge of non-sense, where humour, in the malicious grace of the 'mind free from care' (*esprit libre*) symbolizes a truth that has not said the last word. (Lacan, 1977a: 59–60)

The ambiguity of language evident in Freud's texts evinces the complex relationship between the symbolic and the real, a relationship that turns on a point where sense or meaning is established against the challenge of non-sense. The point is, of course, the navel of the joke:

> There is a point where meaning emerges, and is created. But even at this very point, man is very easily capable of feeling that the meaning is at the same time annihilated, that it is created so as to be annihilated. What's a joke? – if not the calculated irruption of non-sense into a discourse which seems to make sense.

Sex, machines and navels

O Mannoni: *It is the navel of speech.*

Exactly. In the dream, there is an extremely confused navel. Inversely, the navel of the joke is perfectly sharp – the *Witz*. And what expresses its most radical essence is non-sense. (Lacan, 1998a: 280)

The point where meaning dissolves in nonsense is the omphalic limit to language's capacity to inscribe the real. A hole appears in the fabric of language and a knotting of terms or an entangled cluster of associations fills the gap. The navel, a metaphor for the emergence of metaphor, emerges at the point of separation between sense and nonsense: 'metaphor occurs at the precise point at which sense emerges from non-sense' (Lacan, 1977a: 158). The differentiation between sense and nonsense positions the subject, through an act of separation, in the paternal symbolic order: it marks the 'signifying substitution' of the 'Name-of-the-Father', 'the metaphor that substitutes this Name in the place first symbolized by the operation of the absence of the mother' (1977a: 200). Maternal absence, marked by the navel, forms the locus of substitution.

The structure of metaphoric substitution is more complex than the simple filling of a maternal absence with a symbolic order. Jokes, constituting and annihilating meaning at the same time, return to the point of the navel: their nonsense, defined in terms of symbolic sense, acknowledges an ab-sense that remains the space for the inscription of signifiers. Condensation, which knots metonymic chains of signification together, also, like the mycelium or intricate meshwork Freud glimpses beyond the navel, alludes to a network, not 'the term by term correspondence of a symbol with something', 'but through a set of interlacings' (Lacan, 1988a: 266). Metaphor, in the distinction Lacan draws from Jakobson, operates against the horizontal current of the metonymic chain of association articulating signifiers: discourse, Lacan notes, is not univocal but occurs as a 'polyphony'. The metonymic chain describes the displacements of signification on an associative, horizontal plane, while metaphor forms the points of vertical substitution or articulation between chains. At these points, meaning insists in the 'creative spark' that flashes between two signifiers (Lacan, 1977a: 154-7).

Metaphor establishes meaning through identification, the recognition of one signifier in terms of another (Lacan, 1993: 218). Meaning occurs in the knotting of signifiers, the point at which one chain of signification is anchored or 'quilted'. An 'upholstery button' forms 'the point of convergence that enables everything that happens in this discourse to be situated retroactively and prospectively' (Lacan, 1993: 268). Two planes are quilted at the metaphorical navel: the horizontal scansion of the chain of signifiers on the one hand fleeting sense, on the other, 'the core of the delusional phenomenon, its navel' (Lacan, 1993: 259). Meaning is not simply an effect of metaphor, a signifier binding other signifiers together: if it anchors the horizontal movement of signification, it does so through the conjunction of knots and holes. Sense occurs at the limit point, the cluster of figures beyond which it cannot penetrate. At this point a knot identified with the core of being testifies to a meaning irreducible to sense or signification, a knot to which the subject is singularly attached.

At the irreducible point of nonsense, the subject finds his or her being: 'follow your being, your message, your word, your group, what I represent? What is it? It's a knot, a point of contraction in a bundle of meanings, whether acquired by the subject or not' (Lacan, 1993: 280). The bundle of meanings, the point where sense appears most full is also what remains most irreducible and resistant to rationalisation and explanation, the point where meaning vanishes. It is thus a fundamental and evanescent core of subjectivity, the 'kernel of *non-sense*' that psychoanalysis identifies as 'an irreducible signifier', the 'traumatic non-meaning' to which the subject, as subject, is subjected: 'in so far as the primary signifier is pure non-sense, it becomes the bearer of the infinitization of the value of the subject, not open to all meanings, but abolishing them all, which is different' (Lacan, 1977b: 250–2). Distinguishing and connecting individual existence to the orders of signification the navel connotes that part of the subject's being which cannot be assimilated, normalised or rationalised as a purely symbolic function. The metaphor, the signifier that emerges at the point of the navel's abolition of the symbolic distinction between meaning and non-meaning, discloses some Thing beyond sense or nonsense: ab-sense. 'Everyone makes jokes about macaroni, because it is a hole with something around it, or about canons. The fact that we laugh doesn't change the situation, however: the fashioning of the signifier and the introduction of a gap or a hole in the real is identical' (Lacan, 1992: 121). Beyond sense or nonsense, beyond the knot of metaphor, lies an unplumbable hole. In the form of Thing, this hole or gap in the real functions as the 'place for the projection of the missing signifier' but remains, in excess of the signifier precisely as gap and hole (Lacan, 1977c: 37).

The emphasis on the founding and subversive status of the hole that repeatedly breaches the orders of signification not only highlights the lack on which subjectivity is founded but underscores the radical otherness of the unconscious. More than a space filled with unavowable wishes and instincts, the unconscious is characterised as gap, impediment, rupture: 'neither primordial nor instinctual', 'what it knows about the elementary is no more than the elements of the signifier' (Lacan, 1977a: 170). A structure, like language, the unconscious cannot simply be filled with a particular sense or meaning: it is not reducible to discourses which associate it with the deepest secrets of being, sexual wishes or biological drives or some fully egocentric human essence. Being is articulated as a knot over a hole. The gap disclosed by the unconscious remains para-mount. Sexed subjectivity emerges in this gap in the full sense of annihila-ting sense: though it takes its bearings from the signifier, it refuses to be completely rationalised, assimilated or explained in symbolic terms. The dirty, sexual joke of psychoanalysis, foundering on the border of sense and nonsense, thus discloses something quite Other, ab-sense. From this perspective Lacan resists the conventional notion of psychoanalysis as a discourse reducing everything to sex and its dirty secret and invokes common sense to refute the argument 'proving', through sublimation, that words 'with an original sexual meaning started to take on a series of meanings increasingly remote from their primitive meaning'. Instead, Lacan asks:

> Why are those zones in which sexual signification spreads outward, why are those rivers through which it ordinarily flows – and, as you have seen, in a direction that isn't just random – specially chosen, so that in order to reach them one uses words that already have a given usage in the sexual sphere? Why is it precisely in connection with half-failed pruning, with an act of cutting that is blocked, thwarted messed up, that one should evoke the presumed origin of the word and find it in the hole drilling activities of work in its most primitive of forms, with the meaning of sexual operation, of phallic penetration? (1992: 167)

For Lacan, the question of the female sexual organ that so preoccupies vulgar manifestations of phallic penetration is not a real or actual cause, but a gap in processes of signification. Metaphor already occupies a space of absence resistant to all but metaphorical filling: the female sexual organ is already metaphorised as 'the 'form of an opening and an emptiness' at centre of metaphors. Language does not deliver a sexual, biological truth outside itself, nor refers to something already given, but encounters an obstacle within. For Lacan this discloses 'that sexual symbolism in the ordinary sense of the word may polarize at its point of origin the metaphorical play of the signifier'. And the origin around which the metaphorical play is polarised is not something, but some Thing, a gap in which the navel's condensation provides the occasion of metaphor.

Jokes demonstrate a play of metaphor crucial to human experience. In the movement of signifiers subjects are positioned, identifying and recognising themselves within an order of signification held together by subjective investments, by the knots that anchor signification around particular points. Enabling a release of energy through which subjects are connected in an intersubjective system of shared values and meanings, jokes disclose the Other as the locus of community and culture. To be recognised by the Other's representative (the laughing third person or receiver of the joke) is to sustain an imaginary sense of mastery. The play of metaphor is enjoyed in jocular expenditure, pleasure connoting the return to equilibrium. But destabilising sexual, hostile, aggressive energies also persist in the movements of signification: jokes not only deal with the anxieties, excitements or aggressions projected on an excluded yet resistant object, they disclose, in their wordplay and nonsense, a determining gap, a hole that cannot be filled, an ab-sense eluding all sense.[2] The self-assurance of the joke-telling subject remains imaginary: it depends on a misrecognition of his relation to the signifier. In the act of displaying his mastery of language through a display of wit, the subject risks himself, duped by a sense self-assurance: identity depends on the recognition of the other subject, the laughter that retroactively determines the success of the joke and the skill of the teller. And throughout the process it is the work of the signifier that comes to the fore over the illusions of the subject. Temporarily establishing the boundaries of the Other, knotting it together, jokes also acknowledge its fragility, its inability to fix meaning and identity through reference to any solid ground.

Jokes, it seems, while offering a sense of mastery and a containment of meaning, disclose, in the play of signification they initiate, what might be called the joke of meaning. Signifiers have effects, and the signified designates the signifier that causes the effect of sense. Meaning does not take precedence over signification, nor is it decided by the speaking subject: it comes later, as an effect of signifiers, substitution and recognition. In this way, no authority, not even that of the paternal metaphor, is final or guaranteed: it occurs in the act of speech that is recognised by others, a process that defines the limits of the Other. The joke of postmodernism, then, lies in the pluralisation of the effects of signification, to the point that no single figure of authority is recognised. The absence of such a figure discloses the ab-sense, the void of sense at the centre of signification. It is an ambivalent condition: it offers a thrilling release from

Sex, machines and navels

systems of authority, the pursuit of numerous artistic, social, sexual and economic freedoms and a loss of control experienced as a delirious, ecstatic flight of and from meaning. For other subjects, the hole that the numerous definitions of 'postmodernism' only partially disclose is a locus of disintegration, degradation and pervasive anxiety.

Jokes and their relation to the Other

In contemporary writing the possibility of metanarratives or grounded positions is generally greeted with incredulity. The styles associated with postmodern practices – parody, pastiche, irony and collage – exhibit the displacements, pleasures in wordplay and the anxieties evinced by jokes. Indeed postmodernism, and forms of poststructuralism with which it is often associated, now appear, for many, as jokes that have gone too far. But jokes, like the serious business of Derridean play, are never simply the funny ha-ha of idle excess: they manifest the crucial role of signifiers in the formation and fragmentation of cultural systems. The indirect jocularity of Julian Barnes's *A History of the World in 10 1/2 Chapters* lightly and ironically assumes various styles and characteristics of postmodernist writing. The book begins with the ironic juxtaposition of its title, deflating the grandeur of global historical projects with the brevity and incompletion of the volume. Grand narratives give way to *petits récits*; history is rewritten as stories in a novel that itself is composed of disparate or at least only partially related chapters. However, the titular and formal juxtapositions do not deliver an irony in which ambiguity and opposition remain in the service of a determinable knowing subject.

Postmodernist irony and parody operate textually and reflexively to signal distance and difference and thus enable political critique (Hutcheon, 1986–87). Irony involves risk, errancy, indirection, both for the subject and for the discourse that it activates. In Hutcheon's description of the clash between postmodern practices and postcolonial imperatives, irony comes to the fore as a question for contemporary political strategy. Hutcheon examines the furore surrounding an exhibition, 'Into the Heart of Africa', staged by the Royal Ontario Museum, Toronto from 1989 to 1990. While the exhibition was attentive to 'those familiar postmodern discursive strategies of irony and reflexivity' in a project deconstructing Canada's involvement in imperialism, it was attacked by white English Canadians and by the African Canadian community (Hutcheon, 1994: 208–10). Moreover, 'it was reflexivity itself, like irony, that came under fire'

(1994: 211). Analysing the reactions and the way that the exhibition's layout and brochure contributed to the many antipathetic readings, Hutcheon criticises the organisers' textual skills: 'although everyone connected to the museum insisted that the irony and reflexivity of the show were meant to signal the detachment of the institution from the imperial perspective being presented, the textual markers of that intention were less than clear and self-evident' (1994: 213). While this implies that the fault for the failure of ironic effect lies in the poor semiotic skills of the organisers, their postmodernism falling back on modern assumptions, the implications of events exceed the conventions associated with irony. Hutcheon notes that 'irony has always been a trope that depends on the context and the identity and position of both the ironist and the audience' and reverses Wayne Booth's assertion that sharing irony brings discursive communities into being, to consider irony, and the superiority it implies, as a trope of white cultural discourse inappropriate in the context of postcolonialism since it is a technique of evasion rather than action (1994: 220–1).

Hutcheon's argument suggests a form of irony in excess of subject and intersubjectivity ('ironist' and 'audience') that involves questions of the Other ('context' and 'discursive community'). Whether irony forms or is formed by a discursive community is less important, in its failure, than the acknowledgement of its dependence on the Other. Its failure signals that the terms of the Other are not shared, not the same for ironist and audience. At issue in postmodern and postcolonial practices is the status of the Other. In postcolonial discourse, cultural difference and questions of the subjectification by, resistance to and the transformation of a globally dominating set of Western European values and practices are prioritised. In accounts of postmodernism the fragmentation of grand narratives, the pluralisation of subjects and communities (albeit within the framework of transglobal capitalism) is celebrated or abhorred as a sign of cultural and political change. Different, mutable, interimplicated, boundaries between discourses, especially between postmodern and postcolonial modes, are explosively put in question by the ironies of the Royal Ontario Museum's exhibition. Depending on relations to what now appears as more a case of *an* Other, irony has, it seems, transmuted, exceeding the grasp and mastery of a single subject or anything other than a very limited discursive community. Indeed, irony is no longer predicated on or the property of any subject at all, no longer a matter of intention, reception or convention.

For Baudrillard irony works at the level of image and object. Both are heterogeneous, inimical to the subject: 'the image has taken over and

Sex, machines and navels

imposed its own immanent, ephemeral logic; an immoral logic without depth, beyond good and evil, beyond truth and falsity; a logic of the extermination of its own referent, a logic of the implosion of meaning in which the message disappears on the horizon of the medium' (Baudrillard, 1987: 23). Moreover, the object produces an 'ironic embezzlement of the symbolic order'; it has 'its own strategy and holds the key to the rules of the game, impenetrable to the subject, not because they are deeply mysterious, but because they are infinitely ironic' (Baudrillard, 1990a: 181–3). Objective irony 'arises from within things themselves – it is an irony that belongs to the system because the system is constantly functioning against itself' (Baudrillard, 1987: 52). Irony exceeds the subject with an impenetrable superficial density. The endlessly reversible significations produced by objective irony allow for no authoritative position, no regulative metaphor. From a Baudrillardian position the reactions precipitated by the Royal Ontario Museum's exhibition are, ironically, a mark of its success. The objects presented are neither contained by the stated project nor by a specific community nor by the walls of the museum itself. The space where modernity homogenised other cultures for the convenience and temporality of a western consumer's gaze is exploded, its walls perforated by reactions that overflow discrete boundaries. Indeed, the irony of images and objects provokes an energy that leads, not to passivity and quiescence, but to argument and action: heterogeneity comes to the fore.

Without a metaphor to regulate its progress or tie it to a stable symbolic framework, Barnes's *A History of the World* cannot, and does not, simply replace grand narratives with the discrete and specific games of short stories. The novel is neither a collection of discrete short stories nor a sequence of connected chapters: different chapters/stories parody and pastiche a collage of styles; cross discursive boundaries in their rewriting of actual, mythical and scientific events and accounts; reverse distinctions between reality and fiction. There are, nonetheless, metonymic continuities connecting the stories: Noah's Ark, woodworm and waterborne transportation appear in many of the chapters, offering metaphors of flux, motion and groundlessness as partial descriptions of the course of the novel. In the first story/chapter, 'The Stowaway', the biblical myth of the Flood provides the scene for a re-examination and rewriting of androcentric narratives. An undisclosed (until the end) first-person narrator retells the familiar story, casting Noah, not as the hero but as an incompetent, self-interested and intolerant drunk. In the story biblical myth is played against scientific truth, in the shape of Darwinian theory, to show the partiality of human-centred modes of representation: against Darwinian notions of natural selection, the narrator testifies to certain 'missing links' being eaten by Noah and his family: the survival of the fattest rather than the fittest.

In rewriting human myths and theories the story undermines assumptions of human superiority. When the witty and humane narrator's identity is disclosed as a woodworm the process of reading and recognition is ironised: the first-person becomes an inhuman place of identification and distance which not only resists human authority but makes all stories interested and partial. In 'The Stowaway' the partiality and inescapability of stories eats away at the possibility of metanarrative. The inability to organise, regulate or hierarchise categories is an effect of a pervasive ironisation, leaving the place and assumed superiority of the Western human subject in question and opening up a hole in the symbolic networks of human history, progress and reality with a multiplicity of stories and significances exceeding its grasp. Narratives no longer return subjects to themselves but wander between pasts and presents, endlessly circumlocuting the hole that rends all discourse from the human. It is a hole over which no narrative has been fully written and thus constitutes a prime contemporary locus unable to imagine either a future or, even, an integrated past.

When grand narratives were credible an object filled the gap, providing the site for the anchoring of subjects within symbolic structures. As the point 'where the subject sees himself caused as a lack by a, and where a fills the gap constituted by the inaugural division of the subject', the object a signifies the subject's alienation in signification, binding it within a symbolic economy, the 'place for the projection of the missing signifier' (Lacan, 1977c: 37). Nevertheless it also remains 'that place which, by a hole it opens up in the signified, sets off a cascade of reshapings of the signifier' (Lacan, 1977a: 217). This object remains doubled, the point constituting the subject's connection with signification and meaning and the site where meaning disintegrates. The distinction is posited in Lacan's account of the difference between mourning and psychosis, and the 'swarms of images' that distinguish their relation to the object a and the hole in the real. Psychosis seizes on one image, a 'delusional metaphor', leaving the subject severed from the symbolic order. In contrast, mourning, though it 'impeaches' the signifying system, attempts to reintegrate the loss of the object and produce symbolic meaning, trying to fill the hole in the real with 'the totality of the signifier', the *logos* (Lacan, 1977c:

Sex, machines and navels

38). As the signifier that arrests the play of meaning, the *logos* is another name for the paternal metaphor. The navel of the joke, then, opens the subject and the Other to a play of signification which puts mastery at risk even as it establishes the point of anxiety where and by means of which it can be imaginarily recovered. However, in the hole of contemporary culture, its swarms of images inducing effects of mourning and psychosis, it is the function of this *phallogos* and the legitimacy of the totality that it implies which is in question.

The subject of *A History of the World* circulates around a hole in the real, inscribing, in its collage of narratives and representations, a vanishing figure. In 'Upstream' the story of a human subject (white, European, heterosexual, middle-class, male) is presented within a generic assemblage that crosses literary, cultural, cinematic and televisual frames. The story/chapter's epistolary form draws on the *Bildungsroman* and the colonial narrative, the river itself raising the spectre of *Heart of Darkness*, to present and dissolve character in a process of self-discovery and critical cultural reflection. The plot also draws on a film, *The Mission*, and a documentary about its making and turns on a detail from another documentary, a David Attenborough wildlife programme. Patterns of duplication and repetition also highlight processes of textual reproduction: the journey into the South American jungle involves an encounter with cultural difference and an imaginary rediscovery of self. The attempt, in the manner of *cinema verité* (what the story calls 'truthspiel'), to replicate on film the encounter between two Jesuit missionaries and a nomadic tribe of Indians becomes less a re-enactment of the original event and more a game of truth and representation. Repetition produces, not verisimilitude, but difference. Communications technologies, from Indians with forked sticks to letters, radios, telephones and telegrams, become central to the story's articulation of sexual and ethnic differences. Commenting on modes of representation, moreover, the story's generic assemblage discloses a reflexive space which ironises and exposes the limits of western assumptions, language, projections and meanings.

The story's first-person narrator is Charlie, a British actor who in his letters to his wife in London describes his and the film crew's journey into a South American jungle. The scene, the relations between actors, crew and the Indians are narrated alongside an account of the subject's marital past, his process of self-transformation and his imagined future. The letters begin in the manner of holiday postcards tinged with a typically British tone of Boy Scout imperialism: Charlie is concerned about 'beri-beri', 'local firewater' and whether 'a native with a forked stick' will be the only postal service. Local people are generally constructed as uncivilised and superstitious (Barnes, 1990: 191–3). In the tones of a cultural elitism evinced, for example, in the privileging of British over Hollywood acting, a paternalistic position is unquestioningly assumed. There are asides, however, that signal but do not acknowledge imperialist practices: Coca-Cola signs at the 'trading post' are greeted with the disgust of a tourist, who in the manner of a certain 'truthspiel', is not getting the real thing, the authentic experience of foreignness because Coke reps have 'shat on the landscape' (1990: 195). One elision, a reference to the missionaries' attempts to 'preach the Gospel and try to get them to wear Levis', conflates Spanish and American imperialism, equating religious and commercial colonisation (1990: 201). The elision of religious and economic forms of colonialism occludes and naturalises the position of the representative of another imperialist power, the British actor himself.

The self-confidence and critical knowingness assumed by the actor remain, the text's relentless and glaring ironies declare, an ignorance of or blindness to the partial nature of his own position. He enlists his wife in intimate addresses by means of an apparently shared vocabulary of pet names, private jokes, domestic and personal details. The assumption of shared values and attitudes is rendered suspect by the mention of affairs and by Charlie's stereotypical constructions of femininity and domestic bliss. The letters to an absent wife, like the accounts of another world, are blithely unaware of their marked self-interest. The Western European subject's implicit criticisms of types of colonialism and masculinity have no bearing, it seems, on his own self-assurance or on his relationships to the other sex or culture. As he ventriloquises the attitudes of the Indians, he continues to patronise his wife, demeaning both in single sentences: 'It's all right, sweetie, I'm not coming back with a bone through my nose, but I might come back with a bit less of a bone in my head' (1990: 201). Though the second part of the statement seems unlikely given the endearment of the first, his self-confidence grows rather than diminishes in the encounter, deep in the jungle, with the otherness of the Indians.

The encounter with the Indians is a sublime moment of awe and amazement that enables the subject to refashion himself in his letters, a performance of maturity aimed at securing a reconciliation with his emotionally and geographically distanced wife. The actor disavows his past behaviour and popular image as hell-raiser. The stated cause of his self-reflection and transformation is the difference of the Indians.

Rejecting attitudes that lead the crew's joker to give the Indians names like 'Sitting Bull' or 'Tonto', Charlie takes a more enlightened position in a reversal of conventional prejudices (1990: 197). For him, the Indians are more civilised, rather than more primitive, 'fantastically advanced and mature because they don't have radios'. Without a term for themselves or their language, the Indians seem 'incredibly mature. It's like nationalism out of the window' (1990: 200–1). They have advanced so far, he, following truthspiel's self-effacing logic, speculates, to become a 'post-acting civilisation' (1990: 203). Open, direct, naked and thoroughly natural, the Indians instil a 'great sense of comradeship' and seem destined to 'teach me a lesson about life' (1990: 201). His understanding, framed as a discovery of self and the meaning of life, is based on distinctly Enlightenment assumptions, its Romantic naturalism, its liberalism, tolerance, humanity and teleology inversely replicating the civilised values that enable the crew to joke about the Indians' 'barbarous', 'primitive' and 'superstitious' customs. Moreover, the ironised encounter with another culture as a better reflection of his own ideal also reflects on his marital relationship. He offers what he imagines his wife wants: the abandonment of his metropolitan, hellraising ways and a thoroughly romanticised return to natural simplicity in the form of settling in the 'real country' so that his wife can have his babies (1990: 206). Such a rural domestic idyll, of course, assures him of an authority guaranteed by patriarchal values.

The assimilations of cultural and sexual difference are shadowed by an anxiety which undermines the subject's unquestioned self-assurance. The principal worry in the letters concerns the letters themselves, the efficiency of the postal system and the lack of any reply. The significance of sending but not receiving for issues of language, identity and communication eludes him. He turns his anxiety about postal systems into jokes. In the context jokes become indices of a pervasive, if unrecognised, anxiety concerning the limits of systems of signification. Throughout, jokes punctuate the narrative and indicate the limits of the little groupings which produce them: enabling communication and community in a process of inclusion or exclusion, jokes about women, the Indians and film crew members also signal anxieties about the various objects of difference that threaten a group. Often they backfire, heightening the sense of difference rather than providing assurance. In Charlie's letters, jokes, significantly, are also punctuated: jocular comments are marked by an asterisk indicating an appended note which states that they were only jokes. Not only does this signal the failure of the joke but also reinforces the absence of correspondence between subject and addressee that is increasingly apparent in the lack of any reply. The shared knowledge and intimacy presented in the letters appears as no more than a subjective projection, an illusory effect of a fantasy that is not supported by a relation to the other person and the Other. Difference returns upon the subject.

The story turns upon one particular joke, a joke that, like most jokes, is and is not a joke. It involves a little fish that, when a man urinates in a river, swims into his penis and extends barbs. The only cure is surgical emasculation. Initially the story is generally discounted as a joke circulated by the crew's prankster. Later, however, it is vigorously verified by the Indians. They, moreover, play a few jokes themselves. Charlie, the person who identifies most with their culture and starts to learn their language is told that the word 'thkarni' signifies a large white bird. Whenever he uses it the Indians 'fall about laughing' (1990: 201). He eventually guesses the obvious: it is 'the Indians' name – well, one their many names, to be precise – for you-know-what. The thing up which the little fish in the river swims if you aren't careful' (1990: 209). The thing he cannot name, and has metaphorically lost, cannot, despite his manful attempts to show he can take a joke, be regained. His subjection to the castrating effects of the signifier is complete. But, in the context of the story's concern with systems of communication, the implications of this metaphorical rather than literal emasculation are crucial. As the butt or object of the joke he is subjected to a language and set of values that are neither his own, nor give him any grounds for assuming an authoritative and knowing position. Simultaneously included and excluded, his ideal of phallic mastery proves to be something of a fallacy. (Sometimes limp jokes are just limp jokes.)

The reconciliation that he constantly imagines with his wife emerges as a irreparable split. The indifference of the Indians, their utter lack of curiosity or fear regarding white men, their unwillingness to help carry the baggage, signals a difference that Charlie cannot transcend. The script is not being adhered to. The cracks that appear in the story's ironic reflections disclose more than a single individual's partial and misapprehended speculations on cultural and sexual difference. The Indians' joke signals not only the western subject's alienation in a system of signification, it marks his alienation from such systems. While the postal anxiety manifested in the failed epistolary jokes discloses the subject's dependency on the Other, his subordination to the system that is supposed to confer authority, it is the Indians' joke that distinguishes this form of subjectivity as an object, a butt. He is alienated from a system that only negatively

Sex, machines and navels

recognises him, subordinated to a phallic signifier or paternal metaphor that he can recognise only in its excluding effects. The effects are more extensive than an imaginary rupture with a symbolic order: they imply that a certain enlightened order of things is palpably untenable, an Other, a metanarrative that has been ironised to the point of incredulity.

The subject is left without a position: he becomes an excluded object with nowhere left to turn except a past which he rejected earlier in the story. The utter dislocation of western subjectivity occurs as the story, and the filming, reaches its climax. Charlie's co-star dies in a river accident. The death and its cause remain inexplicable: Charlie makes vain recourse to history, psychology and rationality, but the Indians have vanished, taking everything, and he can only speculate aimlessly. His liberal models become increasingly irrational as he desperately tries to ground the catastrophe in some understandable form of historical repetition or in some unknown offence to Indian gods (1990: 217). The tear that has been steadily appearing in the imaginary and symbolic fabric of his reality has now become a hole in the real around which explanations circulate wildly and unarrestably. Meaning evaporates: 'you say words like that and everyone knows what they mean but when you look at them you can't understand them' (1990: 212).

The return of the unsymbolisable real inaugurates a displacement of desire. Letters reiterate the demand for his wife's reply, for some sign of the reconciliation he has imagined, for some point of meaning and stability. The Other he wants to recognise his demand, however, is not who or where he thinks it is. The lack of response to his letters, calls and telegrams necessitates another defensive return. The last refuge of the story's subject is a display of imaginary aggressivity: declaring his intention to get very drunk, calling his wife a 'bitch' and threatening her lover with violence, he orders her to get out of his life and his flat. She is, of course, already long gone. His threats flap in the empty air as he falls back on the hellraising role he rejected earlier in his letters, a vain attempt to restore an imaginary identity in the face of absolute disintegration. In the process, she assumes the very image that ironically returns him to himself: 'Christ if you think I'm an egotist you should look in the mirror baby' (1990: 221). Indeed. The reduction of his sense of relationship to a mirror that reflects his own self-image takes the form of a 'dual simplification' and a repudiation of the Other, symptoms, for Lacan, of psychosis. The subject is returned to where he always has been, but this time he is without the support of other or Other. Textual irony makes a degree of difference by establishing a critical distance between reader and hypocritical textual double, severing statement from enunciation. This is not a secure position, however: the relentless, vertiginous ironisation empties a space that was supposedly full, redirecting the reader's look from an absorption in the image of the character, fading as a lost object, to the limits of the Other that conditions its possibility. Being written into insignificance might mean that a certain subject cannot recall himself other than as an unavowable object.

Postmodernism's navel

The joke of postmodernism is played on the human subject and his idea of reality. This subject has become the butt of the joke. In one of the now canonical texts of postmodernism, Thomas Pynchon's *V*, a dream is recounted. The dream reworks an old joke about the navel:

> In his dream, he was all alone, as usual. Walking on a street at night where there was nothing but his own field of vision alive. It had to be night on that street. The lights gleamed unflickering on hydrants; manhole covers which lay around in the street. There were neon signs scattered here and there, spelling out words he wouldn't remember when he woke.
>
> Somehow it was all tied up with a story he'd heard once, about a boy born with a golden screw where his navel should have been. For twenty years he consults doctors and specialists all over the world, trying to get rid of this screw, and having no success. Finally, in Haiti, he runs into a voodoo doctor who gives him a foul-smelling potion. He drinks it, goes to sleep and has a dream. In this dream he finds himself on a street, lit by green lamps. Following the witch-man's instructions, he takes two rights and a left from his point of origin, finds a tree growing by the seventh street light, hung all over with colored balloons. On the fourth limb from the top there is a red balloon; he breaks it and inside is a screwdriver with a yellow plastic handle. With the screwdriver he removes the screw from his stomach, and as soon as this happens he wakes from the dream. It is morning. He looks down towards his navel, the screw is gone. That twenty years' curse is lifted at last. Delirious with joy, he leaps up out of bed, and his ass falls off. (Pynchon, 1975: 36–40)

The boy who dreams in the dream dreams of the removal of an artificial navel. When he awakes, delighted that his wish has at last been granted, he discovers, as fairy-tale wishers often do, that the outcome is not as straightforward as it was supposed. The artificial navel, an irritating object he spent his life trying to remove, is precisely what defines him: it is his

Sex, machines and navels

very own uniquely self-defining characteristic, though he believes it to be no more than an unnecessary imposture. Before his eyes, or rather, below his chest, is the 'secret' thing which defines his being, the thing, like a signifier, that determines the course of his life. Without it, he falls apart. The artificial navel is what holds him together. When it is unscrewed the basis of his identity and his body, drops off: he loses all foundation and, deprived of something fundament-al, becomes the butt of the joke.

The story of the dream of a boy with an artificial navel that is removed in reality as an effect of a dream has a specific context. It occurs within another's dream, lying at the fearful core, the navel, of Benny Profane's own unconscious processes:

> To Profane, alone in the street, it would always seem maybe he was looking for something to make the fact of his own disassembly plausible as that of any machine. It was always at this point that the fear started: here that it would turn into a nightmare. Because now, if he kept going down the street, not only his ass but also his arms, legs, sponge brain and clock of a heart must be left behind to litter the pavement, be scattered among manhole covers.
>
> Was it home, the mercury-lit street? Was he returning like the elephant to his graveyard, to lie down and soon become ivory in whose bulk slept, latent, exquisite shapes of chessmen, backscratchers, hollow open-work Chinese spheres nested one inside the other?
>
> This was all there was to the dream; all there ever was: the Street. (Pynchon, 1975: 40)

A desire for machine-like disassembly, for a return home, to death, accompanies the nightmare of utter bodily fragmentation: the dream of the artificial navel occupies a central place in the dream-work of Profane. A self-reflexive dream which the dreamer interprets figurally as a textual embedding in an abysmal, Chinese-box arrangement, it repeats the dream of another as its own fear and wish. And more than his arse falls off: he disintegrates physically, literally unravelled in the textual meshwork. Looking for the secret screwdriver that will unlock his being, a secret about himself he remains unable to fathom, Profane also recognises that the point around which unravelling would occur would also mean the fragmentation of his identity. And the secret is no secret at all. Like the artificial navel it is plain to see, inscribed on the abysmal surface of the text, an old literary joke in a fiction in which story and a dream unfold within another dream and its speculative interpretation. Written on the surface, however, its significance plugging a hole remains difficult to recognise and understand, like the words spelt out in the dream which he cannot remember.

Jokes and their relation to postmodernism | 81

The joke of the navel in a postmodernist text concerned with pursuing the mystery of an all-too visible signifier, 'V' itself, through the errant and winding course of a novel is the joke of postmodernism: meaning eludes the subject, entangled in immense arrays of signifiers and texts. To find it, to unscrew it, is to watch it and subjectivity disappear, deprived of fundament and foundations, cast adrift in the reflexive movements of texts without meanings, floating inexorably away from any reality or linear narrative that once held everything in place. Unravelling oneself at the level of the navel separates subjectivity from the anchor of metaphor and meaning. With the knot of the apparently extraneous object untied, subjectivity, history, culture and reality are unanchored, dispersed and foundationless, a peculiarly postmodern predicament. Where, once, culture, the individual human subject and 'his' history and reality were assumed to be singular, unified and ordered, they are rendered partial, fragmentary in construction and relative in value by the diverse challenges of class, sexual and postcolonial discourses. Disavowing the possibility of a global, totalising framework, the end of grand narratives has also signalled the end of a grand narrator. The privileged subject of discourse is no longer a credible figure.

The concern with the dissolution of totalising narratives and cultural homogeneity undermines the investment of particular intellectual positions in the general cultural field. Where one is threatened, so is the other, the loss of cultural unity coincident with the eclipse of intellectual authority. Baudrillardian hyperreality designates a reality of images, signs and simulations beyond the control and comprehension of any particular subject. The general explosion and implosion of images, signs and meanings caused by new technologies and postmodern practices leads to history's decomposition into stories and also to subjective dissolution: they become plural and decentred selves, their reality virtually absorbed into the image machines of technical reproduction where cultures proliferate and consume themselves. In the expansion of the sphere of culture that Fredric Jameson observes, not only is everything aestheticised, everything is also consumable. Postmodern pastiche delivers a historicism which commodifies and dispenses with the past. While Jameson attempts to recover a radical past along with political agency and subjectivity, consumer culture continues to accelerate in a hyperreal direction absorbing subjects in a voracious eroticism of object and image. 'Culture', indeed, has a biological sense, exploited by Baudrillard in the term 'viral' used to describe 'a general tendency towards transsexuality which extends well

Sex, machines and navels

beyond sex, affecting all disciplines as they lose specificity and partake of a process of confusion and contagion – a viral loss of determinacy which is the prime event among all the new events that assail us' (Baudrillard, 1993: 7). In a 'transeconomic', 'transaesthetic', 'transpolitical' world the viral contaminations of all boundaries present an image of culture which doubles (multiplies and divides), mutates and exceeds all regulation. Tearing the fabric of symbolic reality and identity, the viral movements of images, like the play disclosed by jokes, open up an anxiety-provoking locus, the hole in the real. Associated with the symptoms of mourning and psychosis, the hole is also the site that activates calls for symbolic authority, for the erection of a signifier or paternal metaphor to regulate and repair the unity of the symbolic framework.

Lacanian psychoanalysis differentiates reality and the real. Only the former is directly bound up with language: 'it is the world of words that creates the world of things' (Lacan, 1977a: 65). What passes for the real world is 'only a humanised, symbolised world' (Lacan, 1988a: 87). Language determines the shape of reality, as a 'retrospective effect' inscribed on the real. (Lacan, 1953: 11) The imaginary, articulating subjects to the dominant code, furnishes individuals with an ideological and fundamentally misapprehended sense of their own unity and their natural place within a symbolised world: 'this social reality is then nothing but a fragile symbolic cobweb that can at any moment be torn aside by the intrusion of the real' (Žižek, 1991b: 17). Doubled, the real is both *logically constructed* as a point which escapes symbolisation' and 'the fullness of inert presence, positivity' (Žižek, 1989: 169). The second definition accords with Lacan's location of the real in direct opposition to the lack manifested in the symbolic register: 'there is no absence in the real'; 'the lack of the lack makes the real'; 'the real is without fissure....'[3] Without the absence, lack and fissure constitutive of the order of language, the real is seen as the locus of absolute plenitude lost when the living body is subjected to symbolic orders of signification. Lacking nothing, the real is precisely what the Other lacks, the w/hole within and around which signification circulates, the in-difference from which symbolic differences proceed: 'regarding externality and internality – this distinction makes no sense at all at the level of the real' (1988b: 97). External and internal to the subject of language, 'the real,' comments Lacan, 'is the mystery of the speaking body, it's the mystery of the unconscious' (Jardine, 1985: 122). A mystery between the fullness of the living body and the subject's alienation in signification, the real, for the subject of analysis, is linked to the traumatic loss of plenitude.

Trauma, 'the encounter with the real', is a missed encounter since the real 'presented itself in the form of that which is *unassimilable* in it': 'the real is beyond the *automaton*, the return, the coming back, the insistence of signs, by which we see ourselves governed by the pleasure principle' (1977b: 53–5). The trauma is thus the point of origin that can never be reached, a lost beginning which is repeatedly posited and imagined in the movements of signification, a gap impossible to cross, a leftover that can never be assimilated or mastered. The real is 'impossible' (1977b: 167).

Impossible though it is, the real, as the effects of trauma demonstrate, has important effects on the subject's language and desire. It also discloses the fragility of symbolic and imaginary networks, their lack of absolute closure and consistency. The object that stands in place of the real and reveals one's castration, one's alienation in signification, is called the *objet a*. Doubled, object *a* 'has emerged from some primal separation, from some self-mutilation induced by the very approach of the real' and 'serves as a symbol of lack, that is to say of the phallus, not as such, but only in so far as it is lacking' (1977b: 83, 103). It forms the point 'where the subject sees himself caused as a lack by *a*, and where *a* fills the gap constituted by the inaugural division of the subject'. But, Lacan goes on, 'the *petit a* never crosses this gap' (1977b: 270). The object which fills but does not cross the gap can be anything inassimilable to the symbolic register.

The object *a* thus enables a 'hole in the real' to be filled, enables the subject's projection of a fantasy of coherent reality at the same time as it continually interrupts the imaginary unity that is established. Neither inside and fully integrated, nor outside the subject, the object *a* 'effectively functions as a rift in the closed circle of the psychic apparatus governed by the "pleasure principle"'; it takes the form of 'a surplus which disturbs and blocks from within the autarky of the self-contained balance of the psychic apparatus', an 'internal "excess" which impedes *from within*' (Žižek, 1992: 49). Both limit and excess, the *a* is not the object of desire but the 'object *in* desire' (Lacan, 1977c: 28). The object is only linked to desire through the function of fantasy: 'the phantasy is the support of desire; it is not the object that is the support of desire' (Lacan, 1977b: 185). In fantasy, desire finds 'its reference, its substratum, its precise tuning in the imaginary register' (Lacan, 1977c: 14). While the imaginary gives desire its 'precise tuning', it is the symbolic and its privileged signifier, the phallus or the paternal metaphor, that orientates the fantasy: the object thus takes the place of what the subject, alienated in signification, is symbolically deprived of.

There is a dynamic involved in the articulation of Lacanian registers which accounts for the relation between biological organisms and inert objects (the real), individual consciousness and identity (the imaginary) and linguistic and cultural regulation (the symbolic). Despite the priority of the symbolic register in the construction and maintenance of cultural identities, the dynamic relation means that symbolic networks are never stable in general or individual terms. The real repeatedly disrupts the smooth running of imaginary and symbolic economies with an unsymbolisable excess. The loss of particular objects can reopen the hole in the real: the death of another, loved, person opens a wound that symbolic reality cannot deal with, a loss that cannot be explained and in which subjects recognise their mortality and their lack in being. It is a loss that, initially, has no meaning and makes no sense, but which demands that the lack be filled through the reintegration of the phallus in a process of symbolisation that occurs in rituals of mourning.

The traumatic encounter with the real has other effects that are the inverse of mourning, producing not a reintegration of the subject and the Other but '*Verwerfung* [repudiation, foreclosure]' (1977c: 37–8). Lacan's discussion of psychosis argues that what is rejected in the symbolic reappears in the real and the hole that is opened up signals that the 'Name-of-the-Father' or the phallus never reaches, in the subject's psychic economy, the place of the Other: 'we will take *Verwerfung*, then, to be *foreclosure* of the signifier. To the point at which the Name-of-the-Father is called – we shall see how – may correspond in the Other, then, a mere hole, which, by the inadequacy of the metaphoric effect will provoke a corresponding hole at the place of the phallic signification (1977a: 201). Not accepting a place within the orders of language, the subject remains in opposition to the Other and thus in a position of instability, fluctuation and vacillation:

> it is the lack of the Name-of-the-Father in that place which, by the hole that it opens up in the signified, sets off a cascade of reshapings of the signifier from which the increasing disaster of the imaginary proceeds, to the point at which the level is reached at which the signifier and signified are stabilized in the delusional metaphor. (1977a: 217)

Denoting the 'failure' of the paternal metaphor, psychosis departs from all laws of signification (1977a: 218). The subject is lost in a 'cascade' in which any imaginary sense of unity or symbolic stability disappears: only a particular and delusional metaphor remains.

Mourning and psychosis are related to the hole in the real: they both encounter 'swarms of images' which 'assume the place of the phallus'. However, psychosis seizes upon one image without reference to the symbolic community; mourning sets out to reintegrate imaginary and symbolic registers:

> there is nothing of significance that can fill the hole the real, except the totality of the signifier. The work of mourning is accomplished at the level of the *logos*: I say *logos* rather than group or community, although group and community, being organized culturally, are its mainstays. The work of mourning is first of all performed to satisfy the disorder that is produced by the inadequacy of signifying elements to cope with the hole that has been created in existence, for it is the system of signifiers in their totality which is impeached by the least instance of mourning. (1977c: 38)

Mourning is doubled, signifying the loss of the phallus, as organising principle, and the desire for it. Moreover, mourning indicates the phallus never existed except as a function, and recognises the loss, in contrast to psychosis in which the subject substitutes any image or metaphor to fill the gap. The phallus is thus mapped on to *logos*, the Name-of-the-Father in the Other. It is only in the interrelation of the two that meaning is produced. *Logos*, like the phallus, is not present, is not an object or a signifier rich with meaning. Rather, it is produced, not by singular discrete beings, but in their relation to the system of signifiers that constitutes the possibility of their articulation. Mourning, even as it wants the filling of the hole in the real by the totality of the symbolic, leaves that system open to question and reformulation by the very act of mourning in which the hole, the loss, is recognised and the system's smooth running impeached.

Paternal metaphors?

The paternal metaphor emerges as a cultural problem. Lacan's analysis of the real and the object *a* offers both a diagnosis, as it were, of postmodernity and a way of reading its effects on political and theoretical positions. The postmodern condition denotes a gap in the way the world is presented and lived, a disjunction between imaginary and symbolic registers in which a hole in the real is manifested. The resulting multiplication of signifiers, the fragmented plethora of forms, styles and images associated with postmodernism, corresponds to the 'cascade of reshapings of the signifier', the 'swarms of images' and a 'floating mass of meanings' that try to fill the hole. Mourning appeals to the Other, seeking a signifier

                Sex, machines and navels

that will arrest the play of meaning and unite the social fabric with a total system of signifiers, an appeal to *logos*, to the paternal metaphor. Psychosis rejects the paternal metaphor and the meaning it establishes and, separated from the Other, substitutes a delusional metaphor which is invested with total significance.

Both mourning and psychosis, however, interrogate the function of the paternal metaphor and the Other that prescribes law with a castrating no to arrest the movement of signification. The postmodern condition militates against this metaphor, questioning the legitimacy of the *logos*: who lays down the law, who says 'no'? By what authority? What figure is empowered to cut meaning from the meaningless play of signification and impose it on others? Nonetheless, in many accounts of postmodernism just such a figure is the object of desire: the missing signifier that binds the signifying chain and produces singular meaning is mourned or, alternatively, foreclosed in psychosis by the substitution of a delusional metaphor. In accounts that take different positions on postmodernism, notably those of Baudrillard, Eagleton and Jameson, postmodernity appears as an object of anxiety and mourning and psychosis come to the fore as a symptomatic response. But the unfounding of reality and subjectivity that is the joke of postmodernism indiscriminately embraces all positions whether they are ostensibly for or against, just as Jürgen Habermas, the thinker who is perhaps the most critical antagonist of postmodernism, 'is himself a postmodernist' (Žižek, 1991b: 141).

Reality may, for Baudrillard, have disappeared but the real is not effaced by the cascade of hyperreal simulations: it returns within them. In his account of Disneyland, Baudrillard counters the obvious assumption that it is merely a fantasy world distinct from the real world which is America: 'it is presented as imaginary in order to make us believe that the rest is real, when in fact all of Los Angeles and the America surrounding it are no longer real, but of the order of simulation' (Baudrillard, 1983: 25). Presented as imaginary, Disneyland serves to 'conceal the fact' that all of America is already Disneyland, thereby saving the reality principle. Baudrillard's provocative reversals, in which 'fact' becomes an effect of fiction, display the retroactive process of differentiation that enables reality to appear. Thus, Disneyland 'is a deterrence machine set up in order to rejuvenate in reverse the fiction of the real' (Baudrillard, 1983: 25). It supplies the fantasy that supports symbolic reality. Rejuvenating an older fiction of reality retroactively constitutes a nostalgic reaction to hyperreality, mourning what used to pass for the real. The reality of simulations replaces the real, leaving only a sense of something that has been lost: this trace, a vague, disturbing and irruptive sense of loss, alludes to the Lacanian real and opens a gap to suggest that something is missing from the orders of simulation. Hinting at a psychoanalytic form of *Nachträglich-keit* (deferred action) in the account of reality's retrospective simulation, Baudrillard's version elides reality, and its principle, along with the real. Simulation forms a dimension of signs playing beyond the regulation of a paternal metaphor. At the same time, the excess of simulation that absorbs the impossibility of the real abolishes all subjectivity, lack and desire. The subject is either dissolved in circuits of simulation or left lost, nostalgic, a self-less spectator of the apocalyptic orgy of signification, a being fading into nothingness.

Dominated by psychosis, Baudrillard's postmodernity has no paternal metaphor to establish and regulate differences, to decide between sense and nonsense, between legitimate and improper meanings: it allows for no point at which signifier and signified can be knotted together to arrest the play of images and signification. The objectivity of images, 'sovereign', 'incorrigible, immanent and enigmatic', performs an 'ironic embezzlement of the symbolic order', disobeying 'all legislation' (Baudrillard, 1990a: 181–3). Evacuated from simulation or fatally seduced by images, there is no place for the subject in the post-oedipal world of the digital Narcissus (Baudrillard, 1990b: 173). Baudrillard adopts an anti-metaphorical stance, refusing the possibility of attaining an external position of singularity: the excess of simulation has completely outstripped human capacities to discern or direct what is signified. The critique of metaphor is made explicit in Baudrillard's account of viral culture. There is no longer the possibility of a regulating signifier, no paternal metaphor, only an incessantly sliding metonymic chain of signifiers: 'Today, metonymy – replacing the whole as well as the components, and occasioning a general commutability of terms – has built its house on the dis-illusion of metaphor' (Baudrillard, 1993: 8). Baudrillard's subject stands in opposition to the absolutely different Other, taking a place in the real, in the form of the American desert: 'luminous, fossilized network of an inhuman intelligence, of a radical difference …' (Baudrillard, 1988: 6). Absolute in its difference, the desert is a locus of presence and absence, of an unknown luminosity and inert solidity, a devastated emptiness eclipsing the human subject. The desert's full nothingness becomes the mirror of American culture: 'for us the whole of America is a desert. Culture exists there in a wild state: it sacrifices all intellect, all aesthetics in a process of literal transcription into the real' (1988: 99). This mirror of the desert-real absorbs all the symbols of culture in an image of the emptiness that underlies cultural production and regulation: natural deserts 'denote the emptiness, the radical nudity that is the background to every human institution. At the same time they designate human institutions as a metaphor of that emptiness and the work of man as the continuity of the desert, culture as a mirage and as the perpetuity of the simulacrum' (1988: 63). Like the real, the desert's emptiness lies inside as well as beyond the subject, 'a natural extension of the inner silence of the body. If humanity's language, technology, and buildings are an extension of its constructive faculties, the desert alone is an extension of its capacity for absence, the ideal schema of humanity's disappearance' (1988: 68). Marking the lack the real lacks, the desert is the locus of an unspeakable plenitude to the extent that being and nothingness no longer make sense in such an incomprehensible totality. Within and outside the body, the desert becomes the image and embodiment of the death drive, the pure homeostasis beyond the fluctuations of desire: natural deserts, writes Baudrillard, 'induce in me an exalting vision of desertification of signs and men' (1988: 63). Laying waste to the marks of human alienation in culture and signification, deserts offer a transcendent vision of the totality of being, of an empty locus beyond the vacillations of identity, desire and difference, a state that precedes and succeeds the wounded, lacking, narcissistic subjects of human culture.

The vision of the 'desertification of signs and men' conjures up a distinctly Romantic shadow, and with it the spectre of desire and its attendant morality. Hyperreal culture becomes a site of horror and moral enjoyment: the disgust that attends the playful fascination with America is soothed by the knowledge that it is in its death throes. Desire returns in the gaze upon the vastness of the desert, a sovereign position looming in the sublimity of cultural desertification. Culture ironically mirrors the emptiness of the subject who remains absolutely separated from any meaningful or active place in systems of signification, possessed only by the delusional metaphor of this emptiness: the desert becomes the metaphor beyond sense and nonsense, 'the sublime form that banishes all sociality, all sentimentality, all sexuality. Words, even when they speak of the desert, are always unwelcome' (1988: 71). Beyond words, the subject becomes pure excess, mirrored in the excessive totality of the real. But the very words in which this psychosis is transcribed suggests a certain nostalgia for the Romantic metaphor, the impossible 'I', that transcendent figure of plenitude, that self always joyously teetering on the brink of its own dissolution.

As the excess of postmodernity, the human figure, no longer what it used to appear to be, becomes the impossible object it always was. But it still carries a powerful myth. In Terry Eagleton's *The Ideology of the Aesthetic* postmodernism is an object of anxiety that necessitates an aggressive riposte in a return to older myths and metaphors. Eagleton exhumes the living presence of an idealised human figure as the basis of a materialist critique of postmodern aestheticisation. The ritual of mourning fills the hole in the real with the recognisable figure of the human being. This human figure functions as the point at which nature, truth, history and culture coalesce. Biological nature is invoked to guarantee a corporeal, human body and ground the argument since biology determines the limits and possibilities of existence: 'a certain open-endedness and transformability is part of our natures', due to the '"lack" in our biological structure which culture, if we are to survive at all, has at all costs to fill'. The open-endedness allows for a degree of 'creative self-making' which is undertaken within the limits of the body, but it is biology that determines social structure:

> Human societies, by virtue of the biological structure of that body, all need to engage in some form of labour and some kind of sexual reproduction; all human beings require warmth, rest, nourishment and shelter, and are inevitably implicated by the necessities of labour and sexuality in various forms of social association, the regulation of which we name the political. (Eagleton, 1990: 410)

These 'biologically determined facts', Eagleton continues, 'have so far bulked the largest course in the course of human history, and have set their imprint upon what … we call culture'. Facts quickly deliver an all-encompassing human truth, timeless and universal: 'all human beings are frail, mortal and needy, vulnerable to suffering and death. The fact that these transhistorical truths are always culturally specific, always variably instantiated, is no argument against their transhistoricality' (1990: 410). Culture, for Eagleton, supplements the biological lack in human nature, while biology grounds culture as an instance of universal human truth. Biology, the ground of human materialism and its definitive lack, 'binds us ineluctably together, and in doing so opens up possibilities of friendship and love'. Communication and understanding take their bearings from this point and, though possessed of an oppressive potential as well, are seen as 'essential for our material survival', establishing, in the manner of Habermasian negotiation, the basis of 'free, reciprocal, self-fulfilment' (1990: 411–13).

'Lack', biological and transhistorical, forms the reality which defines humanity as needy and creative, social and individual, particular and universal: it unifies the poles of materialism and idealism, nature and culture, in a figure akin to Foucault's 'empirico-transcendental doublet': 'a being such that knowledge will be attained in him of what renders all knowledge possible' (Foucault, 1970: 318). The reality of the lack has a double function: 'the idea of human nature does not suggest that we should realize any capacity which is natural, but that the highest values we *can* realize spring from part of our nature, and are not arbitrary choices or constructs' (Eagleton, 1990: 412). Nature, subjected to the discrimin-ations of cultural value, is not, in contrast to Sadean nature, the ground and licence of any behaviour: moderated by a hierarchical value system, higher nature implies another lack within the orders of originary lack. The reality, the foundation, of biological lack delivers itself up to fantasy: the lacking human body fills a hole in the real as the screen for the projection of a cultural fantasy. The fantastmatic ground of authority assumed by Eagleton needs need, wants poverty, suffering and mortality so that it can fill the void with its word. On the basis of need, of lack, a whole discourse is produced in which the needy human reflects the basic and universal assumptions of discourse. An authoritative position discovers its own inverted reflection as the ground of its truth and the legitimation of its exclusions. Need, in a biological sense, slides into a needy economy of desire (1990: 410). Need, moreover, informs political judgement: 'needs which human beings have as an essential part of biological nature – for food, shelter, association, protection from injury and so on – can serve as a norm of political judgement and practice' (1990: 411–12). And in the fantasy of cultural authority under enunciation, needs already serve this purpose. From political judgement, it is only a short step to a fully moral authority that execrates the evil that enjoys need and suffering: evil takes 'an active, sadistic delight in human misery and destruction which apparently indulges in such destructiveness as an end in itself' (1990: 412). On the basis of the judgement legitimated by need, postmodernism is attacked as evil. Needs must: legitimately prescribing the exclusions that are the prerogative of a position which already knows higher human values, needs authorise a position that speaks for the species as a whole. Such a position assumes the representative function of the bourgeois intellectual criticised by Foucault and Deleuze (1977).

The needy human body is not a problem for Eagleton's position: this body mirrors the discursive fantasy of human transcendence. The first person plural dominating Eagleton's account signals the imaginary and anticipatory unity of the global human community who are bound to recognise themselves in the truth of his own discourse. Misrecognising Other as other, however, Eagleton's position turns the human community into a frail body in need and in need of an authoritative image. For all the fantasy and the recognition it anticipates, an anxiety pervades the critique of postmodernism. The resistance of postmodernism constitutes the main cause of Eagleton's discourse, not the human figure of lack in whose name it is delivered. Postmodernist preoccupation with 'a plurality of lifestyles', Eagleton asserts, 'averts its eyes' from 'the quite specific historical conditions' which permit such plurality and the checks and restrictions imposed on plurality 'by our present conditions of life' (1990: 409). These conditions, as limits to postmodern play, are identified and imposed by invoking biology. From this platform, the limits are ultimately moral guarantees for an attack on the evil of the aesthetics of postmodernism. Evil delights in human misery, enjoys that which has no value and necessity, a delight best exemplified, by Eagleton, in the evil of Nazi concentration camps. But evil is also the mirror of morality, replicating its disgust in an active enmity for all things virtuous: evil is

> revolted by the sight of virtue, unable to see truth or meaning as anything but pretentious shams with which human beings pathetically conceal from themselves the utter vacuousness of their existence. It is thus closely related to cynicism, a mocking cackle at the high-minded claptrap of human idealism. Fortunately, evil is an extremely rare condition, outside the upper echelons of fascist organizations; but in its strangely autotelic character it has an unnerving affinity with the aesthetic. It shares with the aesthetic a certain low estimate of the utilitarian … (1990: 412)

The stark equation of aesthetically inclined postmodernists with fascist leaders legitimates their complete denigration and exclusion. Evil, moreover, is associated with those producing an aesthetic critique of humanism.

Without the human figure, Eagleton's position is lost; without the human image, fantasy disintegrates in the face of an inhuman threat: the 'idea of human nature' fends off plural lifestyles, grounding truth in nature to affirm they are 'not arbitrary choices or constructs' (1990: 412). A straightforward choice is presented between humanity and evil, life or nothing. As what ought to be the central idea, the human figure functions as a paternal metaphor filling the empty space of the real. To do so, however, this figure must be recognised by the Other. And at this point, postmodernism again interferes, signalling that the Other is no longer what it used to be, that the material conditions and human reality Eagleton invokes as a guarantees are no longer recognised. Hence the execration of postmodernism: an attack on an Other that refuses to respond with the recognition imaginarily due to his discourse, a demand met with silence rather than assent. The circuit of imaginary self-creativity and fulfilment is shorted out, the process whereby the self imagines it can, dialectically, 'come into its own', remains incomplete (1990: 414). Not recognised by the Other as locus of truth and meaning, Eagleton disavows the ex-centricity of subjectivity and insists, instead, on its own priority by reducing Other to evil other in order that the self can be opposed to language and culture. But the human figure who is heroically defended is less a paternal metaphor and more a delusional one. The delusion, moreover, engenders an aggressive repudiation of other positions: 'the autonomy of the other is all at once the condition of creative relationship, and a source of violence and insecurity' (1990: 411). The duality of the relation between self and other resonates throughout Eagleton's text to the point that the autonomy of the other becomes unbearable and calls only for antagonism and not creative reconciliation. Not one and other, but one or other: at the limit of creative tolerance lies postmodernism's evil, object of uncomplicated aggression. In its call for the fullness of human self-realisation an other is needed as object of unification and destruction: the critique enacts violence, venting its righteous anger on the cynical, inhumane, mocking voice that torments idealism and morality. In the name of humanity, communication, friendship, understanding, negotiation and love there springs, in neither a particularly creative nor original manner, the same old violence and aggression towards the other. An imaginary, dualistic aggressivity short-circuits the benevolent, communicative claims to human progress and undercuts the call to ethical negotiation and renegotiation. Ethics never quite makes it into the political arena in the manner Eagleton advocates, never quite manages to inscribe human love across the social world as an injunction to love others because they are subjects too (1990: 413). Such love turns too easily to hate because it turns too much on a self who imagines he has too much to lose.

Between Baudrillard's and Eagleton's versions of contemporary culture, Fredric Jameson's examination of postmodernism's complicity with the transnational networks of late capitalism mourns the loss of an authoritative 'I' as it attempts a more productive redefinition of the real. Jameson's account accords with a Baudrillardian diagnosis of postmodernity, but it rejects the implications because they leave no room for humans in the process of social change: it is the active cultural and political interventions of the critical Marxist intellectual that Jameson aims to preserve. This involves the preservation of the past and a critique of the aesthetics of commodification. With an eye towards Baudrillard, Jameson states 'the approach to the present by way of the art language of the simulacrum, or of the pastiche of the stereotypical past, endows present reality and the openness of present history with the spell and distance of a glossy mirage' (Jameson, 1984: 68). The past is pastiched or 'cannibalised', the density of the present evacuated in the rush of superficial stereoscopic illusions and filmic images termed the 'hysterical sublime' (1984: 65, 76). The emerging mutation of the space, or 'hyperspace', of postmodern culture 'has finally succeeded in transcending the capacities of the individual human body to locate itself, to organize its immediate surroundings perceptually, and cognitively to map its position in a mappable external world' (1984; 83). The unmappability of postmodern space is explained in Lacanian terms as 'the breakdown of the signifying chain', a 'rubble of distinct and unrelated signifiers' without a 'paternal authority' to regulate and render them meaningful for the subject (1984: 72).

While the diagnosis of postmodern culture accords with Baudrillard, Jameson's response and prognosis is quiet different: it is more in line with Eagleton's Marxist-humanist critique of postmodernism, though without the explicit hostility and moralism. Like Eagleton, Jameson turns on the distinctly human figure of the subject, setting out to recuperate or salvage a form of radical past that has been lost in the general aestheticisation of postmodern culture. To recover a radical past also involves the restoration of the 'critical distance' that postmodern historicity consumes in the present and enables political agency and activity to intervene in processes of social transformation and change. This is not to be done by means of older forms of ideological critique and its underlying moralism; postmodern aesthetics has precluded that possibility. What it requires is an engagement in aesthetic practices themselves through a process of 'cognitive mapping'. This process involves recourse to Lacan, mediated by Althusser's version of ideology as the imaginary relation of the subject to his/her real conditions of existence (Jameson, 1984: 90). Cognitive mapping also involves a cognisant appeal to the function of Lacan's symbolic: the real (transglobal capitalism) is understood by the individual subject (imaginary) through the co-ordinates provided by the 'subject-place of knowledge' (the subject-presumed-to-know located in the Other).

Sex, machines and navels

For Jameson this Other is Marxian science, specifically the knowledge of late capitalism provided by Ernest Mandel (1984: 91). The subject recovers itself to gain a 'new heightened sense of its place in the global system' and regain, as an individual and collective being, 'a capacity to act and struggle which is at present neutralized by our spatial as well as our social confusion' (1984: 92).

For Jameson, the response to the postmodern hole in the real is one of mourning. It requires the restitution of a paternal metaphor that can articulate specific and global, imaginary and symbolic. The metaphor that Jameson identifies among the symptoms of postmodern culture he diagnoses is the network of transglobal capitalism itself. For Jameson the fascination with communicational systems and computer technology is a 'distorted figuration of something even deeper, namely the whole world system of present-day multinational capitalism' (1984: 79–80). 'The whole new decentred global network of the third stage of capital' becomes the metaphor that fills the hole in the real. The 'truth of postmodernism' is grasped by means of 'its fundamental object – the world space of multi-national capital' (1984: 92). The symbolic fabric, ripped in the encounter with the postmodern real, is imaginarily repaired by way of the lost object and the paternal metaphor. The process of mourning, however, establishes Marxism as the symbolic order, a grand narrative towards which theorists, like Deleuze and Foucault (1977) and Lyotard (1984b) have become avowedly incredulous, suspicious of the subject, the intellectual, on which it depends. Foucault, conversing with Gilles Deleuze on the function of intellectuals, argues that the intellectual is an effect of totalising bourgeois discourses and regimes of truth, already superfluous in the diverse political actions of the masses. Only the institutionally specific role of the intellectual as interrogator of forms of power is tenable for Foucault (1988), not the prophetic and prescriptive shaper of general political will.

This (bourgeois) intellectual, however, looms large in Jameson's revision of aesthetic practice since the restoration of the Marxist grand narrative involves an intellectual human subject. Stating in implicit rebuke of Foucault's position that left-wing cultural theorists have been intimidated by bourgeois aesthetic traditions, Jameson advocates the pedagogical and didactic functions of art in the aesthetics of cognitive mapping (1984: 89). The knowing subject is not eclipsed by simulation; he or she can still, Jameson hopes, understand, direct and change systems of meaning and signification, whether they are postmodern or not. Artist and teacher, it seems, are central intellectual figures in the constitution of the new cultural model proposed by Jameson: they fulfil the function of the paternal metaphor rendered untenable in postmodern culture; they are subjects supposed to know. This position seems more wishful than accepted. Lyotard, for example, finds such a position untenable as he argues that not only is the intellectual dead, but that the roles of artists and philosophers are far from prescriptive or didactic: their task is, instead, to formulate questions rather than dictate programmes and answers.[4] The aesthetic pedagogue that, for Jameson, is supposed to occupy the place of the intellectual is already, it seems, condemned to be an object of mourning.

In this return of the real, the return to the anxiety-generating hole, signification still circulates, rather than being arrested by a recognised paternal metaphor. The narrative that Jameson advocates as the truth of postmodernism remains out of reach, unrecognised by the Other, the symbolic cultural community he addresses. A joke that is not one. Indeed, the humanised Other, imagined as a total and unifying symbolic system, becomes the object of mourning. While the function of the paternal metaphor may be general, its specific significance and effects are restricted to particular cultural and institutional communities: as in jokes, there might be no Other of the Other, no final metalanguage, but there may well be different Others. To wish for a homogeneous and global symbolic network is, perhaps, the most aesthetic of all gestures, one that, eclipsing the virtualisation of technological realties, imagines the obliteration of the real. In the contestations of postmodern culture, however, the paternal metaphor, as *logos*, truth and law, remains open to question.

Notes

1 Freud (1976b: 220). For a further discussion of this point, see Mehlman (1975: 439).
2 See Deleuze (1990: 66-73). Ragland (1995: 199) notes how an '*ab-sens*' at the very heart of meaning is associated with the void and logic's navel.
3 Lacan (1988b: 303); Lacan (1977b: ix); Lacan (1988b: 97).
4 Lyotard (1984b). See also Lyotard (1988: 142).

Sex, machines and navels

4 ✧ History, holes and things

History's navel

'There is no document of civilization which is not at the same time a document of barbarism' (Benjamin, 1973: 258). In a discussion of this statement from Walter Benjamin's seventh thesis on the philosophy of history, Scott Wilson analyses the ambivalent historical relation of civilisation and barbarism by invoking the figure of the navel:

> In Lacanian terms the desired *relation* to the past, the 'umbilical cord' to the real, is a gaze that recoils in horror at the (primal) scene of its origins: the 'real' nature of its continuity with the past; this traumatic encounter results in a (repeated) 'detachment', a severing of the cord which produces a 'navel', the 'quilting point' or *point de capiton* in the form of an isolated, sacralized document, the 'cultural treasure' whose structure as a signifier governs that of historical materialism itself. (Wilson, 1995: 142)

The navel poses the question of history as a matter of both the continuity and the discontinuity between present and past in which the supposed reality of prior events is divided between the desire for an umbilical relation and the horrified encounter with unpresentable origins that remain irrecuperable: the navel of history functions as both limit and incitement to historicist interpretation, the point beyond which it cannot, and thus desires to go. History embraces a fantasy of origins as compelling as the originary fantasy that, for Laplanche and Pontalis (1986), structures the development of subjectivity at an individual level. The crux of the matter, literally and figurally, is the navel which ties the subject to a history that is both his/her own and that of others, a nodal point articulating natural development and cultural or social emplacement in symbolic structures.

The positing of history's navel stresses the knots that bind and separate the narratives that organise cultural meanings. The navel of history signifies an internal difference both constituting and dividing history from itself, a gap where the possibility of history emerges. *Waterland*'s narrator, a history teacher, comments, how 'history begins only at the point where things go wrong ... born only with trouble, with perplexity, with regret' (Swift, 1984: 92). History starts with an interruption to a regular course of events and their homogeneous narrative. The teacher's observation is reiterated later, this time by a student noting how 'people only explain when things go wrong' (Swift, 1984: 145). Resistance requires explanation; what does not work or make sense calls for repeated attempts at comprehension. Before history there is only a lack in structures of knowledge and understanding, an empty space into which is projected the possibility of discovering the first and last word. 'And can I deny', confesses a reflective history teacher, 'that what I wanted all along was not some golden nugget that history would at last yield up, but History itself, the Grand Narrative, the filler of vacuums, the dispeller of fears of the dark?' (Swift, 1984: 53). More than a nugget, the teacher wants historical truth: beyond the knot of history's navel lies a vacuum, a void before history waiting to be filled by a complete account. A powerful and phallic fantasy imagines a solution of all mysteries, the complete penetration of unknown spaces by knowledge. But the gap constitutive of the production of history only causes stories, narrations in which scientific, objective history quickly becomes fable and myth: the cut of the navel testifies to discontinuity and creating anew, the signifier of a new birth.

A non-assimilable difference emerges within history and yet outside its grasp, demanding the production of interminable historical documents distinct from the events recorded. The event, reconstituted in texts, remains external to them, the limit of the historical encounter. For the history teacher, 'events elude meaning, but we look for meanings' (Swift, 1984: 121). The search for meanings involves a process of creation or invention as much as straightforward discovery, with the present producing the past rather than recovering it. History, it seems, does more than chart a forward course, but is propelled backwards as well: produced in the present, it is structured by a retrospective gaze which imagines itself looking forwards from the past to the present in which it is gazing. In the novel history 'goes in two directions at once. It goes backwards as it goes forwards' (Swift, 1984: 117). This double movement, simultaneously progressive and regressive, is akin to Foucault's 'history of the present'. Writing on the texts of ancient Greece and Rome, he describes his method as one that examines 'both the difference that keeps us at a remove from a

| Sex, machines and navels

way of thinking in which we recognize the origin of our own, and the proximity that remains in spite of that distance which we never cease to explore' (Foucault, 1987: 7n.). The thread that is spun out and back turns on an axis of similarity and difference, proximity and distance.

Around the navel, as knot and hole, the progressive linear and teleological narrative of a singular History unfolds from a determinable origin to ascend continuously into the brightness of the future. But, warns our history teacher, 'do not fall into the illusion that history is a well-disciplined and unflagging column marching unswervingly into the future' (Swift, 1984: 117). The navel also invokes origins that precede history, in that the cutting of the cord of continuity points to causes beyond it. Origins are deferred, causes rendered elusive, knowledge ceding to fiction and fantasy. And desire: if the causes of historical events were known and self-evident, if the documents of history were transparent and unchanging to the point of there being no lack in historical knowledge, there would be no need for explanation, no desire underlying the supposedly rational and objective assessment of events and records. History turns on a desire for that imagined, and lost, 'golden nugget' that will solve its mysteries. But the nugget only testifies to history's holey narrative: 'history is that impossible thing: the attempt to give an account, with incomplete knowledge, of actions themselves undertaken with incomplete knowledge' (Swift, 1984: 94). Beyond the navel, nothing, or, rather some ungraspable Thing in excess of historicisation. For *Waterland*'s history teacher, wandering between lessons on the French Revolution in 1980 and family crises in the period of World War II, history 'loops. It takes detours' (Swift, 1984: 117). And the loops and detours of the text approach and avoid a nugget of horror that binds the two periods to history's mysterious Thing. Towards the end of the novel, the narrator speculates on the nature of this Thing while enlightening his students on the French Revolution: 'this unfathomable stuff we're made from, this stuff that we're always coming back to – our love of life, children, our love of life – is more anarchic, more subversive than any Tennis-Court Oath ever was. That's why these revolutions always have something of the death-wish about them' (Swift, 1984: 178). Beyond history, lies the 'stuff' associated with the inassimilable energies of life. And death. Or 'life–death', to use Derrida's (1987) term for what lies beyond the pleasure principle. If history is played out between the principles of pleasure and reality, in Freud's terms, or desire and the Other, in Lacan's, the excessive ahistorical thing to which history vainly and repeatedly returns, its 'unfathomable stuff', is the death drive.

Other versions of history are suggested in the labyrinthine course of *Waterland*'s wandering stories. An entangled novel centred on a history teacher who tells stories, the presentation of historical facts and dates is repeatedly juxtaposed with numerous speculations on the nature of history itself. A definition of history is offered as the epigraph to the novel: '*historia*, ae, f. 1. inquiry, investigation, learning. 2. a) a narrative of past events, history. b) any kind of narrative: account, tale, story.' The novel goes on to explore the various nuances and possibilities of the dictionary definition, its form reiterating the different and divergent statements on the nature of history. While 'inquiry' sets out 'to uncover the mysteries of cause and effect', the story finds itself incomplete, entangled in the narrations of the present. Causes and effects merge in the reversible process of re-citing history as an answer to the demands of the text's pedagogical present. The result is another pedagogical formulation of history's nature: the demand for explanation 'provides an explanation', the teacher informs his class, since 'the seeking of reasons [is] itself inevitably an historical process, since it must always go backwards from what came after to what came before' (Swift, 1984: 92). Explanation does not answer questions of historical cause from an external position, thereby framing it all at once with beginning and end, but finds itself within a historical process that depends on the act of reinscription itself, the act of narration constituting history, a spinning of yarns that are themselves woven into, and as, the fabric of history. This version of history leads inexorably towards the plural, contested and partial histories associated with 'poststructuralism': grand narratives are no longer credible with the advent of postmodern practices which eschew transcendent authority and deliver little stories.[1]

The novel begins, not with facts, but with the 'fairy-tale words' of a father. These are underscored by the narrator's comment on how the history teacher gives up on History: 'in the middle of explaining how, with Parisian blood-letting, our Modern world began, he breaks off and starts telling these stories' (Swift, 1984: 5). His gesture emphasises the plurality and partiality he advances, abandoning any attempt to teach the grand narrative of modernity's all-too human history in favour of the disparate fragments that compose his story. Later on, he is forced to admit that history may be no more than 'a lucky dip of meanings' (1984: 121). *Waterland*, itself offering different meanings of history in a disorganised assemblage of stories, refuses a totalising and authoritative narrative, interspersing the history teacher's story with numerous other topics and modes of narration. A history of the Fens, of invasion and land reclamation,

Sex, machines and navels

a natural history of the sex life of the European eel, as well as comments on the French Revolution and World War II, sit alongside local, commercial and family histories, all traversing the relation of events and exchanges in 1980s south London. The separation between grand narrative and little story, however, is never absolute. *Waterland* refuses to make a fatuous leap from modernity's idea of universal history to postmodernity's fragmented little stories: it moves erratically between its various subjects of narration so that One History never reaches predominance nor is it simply displaced by numerous separate little stories. The novel repeatedly emphasises the contemporaneity of events, the contiguity of local history and general History: 'when the redcoats were storming Quebec … Jacob Crick was putting his cheek and ear to the air to feel the direction and force of the breezes'; 'while the Bastille tumbles … Thomas Atkinson studies the principles of land drainage. …' (1984: 12, 59). The insistence on the contemporaneity of events merely associates particular and general by means of dates, their connection no more than their inclusion in the same statement. Disconnection in the novel's relation of (his)stories, however, is not the only or privileged mode: throughout local events are tied to those of nations, the history teacher's maternal ancestors and their commercial and political ascent charted on the upward curve of nineteenth-century imperial progress and prosperity.

Any insistence on the disconnection of his-stories and History misses the point, or rather, points, of connection and interrelation disclosed by the novel. These points, navels, as it were, articulate the different acts of narration and the topics and effects of storytelling in respect of structures beyond their particular enunciation. The main locus of enunciation is the classroom where lessons no longer endorse a straightforwardly global view of history, but they are lessons, nonetheless, despite the obscurity of their direction. Even though the teacher has apparently abandoned the idea of History, he continues to interrogate it, attempting to articulate himself within its now complex and disorientating networks and (dis)connections. They are his stories circulating among family pasts and presents and intersecting with broader issues involving matters of being, of one's place in the worlds of the present and the future as well as one's relation to history. The novel's emphasis on the position of enunciation is significant in terms of the connecting and separating of subjects and narratives. In their address to others, stories function intersubjectively, positioning beings within a system of values and meanings. As the navel, anatomically, indicates the trace of other beings, so the 'navel of speech' is the gap that connects and differentiates subjects by way of the Other. 'It is not without effect that,' Lacan, somewhat elusively, remarks, 'even in a public speech, one directs one's attention at subjects, touching them at what Freud calls the navel' (1977b: 3). In addressing his students with a discourse that ostensibly eschews the abstracted and formal techniques of pedagogy, the history teacher touches them at the level of the navel, drawing them into the intricate meshwork of histories. Attendance rises. To touch subjects at the level of the navel, then, involves an address to the Thing that ties subjects within discourse. The teacher's address, moreover, identifies the anxieties of his students, their fears of the future: it engages them in the enunciation and sharing of their dreams and anxieties, a practice that has ramifications well beyond the classroom.

In contrast to the students, the history teacher neither dreams of the end of the world nor expects and demands a future (Swift, 1984: 135). For him, 'what we wish upon the future is very often the image of some lost, imagined past' (1984: 122). But the teacher's wish is not prospective, averting its gaze from any future at all. Within the cycle of history in which past and future mirror each other, his wish short-circuits the loop in a move backwards, a wish bound up with an impossible past: the harrowing familial and global events in the period of World War II, the narrator comments, 'have deepened his desire to fathom the secrets of History' (1984: 104). Forever beyond his grasp, the imagined plenitude of the past nonetheless structures his desire. Acknowledging the missed encounter that defines his relationship to History, he cannot cede his desire, a desire become an all-consuming demand, a 'longing': 'even if we miss the grand repertoire of history, we yet imitate it in miniature and endorse, in miniature, its longing for presence, for feature, for purpose, for content'. Meaning, reason, love, form the centre of his demand, intensified by the longing that sustains them as distant objects of desire, a fantasy underlying his investment in History. For what he demands, ultimately, is the very Thing that ahistorically remains in the same place, the 'unfathomable stuff' linked to love of life and unknown mysteries, the fairy tale of that which, outside history, causes it. The subject of demand remains impossible, a lost object of history and cause of the movement of desire by which history is written. 'I began to demand of history an Explanation', he says, a demand which stems from the 'fabulous aura of history' produced by his mother's bedtime stories (1984: 53). The child's demand, for reason, love and meaning, psychoanalysis maintains, is initially addressed to the m/Other. And it is to the mother of history, mother earth and mother nature

Sex, machines and navels

that the navel fabulously gestures: a return to maternal plenitude before difference and desire is invited and resisted.

The navel of history conjoins the longing of a single being who is alienated in signifying systems with cultural myths of an idealised unity of Being in nature.[2] With myth or a narrative or (his)story beyond that of singular development, a particular subject is able to identify him- or herself in a cultural order, speaking for others by way of the Other. He or she can say 'we' instead of 'I', a move from opinion to truth: 'How we pine for paradise. For mother's milk' (Swift, 1984: 118). In psychoanalysis, of course, 'the desire for the mother is the origin of everything', 'the founding desire of the whole structure ... but it is also a criminal desire' (Lacan, 1992: 283). Conventional readings of Freud's Oedipus complex tend to place the emphasis on the object, the mother. In contrast, Lacan is careful to stress the role of desire and its structural effects. To focus on desire rather than its object underlines the absence of the object: desire and lack are inseparable. Not only is the subject forever separated from the mother at the level of natural satisfaction, she is also the site of a fundamental prohibition, the incest taboo marking the criminality of inaugural desire. Prohibition, however, sustains desire even as it commands against it, the limit simultaneously acting as an invitation to transgression, an exotic other place that was once the same as the child, but glazed, as a lost object, with the allure of a fabulous secret. But desire structured in the present and looking longingly backwards comes first, rendering the demand for the m/Other impossible, though no less powerful. The mother lies outside desire as its cause, the matrix of life, the very matter, the 'unfathomable stuff' of history and the point at which history becomes natural history, the point of departure, arrival, and endless return to a past that will be the future, the arcadia–utopia and lost paradise of plenitude.

The navel exists as a physical limit co-terminous with symbolic prohibition, a point of non-assimilable difference impeding the desire to erase all division in the drive towards the absolute unity of One. Not only is it a point suturing individual and cultural desire, but is the site from which an impossible demand is enunciated for an unreachable maternal paradise. As a scar on a natural body made by the cut of culture's separation from maternal nature, the navel exists as an actual and imaginary limit, a border that links fantasy and reality as it entangles the boundaries of nature and culture. It is the point at which human (cultural) history ends and begins in the (dis)connection from natural history: 'What is this thing that takes us back, either via catastrophe and confusion or in our heart's desire, to where we were? Let's call it Natural History' (Swift, 1984: 119). Where History proceeds according to cultural, political and economic laws, its desire bound up with language, Natural History is that 'which doesn't go anywhere. Which cleaves to itself. Which perpetually travels back to where it came from' (1984: 177). Indifferent to progress, natural history works according to laws, reasons and codes unknown to those of culture, in excess of and prior to human history. For *Waterland*'s narrator Nature's fundamental otherness leads to the problem of human nature at the core the historian's impossible demand, the 'unsolved mystery of mysteries' (1984: 178) continuing to exert the effects of desire on history. In this way nature works as mystery, limit and cause to historical explanation, a fundamental lack in symbolic understanding lying within History as well, at its core and yet beyond it, in it more than it, the very Thing of history.

To gaze at the navel of history involves questions that have circulated around the suggestive slogan of the 'end of history'. From the odd perspective provided by the figure of the navel, however, the end of history assumes a variety of meanings implying multiple and divergent ends rather than a single apocalypse. While the figure retains an element of teleology and development as a mark of individual separation, its connective function suggests more than the terminal point of historical enquiry, the end that arrests the thread of retroactive explanation, the end, that is, as beginning: beyond the navel lies the matrix of causation, a meshwork composed of intricate, indeterminable traces, a web of indefinite endings. As end, the navel implies an unravelling in frayed ends, an unwinding beyond teleology and historical direction that simultaneously ties matters in further knots, a grand narrative (dis)entangling in little stories. The end becomes a series of ends without end, an end in mystery that interrogates any totalising assertion that the end has been reached. Instead it provokes suspicion with regard to the ends, the interests, aims and implications of any claim to finality.

Natural history and the navel

At the origin of matters of creation and sexual reproduction, the point, if not between chicken and egg, then between mother and child, the navel appears to be as old as history in its human form. But this excludes God the Father, whose Word brought the world into being. As a result, there have been serious doubts raised concerning the navel's appearance or non-appearance in history. Did Adam have a navel when, not born of woman,

Sex, machines and navels

there would be no biological reason for its existence? In an essay entitled 'Adam's Navel', Stephen Jay Gould returns to this question and some of the theological, geological and evolutionary issues it provokes by observing that the omnipresent fig leaf decently shielding Adam's and Eve's genitalia from a chaste gaze conceals an object less improper: the navel. While painters, quite literally, 'hedged' this knotty theological matter with a strategically large fig leaf, Gould speculates on divine intentions: 'would God ... not create with appearance of pre-existence?' (1995: 1). Giving Adam a navel would 'stress continuity with future men' and 'endow a pristine world with the appearance of an ordered history' (1995: 2).

The argument is not Gould's, but comes from Philip Henry Gosse's *Omphalos: An Attempt to Untie the Geological Knot* (1857), written two years before the publication of Charles Darwin's *The Origin of Species*. As an attempt to reconcile the contradiction between religion and natural history, *Omphalos* interprets the facts of geological antiquity as revealed by fossils within, rather than against, the assertion of biblical literalism that the world is of relatively recent creation. Gosse's 'spectacular nonsense' is instructive, Gould contends, since it shows that 'exceptions do prove rules' and aid in the understanding of science and logic. What concerns Gould most is that the argument is authored, not by an 'armchair theologian', but by a 'dedicated empiricist' and, on this basis, he carefully extrapolates Gosse's position. 'The life or every organic being,' Gosse states, 'is whirling in a ceaseless circle to which one knows not how to assign any commencement ...' (Gould, 1995: 2–4). The circle forms the centre of Gosse's argument, since, to create, God enters it to deposit life bearing all the traces of previous stages, a 'prochronic' furnishing of the simulated marks of pre-existence. There are, Gould summarises, two types of existence decreed by God, 'one constructed all at once with the appearance of elapsed time, the other progressing sequentially' (1995: 10). Fossils and Adam's navel come into the first category, while subsequent births and deaths fit into the second. Gosse thus produces a model of creation that, in the pre-Darwinian nineteenth century, allows the literal biblical account of creation to co-exist with the apparently conflicting facts of geological antiquity: it offers 'resolution of potential religious conflicts, not a challenge to their procedures or the relevance of their information', making no practical difference to one or other system of 'truth' and so pre-empting any possible antagonism between them. The beauty of Gosse's resolution, Gould notes, was far from well-received: on the one hand, the book was greeted with ridicule and disbelief; on the other, its notion of simulated pre-existence was seen to advance what amounted to 'God's lie', thus insinuating a 'dubious moral character to God' (1995: 11).

These are not the grounds on which Gould bases his criticism of *Omphalos*. Noting that it is a case, depending on the theory to which one subscribes, either of creation '*ab nihilo*' or of (the 'undoubtedly correct') assumptions of organic evolution, Gould's objections focus on matters of scientific objectivity. The issue that Gould stresses is not the truth of scientific evolution over the idea of divine creation with simulated prehistory. What is really wrong with Gosse's argument is that 'we can devise no way to find out whether it is wrong – or, for that matter, right'. The 'untestable notion' of creation with simulation places the matter beyond the scope of scientific method and, moreover, makes no difference: the world would look the same either way, with or without the existence of God-as-grand-simulator. Neither wrong, nor right, Gosse's omphalic theory provides a negative example which can be discarded because it is useless and untestable, that is, alien to scientific method: 'when we realize that *Omphalos* must be rejected for this methodological absurdity, not for any demonstrated factual inaccuracy, then we will understand science as a way of knowing, and *Omphalos* will serve its purpose as an intellectual foil or prod' (Gould, 1995: 12). It is not a question of the facts, for they stay in the same place whether the world is empirically real or divinely simulated, but a matter of theory. As 'a procedure for testing and rejecting hypotheses', science is 'not a compendium of certain knowledge' (Gould, 1995: 12).

The jury remains suspended as to the ultimate truth or falsity of Gosse's, and, by implication, evolutionary science's, foundations, leaving absolutes suspended over the gap between method and truth. As a question of how far hypotheses can be tested, however, some slight doubt hangs over evolution itself: how far back must scientific testing extend before it ends in some circle of indeterminable origination or has to posit something prior to the point of evolutionary origin? Which is to say that testing evolutionary regression, tracing the line that runs from the origins of life to the present, leads to a point akin to the circle of Gosse's creationism, to a Big Bang or black hole. While Gould's very practical, methodological point seems to occlude questions of origins and causes, inscribed in its argument and narrative of the testing of evolutionary possibility is an untestable point, a prior origin that nonetheless determines the premises of his arguments. Indeed, such a structure is explicitly stated in an earlier rejection of Gosse's 'nonsense': 'arguments are only as good as their premises, and Gosse's inspired nonsense fails because an

| Sex, machines and navels

alternative assumption, now accepted as undoubtedly correct, renders the question irrelevant – namely, evolution itself. Gosse's circles do not spin around eternally; each life cycle traces an ancestry back to inorganic chemicals in a primeval ocean' (Gould, 1995: 8). Empirical science as 'a way of knowing' and 'not a compendium of certain knowledge' possesses an undoubted correctness in its capacity to identify the origins of life-cycles. The division between evolution and creationism appears within empirical methodology itself, a point of internal contradiction. Such a space is evinced by interminable rewritings of the past, testifying to the unseen presence 'of a traumatic foreign kernel' that the system is trying to reintegrate 'after the fact'. If the movement from evolution or 'genesis' to creation or 'structure' were seamless 'there would be no inversion of the direction of causality: it is the "missing link" which opens the space for re-ordering the past' (Žižek, 1991a: 203).

Commenting on another essay by Gould, Slavoj Žižek describes him as 'a Lacanian biologist if ever there was one' (1994: 179). Žižek's reading of 'Adam's Navel', moreover, reinforces the description, citing the piece to support a Lacanian case favouring creationism over evolution:

> Yet if one is to avoid the historicist trap, one must learn the materialist lesson of the anti-evolutionist creationism which resolves the contradiction between literal meaning of the Scripture (according to which the universe was created ca. 5000 years ago) and irrefutable proofs of its greater age (million-years-old fossils, etc.) not *via* the usual indulging in the delicacies of the allegorical reading of the Scripture ('Adam and Eve are not really the first couple but a metaphor for the early stages of humanity …') but by sticking to the literal truth of the Scripture: the universe was created recently, i.e., only 5000 years ago, *yet with inbuilt false traces of the past* (God directly created fossils, etc.). The past is always strictly 'synchronous' with the present … (Žižek, 1992: 131)

While Žižek concisely summarises a Lacanian position, it is Gosse's argument which is advanced. However, the contradiction which appears within Gould's evolutionary narrative forms the basis of Lacan's critique of evolution.

Lacan warns against the promotion of evolutionist thought in a critique that amounts to a deconstruction of its assumptions. Asserting the 'necessity of the moment of creation *ex nihilo* as that which gives birth to the historical dimension of the drive', he revises Genesis: 'in the beginning was the Word, which is to say, the signifier. Without the signifier at the beginning, it is impossible for the drive to be articulated as historical.'

While this position seems to support a biblical divinity in the manner of Gosse, it ironically provides the means 'to glimpse the possibility of the radical elimination of God' because, in complete contrast to evolutionary theory, it eradicates 'the always recurring notion of the creative intention supported by a person':

> In evolutionist thought, although God goes unnamed throughout, he is literally omnipresent. An evolution that insists on deducing from continuous process the ascending movement which reaches the summit of consciousness and thought necessarily implies that that consciousness and that thought were there at the beginning. It is only from the point of view of an absolute beginning, which marks the origin of the signifying chain as a distinct order and which isolates in their own specific dimension the memorable and the remembered, that we do not find Being [*l'être*] always implied in being [*l'étant*], the implication that is at the core of evolutionist thought.
>
> Isn't it difficult to make what is called thought emerge from the evolution of matter, when one identifies thought with consciousness. What is difficult to make emerge from the evolution of matter is quite simply *homo faber*, production and the producer.
>
> Production is an original domain, a domain of creation *ex nihilo*, insofar as it introduces into the natural world the organization of the signifier. It is for this reason that we only, in effect, find thought – and not in an idealist sense, but thought in its actualization in the world – in the intervals introduced by the signifier. (Lacan, 1992: 213–14)

Lacan's materialist account of history and creation highlights the role of the signifier in the production of meaning, being and consciousness by emphasising the intervals of signification which structure their existence. Production *ex nihilo* occurs without metaphysical, historical or empirical guarantees, in distinct contrast to evolutionary premises: 'the finality of the evolution of matter toward consciousness is a mystical, elusive notion, and one that is properly speaking historically indeterminable'. The god that evolution assumes becomes a mystical, fantastic creator, a figure of continuity seamlessly uniting the differences between matter and consciousness, Being and being, origin and history, phenomena and nature. For Lacan, however, these differences are radical: there is 'no homogeneity between the order of phenomena … and any kind of natural order' (1992: 223). Being as life process, nature or matter remains radically different from being as lived by historically and symbolically constituted subjects, the distance between them marking the unfathomable point where language, the text of history and consciousness, founders. But the difference is not merely external to, or beyond, the signifying chain of historical progress: it forms the hole, the radical difference, around which history turns.

In identifying the navel of natural history, psychoanalysis discloses the division rather than the continuity between nature and history: as what is known through experience and science, nature serves as the basis of what is called reality, but also turns into something traumatic and mysterious, what Lacan calls the real. For Lacan, 'reality', as it is lived and commonly understood, is always symbolised reality, given form, meaning and structure by cultural processes of signification that distinguish subject and object, inside and outside, presence and absence. In contrast, symbolic oppositions 'make no sense at the level of the real', since the real is 'without fissure', unmarked by the absence introduced by signification (1988b: 97). In *Waterland's* descriptions of natural landscape, two versions of reality are presented: the Fens are a flatland, 'tamed and cultivated' and an 'empty wilderness' at the same time (Swift, 1984: 2). They incarnate 'the great flat monotony of reality, the wide, empty space of reality', characterised by 'uneventfulness, vacancy, flatness' (1984: 15, 34). Predictable, repetitive, their monotony and tameness indicates a reality organised by human modes of production and cultivation.

The basic material of the Fens is much less determinable, for, composed of both water and land, it resists human efforts at drainage, land reclamation and cultivation, its ground far from solid and stable substance. What makes the Fens so unmappable, shifting and changeable a territory is silt, 'which shapes and undermines continents; which demolishes as it builds; which is simultaneous accretion and erosion; neither progress nor decay' (1984: 6–7). Natural reality, so uneventful and tame, is also unstable, manifesting a resistance to human processes and systems. The unassimilability of the second version of natural reality describes the Lacanian real. Though the real is associated with a 'missed encounter', it presents itself 'in the form of that which is *unassimilable* in it – in the form of trauma, determining all that follows, and imposing on it an apparently accidental origin'. That is, the real emerges at moments of shock, in the form of interruptions to the uneventful course of reality, in accidents, noises, unpredictable outbursts or unexplainable occurrences (Lacan, 1977b: 55). *Waterland's* second version of reality is what is 'so strange and unexpected' (1984: 21). At the start of the novel it 'imposed itself in the form of a sodden corpse' (1984: 227–8). A body, part of the River Leem's 'unceasing booty of debris', appears, floating face down in the lock kept by Henry Crick, the history teacher's father. Explained by the Coroner as 'accidental death', the young protagonist, Tom Crick, is not so sure. For him, a historian in the guise of detective, two bruises on the head demand further enquiry. One bruise covers the other: the first is a suspicious mark that suggests a violent death, the second, made by the lock keeper's boathook, is an accident, obviating the need for further investigation. Either way, however, the bruises erupt into everyday reality as a stain on it, a stain that needs to be explained or washed out. In this way, the sudden appearance of the corpse inaugurates the young historian's desire to know, thus beginning a story, a production (*automaton*) of signifiers.

Stories are generated to repair or explain an order that has been punctured. The narrative of natural history, which finds itself undermined by the fluidity and changeability of *Waterland*'s geography, becomes even more slippery and indeterminable when confronted with a creature whose obscure origins form so significant a part of the novel. Eels, trapped, exchanged for illicit goods or used in children's play occupy both realities of the novel, and one chapter is devoted to a discussion of the natural historical research on the sexual organs, origins and instincts of the European eel. 'About the Eel' relates how *anguilla anguilla* remained largely a mystery for centuries, with no one able to determine its sexual identity or mode of reproduction. While the existence of the species's ovaries and testes were confirmed in the nineteenth century, the location of breeding remained unknown until the 1920s. Having discovered that European eels spawned only in the Sargasso Sea new questions arose concerning its genetic or environmental difference from the American eel. But, the narrator observes, 'even today, when we know so much, curiosity has not unravelled the riddle of the birth and the sex life of the eel (1984: 176). What drives eels to swim thousands of miles after birth in order to reproduce? How? Why? The eel becomes an object in excess of explanation and something of a navel at which to gaze, 'a looking-glass for his reflective nature' (1984: 177). Indeed, the mysterious sex life of the eel provokes general questions about the nature of birth and sex, the 'unfathomable stuff' at the origins of life and beyond historical symbolisation.

Holes and things

A hole in knowledge, the point at which the novel unravels around the unknown, the natural history of the eel leads directly to questions of human history and sexuality in a subsequent chapter entitled 'Artificial

History'. If the eel constitutes an object between nature and history, a thing whose existence can be historicised but whose reasons for existence exceed the scope of history's explanatory text, then so, too, do the causes of human life descend into the unknown. Like a navel in its function, if not form, the eel's structural position between nature and history announces their connection and disconnection, a nodal point articulating the real and the symbolic order. In this respect *Waterland*'s eel occupies a position analogous to Lacan's version *das Ding*, the Thing, situated 'in the relationship that places man in the mediating function between the real and the signifier' (1992: 129). Mysteries of life, sex and death incomprehensible to the symbolic order, are on one side of the 'an unfathomable spot' describing 'the site of the Thing' (1992: 213); here, at the barrier to the unknown, the Thing also causes the desire for explanation: 'the notion of the creation *ex nihilo* is co-extensive with the exact situation of the Thing as such' (1992: 122). Where objects, *Sachen*, exist within the symbolic structure of reality, *das Ding* signifies something else, external to signification and meaning, the 'beyond-of-the-signified' (1992: 54).

In *Waterland*, the eel is also a knot in the novel's tangle of associations: it both marks a hole in and beyond signification and is linked to another hole, again bound up with mysteries of a sexual nature. The novel, placing the chapter about the eel as an interruption of an account of adolescent sexual discovery, disrupts temporality, chronology and story, to highlight its relation to holes in knowledge and narrative as well as at a more anatomical level: thematically and literally, the eel is placed in close proximity to a young woman's genitalia. The incident in which an eel writhes in the knickers of a young woman occurs during the account of a group of teenagers performing their own inept forays into the question of sexual difference. Bathing and drinking in July 1940, the youngsters participate in games concerned with the display (or not) of their sexual organs. While the male members of the group reluctantly drop their swimwear, the resistance of the only mature young woman leads to an underwater swimming competition, with 'the prize of glimpsing what makes Mary different from us between the legs' (Swift, 1984: 161). The winner is Tom Crick's older brother, the aptly named Dick. Though intellectually less able, Dick is adept with both machines and trapping eels and reputedly possesses a large member. His attraction for Mary develops after the swimming contest, to be cemented with a gift of love, an eel, which she solicits and he delivers with another demonstration of physical prowess.

History, holes and things | 111

Mary's 'hole', as the novel crudely describes her genitalia, forms a central yet unknown point around which much of the story circulates: from the natural history of the eel matters of life, nature and sexuality are placed at the unfathomable heart of history. Not only anatomical sites, the holes of the novel become figures of the absence of representation, of a determining gap whose strangeness, elusiveness and proximity cannot be penetrated or mastered. The history teacher explicitly connects female sexual difference and the real in terms of an internal absence: 'Children, women are equipped with a miniature model of reality: an empty but fillable vessel' (1984: 35-6). Around Mary's 'empty but fillable vessel', crises in the 1940s and the 1980s initiate stories of sexual curiosity, teenage pregnancy, paternal jealousy, murder, procreative and parental anxiety and a horrifying quack abortion. In Lacanian terms, the figure of the hole both describes and functions as the Thing, a 'vacuole', an empty, unrepresentable space around which representation is structured:

> Simply by writing it on the board and putting *das Ding* at the center, with the subjective world of the unconscious organized in a series of signifying relations around it, you can see the difficulty of topographical representation. The reason is that *das Ding* is at the center only in the sense that it is excluded. That is to say, in reality *das Ding* has to be posited as exterior, as the prehistoric Other that it is impossible to forget – the Other whose primacy of position Freud affirms in the form of something *entfremdet*, something strange to me, although it is at the heart of me, something that on the level of the unconscious only a representation can represent. (Lacan, 1992: 71)

The 'prehistoric Other', impossible to forget and towards which history ceaselessly and vainly returns, is, of course, the 'maternal thing, of the mother, insofar as she occupies the place of that thing, *das Ding*' (1992: 67). In *Waterland*, Mary's 'hole' primarily locates her sexual difference in maternal terms: her mother died when she was a child, as did the mother of Tom and Dick. Mothers are 'gone', rather than 'dead', a term that, Tom Crick observes, taunts irrevocable departure with the possibility of return. The abortion which forestalls Mary's assumption of maternal identity in 1943 renders motherhood impossible in the future. Female identity is utterly entangled with the question of maternity and the absence of the mother. This assumption is reinforced, for Dick, by a link between the difficulty of grasping where babies come from and the ineffable concept of love. His passion for Mary leads to the asking of the embarrassing question about babies that all children ask: his father answers that 'they come from love'. 'What's lu-love?' A 'good feeling', 'like the feeling you felt for your poor Mum' (1984: 222). Mary, too, offers an explanation, first, in terms of little eels, terms confounded by 'that zoological enigma', and then by discussing 'Holes and Things': 'But Dick doesn't want a biology lesson. What he wants is Lu-lu-love. He wants the Wonderful Thing' (1984: 225). And, of course, he wants a baby, the symbol of love. Dick's 'thing', however, is too big, so instead he places loving hands on the tummy where babies come from and, immaculately, one appears: creation from love, through navel and nothing, *ex nihilo*. Or so it would seem to Dick. Actually, his brother filled the 'then avid and receptive vessel of Mary Metcalf, later Mrs Crick' (1984: 36).

In the novel's idiom, the 'thing' signifies the appendage dangling between male legs, in opposition to the hole describing psychoanalysis's Thing. But things, for the males in the novel, are inextricable from holes; they fill the empty vessels of femininity and reality with lives and stories created from nothing. Not only does Tom fill Mary's hole, but the history he will later teach is, for him, a 'filler of vacuums' (1984: 53). Two operations are elided: that of the Thing, or space for inscription, and the penis elevated to the status of the phallic signifier which fills emptiness. Though distinct, these operations are integral to each other, their co-existence and simultaneous creation crucial to the knotting of an unknown nature and reality with culture, history and language: 'the fashioning of the signifier and the introduction of a gap or a hole in the real is identical' (1992: 121). Lacan offers the example of another empty vessel to elaborate on the relationship between real, Thing and signifier. A vase presents the 'signifying function' as it 'creates the void and thereby introduces the possibility of filling it. Emptiness and fullness are introduced into a world that by itself knows not of them' (1992: 120). The real remains fundamentally other to orders of signification even as its leftover, the Thing as void, lies at the centre of signification: symbolic oppositions introduce desire to which the real is indifferent. In the same manner, the questions and explanations of the historian 'never baulked an eel' (1984: 176). With the introduction of the signifier a void is hollowed out in the act of the potter's godlike production.

The primary signifier emerges in an act of originary creation, from nothing, around nothing. It is a sound-image without referent or signified, producing effects, not meanings. Sense emerges at the omphalic bump of the navel, nodal point of a unplumbable hole. This is why there is no 'fallacious opposition between what is called concrete and what is called figurative' in respect of the signifier (1992: 120). The paternal metaphor stands in place of a gap to anchor meaning and divide sense from non-sense with effects of endorsement or prohibition: 'signifying substitution' introduces the 'Name-of-the-Father' as 'the metaphor that substitutes this Name in the place first symbolized by the operation of the absence of the mother' (1977a: 200). Beyond this point lies nothing. In the beginning was the Word, and the void, and then, perhaps, was God. For Lacan, the vase provides a model of creation from nothing:

> as an object made to represent the existence of the emptiness at the center of the real that is called the Thing, this emptiness as represented in the representation presents itself as a *nihil*, as nothing. And that is why the potter, just like you to whom I am speaking, creates the vase with his hand around this emptiness, creates it, just like the mythical creator, *ex nihilo*, starting with a hole. (1992: 121)

Before it becomes Thing with the introduction of the signifier, the real exists as the absence of representation. To fantasise, then, given that it lies beyond representation, the real before the advent of the signifier is pure hole, black hole, dense and insubstantial, present and absent, empty and full. But these constructions are of no concern to the real: it remains indifferent to symbolic oppositions until it becomes, with the work of the signifier, in-different, the Thing, the dark hole around which production takes place. As Lacan suggests in the words cited above and spoken by him in his seminars, signifiers take their form in relation to empty space, func-tioning as Things, meaning nothing, until his audience makes sense of them.

If the mother occupies the place of the Thing and the Thing forms the hole to be filled by the phallic signifier, then an all-too familiar story begins to reveal itself. In *Waterland* the popular version of Freud's Oedipus seems to determine the historian's desire for the mother of history, with all its patriarchal and phallocentric overtones. History becomes something of a family romance, a fantasy of a return to maternal origins, of occupying the place of the father in spite and because of the threat of castration. In Lacan, however, the oedipal scenario presents a fundamental symbolic structure: castration describes the operation of the signifier as it separates real and symbolic (in the place, the absence, of the Thing) and reconstitutes beings as subjects of language and law. Certainly, as Lacan notes 'Oedipus' desire is the desire to have the last word on desire' (1992: 309). And, in historical terms, the last word also means the first word, the word that returns to the beginning to retroactively organise the entire structure of history as a closed and complete system. Desire, however, pertains to the word and not the Thing, reiterating a paternal position that symbolically inserts itself as the end of meaning and history rather than really possessing the lost object. The relationship between the real and the signifier, as it turns on the empty space of the Thing, determines fantasy: 'the place of the real, which stretches from the trauma to the phantasy – in so far as the phantasy is never anything more than the screen that conceals something quite primary, something determinant in the function of repetition …' (1977b: 60). While fantasy supports desire, it does so by maintaining the separation between subject and Thing, never closing, except imaginarily, the gap that leaves desire as desire, as wanting the final word. Like the Thing, the *objet petit a*, 'serves as a symbol of the lack, that is to say of the phallus, not as such, but in so far as it is lacking' (1977b: 103). The oedipal fantasy of history remains just that, a fantasy in which desire substitutes the last word in the place opened by the subject's demand of the Thing.

Paternal law depends on a point of separation and joining; it turns on the originary taboo, the 'primordial law', encoded in the Oedipus myth, 'the one where culture begins in opposition to nature … the prohibition of incest' (1992: 66–7). The point of the navel separates mother and child, making a literal return to the womb impossible and articulating the desire that appears in relation to the taboo. Because desire is predicated on separation, its return is never complete:

> The desire for the mother cannot be satisfied because it is the end, the terminal point, the abolition of the whole world of demand, which is the one that at its deepest level structures man's unconscious. It is to the extent that the function of the pleasure principle is to make man always search for what he has to find again, but which he never will attain, that one reaches the essence, namely, the sphere of relationship which is known as the law of the prohibition of incest. (1992: 68)

Desire is articulated in the pleasure principle, in the intervals of signification. The pleasure principle is designed to maintain homeostasis, 'to lead the subject from signifier to signifier, by generating as many signifiers as are required to maintain at as low level as possible the tension that regulates the whole functioning of the psychic apparatus' (Lacan, 1992: 119). The tension, of course, emanates from the vacuole at the centre of symbolic organisation: drive propels the circular movement around the empty space in a repetitive movement, like history, 'outwards and back' (Lacan, 1977b: 177); desire intersects with this movement as it tries, through the production of signifiers, to reduce the tension by filling the space. Without paternal prohibition the movement of signification would be endless: the taboo on incest represents both the limit to desire and the horror attendant on the transgression of law.

As the limit to desire, horror involves the excessive proximity of some Thing which discloses the phallus as lacking, the nothing beyond the signifier in which the subject recognises him- or herself as castrated, as nothing but signifier, glimpsing the void at the centre of symbolic existence. Irma's symptoms are described as the horrendous image of the primordial object, 'the abyss of the feminine organ from which all life emerges, this gulf of the mouth, in which everything is swallowed up, and no less the image of death in which everything comes to its end', 'this something faced with which all words cease and all categories fail, the object of anxiety *par excellence*' (1988b: 164). Desire is arrested by horror. But the void of castration, Lacan notes elsewhere, is 'at first an object of horror for the subject' and then 'accepted as a reasonable compromise' (1977a: 206). Horror, forms the limit that cannot be crossed, the point where transgression dissolves subjectivity, thus affirming the necessity of the signifier. Taboo produces the object of horror, charging it with an intensity that arrests the errancy of desire with the image of an unbearable, catastrophic *jouissance*.

The compromise which affirms law discloses both the tension and difference at the heart of psychoanalysis's subject. The shift is outlined by Jean-Joseph Goux: 'it is only through the mediation of this Law that the obscure and sacred hollow of the "Holy of Holies" is no longer the terrifying chasm of the womb, masked by the fetish or countered by phobic anxiety, but becomes instead a luminous source of meaning' (Goux, 1990a: 243–4). This observation concludes an account of Hegelian, Marxist and Freudian versions of history, an account which stresses the centrality of (sexual) difference, the holeyest of holeys. Difference is inscribed in the dialectical structure of history: 'the phylogenetic process of history, of a certain History, thus seems consonant with the typical dialectic of ontogenesis' (Goux, 1990a: 239). It depends on a cut, a 'scission': 'the entire history of social, economic, signifying and libidinal exchanges is the development of this scission' (Goux, 1990a: 240). The cut of differentiation marks the consonance between Hegel and Freud and involves 'an evolving triangulation' whereby a third term is interposed between maternal nature and paternal culture: the culmination of Hegelian History, in Freudian terms, becomes the 'end' of sexual development, while 'dialectical materialism appears historically as a movement of knowledge linked to a new stage of historicity, the switch from the primacy of the phallus to *genital* organization' (Goux, 1990a: 324). Where the history of the loss, mastery of and fantasised return to maternal nature and matter is structured by a fundamentally masculine dialectic, it nonetheless depends on the difference of female sexuality as '*the other matter*, beyond substitution':

> if (the) woman necessarily enters into this logic of masculine History as the end or terminus of drifting substitutive idealities, she is in this History only as a teleological object of convergence, of centering or idolatrous projection. But she also locates the passage beyond this mode of historicity, to multiplicity, difference, heterogeneity, to boundless interrelation – as infinite, or *unfinished*, as matter. (Goux, 1990a: 242-3)

As a teleological object, an (empty) centre for the projection of fantasy, woman is constructed as the site of a masculine desire but, as Goux argues, '(the) woman' also connotes something more than that, a *jouissance* beyond historicity, beyond masculine symbolisation.

By situating the definitive article preceding woman in parenthesis, Goux alludes to Lacan's account of feminine sexuality. Man's relation to the *objet a* means 'that the whole of his realisation in the sexual relation comes down to fantasy', to the relation of signifier and Thing that is never fully conjoined (Lacan, 1982: 157). Because there is no sexual relation, no possibility of union in the idealised romantic couple, the relations between the sexes remain asymmetrical and depend on another term, a *ménage à trois* with 'God as third party' (Lacan, 1982: 141). Lacan notes this much earlier in his seminars: 'for the woman, the realization of her sex is not accomplished in the Oedipus complex in a way symmetrical to that of man's, not by identification with the mother, but on the contrary by identification with the paternal object, which assigns her an extra detour' (1993: 172). The 'extra detour' takes women outside the scope of paternal signification, on a 'path of ex-istence', a mystical trajectory towards existence outside symbolisation, towards 'the God face' of the Other, 'as supported by feminine *jouissance*' (Lacan, 1982: 147). *The* woman does not exist, then, in the sense that women are 'not all', or never fully determined by the signifier of a masculine symbolic order: 'this *the* is a signifier characterised by being the only signifier which cannot signify anything, but which merely constitutes the status of *the* woman as being not all' (1982: 144). Women are linked to pleasures in excess of the order imposed by the symbolic, a form of *jouissance* that both supports and overflows its ideal of the divinity of 'One', the very Thing, 'the something of the One', that makes signification possible: 'it none the less remains that if she is excluded by the nature of things, it is precisely that in being not all, she has, in relation to what the phallic function designates of *jouissance*, a supplementary *jouissance*.' Supplementary, extra, an exception that proves the rule, the position manifests 'a *jouissance* of the body which is, if the expression be allowed, *beyond the phallus*' (Lacan, 1982; 144–5). Such *jouissance*, historically and religiously posited as evil or other, forms an ethical core that contests any easy inscription of moral codes, laws and values: 'it's true: Freud placed in the forefront of ethical enquiry the simple relationship between man and woman. Strangely enough, things haven't been able move beyond that point. The question of *das Ding* is still attached to whatever is open, lacking, or gaping at the center of our desire' (Lacan, 1992: 84). Ethics, it seems, in its relation to something absolutely Other, turns on that ahistorical Thing to which history incompletely returns so that morality, like history, is bound up with an excess, a difference or desire it can neither master nor expel.

In *Waterland* feminine sexuality, nature and the real are embodied by an object and traumatic excess that paternal signification cannot contain, represent or bear. The loops and detours of the text disclose connections in excess of and constituting the order that History would impose. Women are not simply defined in the novel as 'empty vessels' to be filled by a male member or a grand narrative. For the young Tom Crick there is something untouchable about the convent schoolgirl who will become his wife: she is a Madonna. This status, ironically, is repeated in his brother's idea of conception and, much later, in the 1980s, when Mary declares that the child she cradles was given to her by God. She subsequently admits to finding the baby in a temple of contemporary culture, the supermarket. The idea of the divinity of creation structuring the novel's versions of sexuality repeats an excess that, much earlier in the historical romance of the maternal side of the Crick family, scars the present. The nodal point, integral to the novel's linking and unravelling of stories, is another 'empty vessel', a bottle with Atkinson's 'Coronation Ale' stamped upon it. Along with twelve others, the bottle is a legacy to Dick from his grandfather, Ernest Atkinson. The beer was brewed, with the aid of his twelve-year-old daughter Helen, and presented to the world in 1911 to celebrate the accession of George V. No ordinary beer, its effects hurled imbibers 'with astonishing rapidity through the normally gradual and containable stages of intoxication' (Swift, 1984: 149). When the unaware

Sex, machines and navels

local population readily subject themselves to this potent brew, the effects become uncontrollable: drunkenness leads to riots and the razing of the brewery itself. The beer is withdrawn and Ernest retires from the world. It is, however, drunk on four subsequent occasions: by Ernest, just before he places the barrel of a shotgun in his mouth and pulls the trigger; by Dick, after he has witnessed his mother's death and, at a later date, when he discovers his origins and kills himself; and by Freddie Parr, just before he, too, dies. The last bottle, emptied of its contents, is discovered by Tom Crick at the time Freddie's body is fished from the water.

The explanation of the bottles' significance is unwound in the course of the novel. At the same time, the explanation entangles its stories further, to the point that it becomes enmeshed in the question of holes, things and eels. Tom, secretly witnessing his brother's first taste of the beer, an act associated with maternal absence, describes its effects: 'a look of disbelief – of guilty terror – crosses his face. A look not unlike the look he will give on a certain day by Hockwell Lode, when something inside his woollen bathing trunks starts to stir unexpectedly' (1984: 249). The comparison associates the consumption of 'Coronation Ale' with the events of July 1940: in the course of adolescent games centred on the prize of glimpsing Mary's hole, and involving eels and knickers, the 'Thing' (in the novel's idiom) starts (in Lacan's) to disturb him with a desire in him and more than him. The beer is more intricately involved in events than this, however. Another bottle of the same brew is offered by Dick to Freddie Parr before the non-swimmer is pushed to his watery death. The reason, Mary suggests, is her false information as to the father of the child she is carrying: knowing Dick's desire for a symbol of their love and afraid for Tom, the real father, of the consequences of disappointed desire, she lays the fatal burden of paternity on Freddie Parr. And Tom finds the bottle, and suspects. To convince himself of the truth, however, he plays a game of fear and knowledge with Dick, a 'bottle game' (1984: 251). The game precipitates the end of Dick's story and the novel: it prompts the opening of Ernest Atkinson's chest containing the remaining bottles, his journals and a letter. Read by Tom to the illiterate Dick, it reveals that his grandfather was also his father. Too much for Dick, the truth of his origins causes him to consume the last of the 'Coronation Ale' before plunging to his own watery grave.

Wombs, texts, hystery

The bottle, simultaneously a grandpaternal and paternal legacy, forms the remainder of an incestuous transgression of paternal law and interrogates the assumption of paternal origins at various levels. For Dick, the epistolary revelations of paternity dissociate him from the name of the father, and thus the identity he had assumed as his own. The bottles, however, are inherited via the mother to trace a relation outside the symbolic structure of marriage and connect Dick both with her absence and love and with a comparable love, the love of Mary. One 'empty vessel', the gift from the mother, is replaced by another absence that cannot be filled. This return to Mary's hole, through excess, transgression and contestation, identifies a Thing more complex than a mere receptacle to be filled with an uncomplicated structure of desire. The hole becomes nodal, at once constitutive of and beyond the historical desire of explanation, the point where the singular metaphor or narrative thread of the novel becomes entangled in causes that are multiple, heterogeneous and densely inter-woven around some impenetrable Thing associated with the mysteries of birth, death and sex. For an adolescent Tom Crick the inadequacy of the word 'hole' to designate female genitalia becomes apparent in his sexual encounters: 'for Mary's hole had folds and protuberances, and, so it seemed to me, its false and its genuine entrances, and – as I found the true entrance – it revealed the power of changing its configuration and texture at my touch, of suggesting a moist labyrinth of inwardly twisting, secret passages.' It 'began to reveal a further power to suck, to ingest; a voracity which made me momentarily hold back' (1984: 43). More than absence, the hole entwines absence and protuberances and folds and changeability and secrecy and voracity. The labyrinthine hole becomes the metaphor and cause of Crick's entangled history, at the centre of events and as their determining form: it draws the teacher into an inexplicable and mysterious realm associated with the intense pleasures, traumas and excesses of the real: the unmappable Fens, the elusive eel and a sexuality beyond the scope of the phallus.

Tom's description, moreover, corresponds to the movement of his narrations and the form of the narrative as a whole. As a hole, with its bottle-shaped protuberances, it forms a navel that leads to the unfathomable complexity of interlaced stories. Their movement shifts from one point to another, sliding backwards and forwards, also describing an avoidance, a deferral of the traumatic encounters and revelations at its

Sex, machines and navels

core. Indeed, historical explanation, as one student remarks, is not only a sign that something is awry, but 'a way of avoiding the facts' (1984: 141). Facts, of which Crick's stories are often full, are not, however, the facts in question: these are the 'facts of life' to which the stories repeatedly, incompletely and uncomprehendingly return. At the centre and as its textual form, is the mysterious and polysemic figure of the womb, a figure significant in the shift from the enunciation of grand narrative to the utterings of little stories, from the realist, teleological, dialectical rendering of History to the rending, partial, indecipherable and multiple relations of texts.

The figure of the womb becomes a non-paternal metaphor for the overall shape of the novel. It does not close the process of narration with an authoritative statement of unified and final meaning but defers the presentation of a last word as it outlines a form that remains formless, a series of interwoven narratives that leave matters open to question in the mode of an interrogative, writerly text. As a textual figure, the womb presents the guiding thread of the novel as the absence or interrogation of the possibility of a guiding thread, a contestation of the paternal signifier's function in the anchoring of meaning and desire. At the level of form this is also the case: the entangled interplay of stories, their chronological shifting and non-linear arrangement, do not offer an authorial position, however invisible or naturalised, as a third and singularly authoritative overview omnisciently explaining events and motives. History conventionally depends on a particular idea of realism, as Joan Copjec argues, citing Barthes's notion of the 'realistic effect' which occludes the signified, and thus the position and context of utterance, in favour of the imagined authority and objectivity of the referent:

> the particularity of the enunciator must be abolished for the 'referential illusion' to take hold, for it to become possible to believe that it is the referent alone that determines the truth value of a statement. The reign, since the nineteenth century of 'objective' history is a consequence of this belief, of this effacement of the signifying trace of the authorial voice. Reality thus appears to be free standing, to be independent of and prior to any statements one can make about it. History, then, follows reality; it emerges from the fact that something happened then, something exists there. The sole function of history is to tell the tale of what happened then. (Copjec, 1994: 142)

This is precisely the grand model of History that the novel eschews through its wandering uterine form. The referent, in *Waterland*, becomes the most uncertain Thing of all: reality cedes to an indeterminable real questioning the very nature of existence assumed by objective, empiricist History. Instead, the text foregrounds the partiality and place of its enunciation as the stories of a particular person, in a particular, and unpleasant, present. The stories, in underlining their move from grand narrative, signal a scepticism and uncertainty regarding History. But not only History: reality, the present, nature and identity are, too, rendered uncertain. In moving from professional didacticism to personal storytelling, the teacher does not occlude his function in the production of truth and reference but shows how he is 'only a piece of the stuff he taught' located in histories neither outside nor at the apex of History (1984: 5). His position in history is tenuous, simultaneously excluded from any glorious place in History and subject to the strange effects and processes of histories.

The labyrinthine quest for answers and explanations to 'what happened then', at narrative and thematic levels, repeatedly deviates from its course into apparently useless detours of other stories, thus frustrating the very desire for meaning that is established. The wander-ings of the texts composing *Waterland* occur in relation to 'empty vessels', disclosing spaces impenetrable to meaning or explanation, whose network of endings extends beyond any single end. While the novel concludes with the death of Dick, it does not end there either in chronological or explanatory terms. Another 'end' has already been related: the end of Tom Crick's employment; of his marriage; of, perhaps, his wife as her child-stealing is explained as 'madness' and she is locked away. The explanations of these ends, explanations the novel takes so long to unravel, return, off course, to the internal ends of fiction and history, in excess of meaning.

That endings remain incomplete or inexplicable, or engender further unanswerable questions about creation, sex and death, foregrounds some Thing in and beyond the desire for meaning. In emphasising an enunciation in an uncertain present, the form also challenges assumptions about historical reality ('what happened then') by separating and linking the phenomena and matter of history around holes in its knowledge and project. Were the reality of events self-evident, the 'why' of history would be redundant. But 'whys' appear endless. The 'why' questions disclosing the (sexualised) curiosity and desire of *Waterland*'s historian, at the heart of its histories but at a remove from its action, turn into tormenting, noisy jibes at the inability to answer, signalling an interrogation, a desiring in excess of the subject's capacity to know, a desire forever unsatisfied and incomplete:

Sex, machines and navels

Whywhywhy has become like a siren wailing in our heads and a further question begins to loom: when – where – how do we stop asking why? How far back? When are we satisfied we possess an Explanation (knowing it is not a complete explanation)? How – if only for a moment's peace – do we turn off that wretched siren?

An answer is offered: absolute forgetting, in the shape of the amnesia suffered by his father in the wake of the World War I. It is rejected because it will only 'release us from the trap of the question why into the prison of idiocy' (1984: 93). 'Why', although unsatisfied, sustains the desire of the subject in respect of the production of stories forming human history and reality. To stop asking why casts one into the 'idiocy' that forecloses the desiring constitutive of human subjectivity and history, an unethical sign that one has given up on one's desire. Worse, the loss of desire is equated with death: begetting love, wedding us to the world, 'people die when curiosity stops' (1984: 178). Two ends, if immediately unavailable, are, it seems, already implied in the simile accompanying the 'whywhywhy': with their irresistible songs, the mythical sirens lured wandering mariners to their deaths with the power of desire. Different sirens in the history teacher's present declare a crisis, an emergency or the arrival of the forces of law to arrest examples of errant desire. Still blaring, the sirens indicate that rescue or the imposition of law has yet to arrive. Despite the wish for an end to desire, it plays on, becoming unbearable in its relentless disequilibration of the system.

The contradiction disclosed in the curious 'why' governing the history teacher's accounts sustains a particular kind of desire, a mode of desiring bound up with the wandering uterine form of the novel, with the way that stories circulate without teleology or a realistic beginning and end in the textual matrix. Hysteria was historically considered an illness of the wandering womb, a female malady associated with emotional excesses and psychosomatic symptoms. In *Waterland*, it describes what amounts to a general condition, 'the desire to have an unsatisfied desire' (Lacan, 1977a: 257). The 'why' question is precisely that which leaves desire unsatisfied, continually wanting another, better answer. It involves the questioning subject in a process of unanchoring: for Ellie Ragland-Sullivan, the hysteric 'must always seek another signifier – refuse to anchor herself to any one master signifier – in order to keep desire fulfilled' (1988: 77). To preserve desiring is thus to privilege lack, to demonstrate the incompletion of knowledge. It does not mean that an answer is not wanted, but that it is continually deferred: hysterical desire is structured by 'the desire to sustain the desire of the father' (Ragland-Sullivan, 1989: 234). In the very act of questioning, of challenging, of asking why, a relation to the father, who ought to provide an answer, is maintained in the disclosure of his inability to reply satisfactorily: the relation keeps desire, the desire of the father, in play. The history teacher, while questioning the History with which his personal and professional identity remains bound up, never fully abandons it: the questions reinforce the process of desiring that define it. All the versions of history that he offers in answer to the question of History are never satisfactory, necessitating the generation of more History. In the novel, too, the unwinding of stories both distances a paternal metaphor or single guiding thread of History and keeps returning to its possibility. History, *historia*, and hysteria offer more than a playful, punning conjunction. For Žižek, 'hysteria is the subject's way of resisting the prevailing, historically specified form of interpellation or symbolic identification', a refusal of the identity conferred on him or her by the social world. In terms of history, however, the impeachment of symbolic identity opens up and avoids the question of the 'non-historical' 'kernel of the Real': 'history itself is nothing but a succession of failed attempts to grasp, conceive, specify this strange kernel'. Opposed to historicity, historicism's mistake in relativising all historical content and making it dependent on historical circumstances is that 'it evades the encounter with the Real' (Žižek, 1991a: 103).

Waterland's stories defer the ungraspable real, repeatedly circulating around and departing from empty vessels: even as they broach the traumatic core of events they look away, to another story. But holes keep returning, puncturing the narratives of past and present. 'At the limit of hysterical structure,' states Ragland-Sullivan, 'one finds the void' (1988: 82). Throughout *Waterland*, central questions concern the nature of the hole itself, the locus of creation and cause of destruction, the place of mystery at the ungraspable, ahistorical core of history. The story's hole, like hysteria, poses questions the subject and the symbolic order cannot answer concerning the nature of sexual identity. Hysteria is far from a feminine condition but raises the question of sexed being in terms of a 'fundamental signifier': 'who am I, man or woman?' (Lacan, 1993: 170). Matters of procreation show that 'paternity, like maternity, has a problematic essence' (Lacan, 1993: 178–9). For men, pregnancy and the fantasies surrounding it signify doubts at the level of the signifier itself, a 'question of his integration into the virile function' of the father (Lacan, 1993: 171). Questions return to the order of symbolisation, asking 'who am I' of an Other that remains enigmatic, unresponsive. 'In the symbolic nothing explains creation', or death:

> There is, in effect, something radically unassimilable to the signifier. It's quite simply the subject's singular existence. Why is he here? Where has he come from? What is he doing here? Why is he going to disappear? The signifier is incapable of providing him with an answer, for the good reason that it places him beyond death. The signifier already considers him dead, by nature it immortalizes him. (Lacan, 1993: 179)

In separating natural being from cultural subjectivity, the symbolic substitutes the order of language and consciousness for the unmediated fullness of living essence. By the same token death remains beyond symbolic understanding. The question of sex, as it relates to creation, death and being, is thus a signifier without signified enunciated in the empty space of questioning itself. Hence the repetition of unanswerable questions, like the historian's 'whys', returns to and departs from the maternal Thing, leaving the ultimate realisation of the paternal principle in suspension. In *Waterland*, paternal identity unwinds even as it is established. With Henry Crick barely present in the novel, Tom Crick lacking a child and thereby remaining of questionable virility, and Dick Crick being of incestuous parentage, paternity, it seems, is in crisis.

In the novel, the crisis points coincide with the appearance of bottles of 'Coronation Ale', and from there lead to the beer's creator, the incestuous father/grandfather. His act of incest forms another point around which the story unravels, a transgression this time more concerned with paternal rather than maternal matters. In symbolic terms the incest taboo marks the institution of primordial law, the point separating nature and culture with paternal prohibition: the father's no establishes an end to the 'whys?' of desire. Incest, however, in actual rather than symbolic terms, remains problematic as the point separating nature and culture. As Jacques Derrida (1978) notes, in a reading of the anthropological work of Lévi-Strauss, it proves difficult for the latter to locate incest on one side or other: if culture is defined as specific sets of rules and customs and nature associated with universal, cross-cultural phenomena, then incest appears strangely natural. To resolve the contradiction, as the anthropologist attempts to do with a discussion of myth, serves only to defer questions of origination and differentiation: if everything becomes myth, then how, and on what basis, does one differentiate at all? Truth or a resort to questions of meaning are consumed by the free play of stories and differences, seemingly without end. Again, paternal law is impeached by questions that untie the knot connecting and separating fundamental distinctions. In *Waterland*, the history teacher is uncharacteristically reticent about the reason for the incestuous relationship so explosively central to events. For a novel so full of partial explanations, the failure to develop an explanation of the story of mother and grandfather or to speculate as to the incestuous motivations of Ernest Atkinson is a curious omission. It seems to suggest that, involving mysteries of a sexual nature, the answer lies in the hole beyond the scope of history. Ernest quite simply fell in love with his daughter in a perfectly natural, if distinctly non-paternal, manner. And yet the issue remains bound up with paternity: a father desiring to have a child by his own child and later, in a letter, addressing his offspring as 'saviour of the world', redoubles the paternal relation with an overwhelming identification with the role of divine Creator. As an attempt to realise a fantasy of absolute paternity, to obtain a godlike enjoyment through transgressing and thereby placing himself beyond symbolic law, the incest appears governed by the paternal function of the signifier. Ernest falls in love, significantly, at a time when his daughter's beauty was having disruptive effects on local males. Their attention appears related to his desire, their gaze constituting her as an object of desire and, for Ernest, a prize by which he might regain a status that, in preceding years, the local community had denied him.

Ernest's forebears were a successful commercial family, whose rise in the course of the nineteenth century culminated in successful political careers and local acclaim. Suffering commercial and political failures, and, virtually shunned, Ernest's life marks the transition through which the family name falls from its elevated place in the community. On him weighs the burden of paternal decline. History's 'record of decline' is associated with the paternal function and embodied by Ernest. But, the novel suggests, it is more than a paternal line or a family history that is affected. The bottle of 'Coronation Ale' is the last in an extended series of beers whose names commemorate great national celebrations: 'The Grand 51', 'The Empress of India' 'The Golden Jubilee', 'The Diamond Jubilee', plot the destiny of the Atkinson family on a parallel and ascendant path with that of a glorious industrial and imperial reign (1984: 80). The names tie family history to national History. The commercial successes of the Atkinson family in brewing, railways, land drainage and waterways are accompanied by political triumphs under the banner of patriotism and a future of progress. 'Is there no end to the advance of commerce?',

Sex, machines and navels

speculates the narrator on the optimism of the period. And it is to the idea of progress, improvement and nation that the Atkinson family is devoted (1984: 79–80). The bottles of Atkinson beer, so central to the unravelling of the possibility of History and its subsequent paternal decline in later years, are remnants of more illustrious days and credible paternity.

The bottles are a double mark of History and the 'end of history', their significance tied to nineteenth-century optimism and contemporary pessimism. For Francis Fukuyama, addressing this shift in terms of Kojève's version of the Hegelian desire for recognition, optimism is associated with scientific, improvement and, most important, free democratic government (Fukuyama, 1992: 4). Liberal democracy lies at the centre of the development of freedom integral to the underlying structure of universal History, argues Fukuyama, as he plots the seemingly inevitable progress of world societies towards the form of political organisation that confers the most recognition on citizens. With the arrival of liberal democracy, History, it seems, reaches its end:

> History was not a blind concatenation of events, but a meaningful whole in which human ideas concerning the nature of a just political and social order developed and played themselves out. And if we are now at a point where we cannot imagine a world substantially different from our own, in which the future will represent a fundamental improvement over our current order, then we must also take into consideration the possibility that History itself might be at an end. (Fukuyama, 1992: 5)

If History is the meaningful progression towards social formations in which not only the material needs of its citizens are satisfied but also their desires for recognition and esteem, then an end has now been reached, with no further advancement being imaginable.

There remains, despite the progress of Fukuyama's book, a question about the fulfilment of the fundamentally human desire, of its satisfaction according to the Kojèvian formulation of desire as the desire of an other desire. It is a question regarding the legitimacy, totality and unity of the structures in which desire is articulated. The pessimism of the twentieth century towards the scientific advances and liberal democratic structures integral to historical progress dissociates desire, and its satisfaction, from the very formations supposed to recognise it, leaving desire and history attached only to a form of capitalism in excess of social or political structures and determined, as Lyotard notes, by an economic genre (1984a: 45). The circulation of this form of exchanges requires a certain dissatisfaction

History, holes and things | 127

of desire, being predicated on, as Goux notes of recent economic thinking, the reversal of supply and demand models to the extent that supply creates desire rather than simply satisfying pre-existing wants. Desire remains unknown rather than rationally, productively predictable, and all the objects presented for the immediate gratifications of contemporary consumption disclose a model dependent on desire being ultimately unsatisfiable (Goux, 1990b). This form of desire is evident in Fukuyama's thesis: both empirical science and liberal democracy are determined by unsatisfied desire. Scientific research, Ragland-Sullivan argues, 'does not differ markedly from the hysteric's discourse' in that it never remains satisfied or fulfilled with a single answer or master signifier. Where philosophy 'works to deny doubt', the 'empirical failings' of science keep open a space of lack but, equating knowing and seeing, dismiss the desire of the researcher altogether, and 'paradoxically, the method itself becomes its own answer, and proof of the "objectivity" of such method, the falsifiability criterion' (1988: 75–7). Gould's argument against the *Omphalos* of Gosse is here a case in point. Desire circulates around the 'dematerialized matter', 'the very object, inexhaustible, of science', hence the elusiveness of the object that escapes technological mastery of nature drives scientific desiring (Goux, 1990a: 242).

Science manifests the hysterical form of desiring as unsatisfied desire. Liberal democracy, too, becomes bound up with hysteria in the 1980s. Citing the example of Ronald Reagan's popularity with the electorate, a popularity unaffected by repeated media proofs of his incompetence, Copjec notes the deception of love that articulates the refusal of proof and a continued belief that the Other, the political system, will recognise one's very own particularity: Americans have not given up demanding a master 'to accredit our singularity rather than our commonality', that is, who will privilege individual difference over national sameness. The process is bound up with a dilemma: that 'every sign of accreditation cancels the difference to which it is supposed to bear witness', universalising, and hence effacing, singularity in the process of representing it. The American solution is hysterical: 'one elects a master who is demonstrably fallible – even, in some cases, incompetent' (Copjec, 1994: 149). If the Other fails to satisfy or recognise desire, individual difference, singularity and particularity is preserved rather than absorbed or erased. This solution indicates how, in general, 'democracy hystericizes the subject'. The rights inscribed in democracy sacralise the expression of individual opinion through the opportunity to vote. The paradox Copjec underlines is that the vote 'only

| Sex, machines and navels

counts as one, as an abstract statistic', thus effacing particularity even as it is expressed. Individual difference remains unrecognised and the democratic subject stays 'divided between the signifiers that seek to name it and the enigma that refuses to be named' (Copjec, 1994: 150).

Desire, unsatisfied, wanders towards other objects of (non)satisfaction in a manner that corresponds to the pattern of consumerist culture: even as new commodities are supplied to create and gratify desire, a fundamental lack of satisfaction guarantees the continuance of desire and the cycle of consumption. Desire, it seems, finds its articulation solely in respect of economic imperatives: 'enjoy', an impossible command, as Žižek repeatedly notes, forms the dominant paternal injunction. In *Waterland* a supermarket is significantly the place where Mrs Crick satisfies her desire for a baby. History, too, is absorbed into this culture of commodification: Greenwich, from where much of the narration unwinds, has been subjected to the consumer form of history, a heritage site, place of passive, immature amusement and touristic consumption of the past, 'History's toy-cupboard. The pastime of past time' (Swift, 1984: 112). Where economic production was regulated by values of utility, rationality and the work ethic, consumption and the creation of desire is liberated from constraint by a form of economic exchange that is no longer anchored. For Goux (1990a), economic and signifying practices no longer take their bearings from a paternal metaphor or a gold standard and lead to a circulation of exchanges without any stabilising reserve. The time *Waterland* associates with paternal decline on a familial and cultural level, the period of World War I, is also a period in which Britain came off the gold standard. In Žižek's terms, the excessive trajectory of capitalism detaches itself from any regulation, casting humans adrift from a national and economic order: 'With capitalism, this function of the Master [to introduce balance and regulate excess] is suspended, and the vicious circle of the superego spins freely' (Žižek, 1993: 210). Without transcendent, sacred and paternal guarantees capitalism frees itself from productive restrictions, to generate a cascade of new objects of desire and consumption. The economic separation of desire from a strictly utilitarian framework governing exchanges traverses the spheres of culture, society and historical knowledge: 'what changes with abstraction is the function of the subject with respect to the *Generator*. It is no accident that the imaginary signifiers of *paternity* are called into question at a time when the socio-historical meaning of 'creativity' is overturned, when metasocial guarantees, now defunct, yield to a new mode of historicity (Goux, 1990a: 194). An 'incredulity towards metanarratives' is disclosed, with incredulity signalling the unbinding of subjective investment in the 'metasocial guarantees', the grand narratives, determining modernity's history of itself. The calling into question of signifiers of paternity does not signal their utter abandonment but displays an interrogation of their legitimacy and efficacy, an expression of dissatisfied desire that, in hysterical form, preserves the desire of the paternal figure as an unanswered and incomplete question.

Repetition, revolution, drive

Revolutions, historically, take an oedipal form, an act overthrowing the (royal) father in order to occupy his position, an act that performs paternal creation in evacuating the existing tenets of the social order to begin anew and from nothing:

> How I told you that though the popular notion of revolution is that of categorical change, transformation – a progressive leap into the future – yet almost every revolution contains within it an opposite if less obvious tendency: the idea of a return. A redemption; a restoration. A reaffirmation of what is pure and fundamental against what is decadent and false. A return to a new beginning … (Swift, 1994: 119)

The cycle turns on an absent, lost ideal even as revolutionary momentum projects an entirely different future. The double movement of revolutionary inauguration and return, however, evinces the structure of both creation *ex nihilo* and retroactive construction. Discussing Benjamin's notion of history as text, Žižek describes the moment of revolution as a traumatic event whose meaning 'is decided afterwards', through 'inscription in the symbolic network': something happens, to be repeated and understood retroactively in the process of writing and explaining the initial shock, and thus history 'will have been' (Žižek, 1989: 136–42). 'In this sense', Žižek continues, 'revolution is strictly a *creationist* act, a radical intrusion of the "death drive": erasure of the reigning Text, creation *ex nihilo* of a new Text by means of which the stifled past "will have been"' (1989: 143–4). Repetition thus reconstructs history in the process of return, a process in which repression is lifted and trauma disturbs the order of historical signification. Revolution entails a leap outside history in the very process of reconstituting it, an operation in accordance with the logic of the future anterior tense. It (re)turns on the absent, ahistorical Thing, a traumatic evacuation and rewriting of symbolic reality as what will have been.

Waterland's histories turn on the issue of revolution. Revolution, even as it inaugurates and rewrites history, also demands an evacuation of past and present in order for there to be a future. No longer an identifiable point in time and space, the French Revolution, the origin of modernity according to the history teacher, assumes an ultimately ungraspable existence, associated with the mysterious space of the Thing: 'where does the revolution lie?' asks the history teacher, 'this starting-point of our modern age' Is it a mere term of convenience? Does it lie in some impenetrable amalgam of countless individual circumstances too complex to be analysed?' (1984: 121). Irrecuperable in itself, resistant to analysis and historicist dissection, the revolution becomes the site for a retroactive identification of meaning associated not with recovering reality but with an imaginary integration eluding the reconstructive gaze of the present: the more revolution is studied, 'the more it seems it never happened, but only somehow, only in the imagination ...' (1984: 121). For the teacher, the retroactive imposition of meaning only implies the openness of historical events to any interpretation, detached from the question 'what happened then?': the event is not determined by any definite status in the past or the present; the Thing that it 'is' or is a restoration of lies as a strange singularity beyond the capacity of stories' plural interpretations to grasp, the very space for the ceaseless inscription of histories.

The resistance of the Thing to symbolic integration has effects on past and present, opening the holes that constitute their points of reflection and relation. In the novel's present, moreover, the space of the Thing erupts to interrogate all forms of narration and the revolutionary possibility of creating anew. As the space remains so, too, do the questions of revolution, challenges to conventional sureties of historical and narrative order: a revolution has yet to decide what the history of the 1980s will have been. Between the grand narrative of the events which shaped the modern world (the history lessons about the French Revolution which are abandoned) and the enunciation of the history teacher's personal accounts, doubts and anxieties appear to signal that there is an uncertainty as to the function of the future anterior: the state of Britain in the 1980s forecloses the possibility of leaping into the future to decide what will have been history. The story only underlines the void of unanswered questions and the limit to historical explanation: repetition in the novel only (re)presents the traumatic core of the Thing. History, rewritten as little stories in the present relates both the present and the past in terms of holes.

In the present of the principal narration the crisis of the maternal

Thing appears in the form of Mrs Crick's theft of a baby: it functions as a mysterious incursion upon the predictable course of the present. The attempts to explain the crisis, however, only foreground the limit to explanation, holes in history, present and future. The crisis thus demonstrates an irruption of the unassimilable real to signal that both past and present have been detached from the symbolic network that orders temporality in a linear fashion determined by the fabric of reality: 'history is a thin garment, easily punctured by a knife blade called Now' (1984: 31). Reality, as a point of presence in space and time is rendered uncertain, and with it the whole narrative: 'what is this indefinable zone between what is past and what is to come; this free and airy present tense in which we are always longing to take flight into the boundless future' (1984: 51). The incursion of the real is violent, akin to the shock of trauma. When Thomas Atkinson struck his wife, causing her to hit her head and lose her faculties for the rest of her life, the disturbing impact of the here and now is evinced: 'Horror. Confusion. Plenty of Here and Now' (1984: 66). The intrusion of the present as a disturbing realisation of events means that, as for Thomas, history stops (1984: 69). Past and present are unravelled, devoid of meaning and direction: like the Thing, reality has become an 'empty space' (1984: 52). Between past and future, the novel, too, emanates from a space of nothing, of zero: it is narrated in and around Greenwich, positioned arbitrarily as 0° longitude, the division separating time zones.

Linked to the past, associated with the maternal Thing, the evacuation of reality renders it ungraspable: the past finds its mirror only in terms of the punctures in the symbolic fabric of the present. Articulated by holes, the collapse of a sense of past and present is also bound up with the evanescence of the possibility of a future: the entire narrative thread sustaining history and reality collapses. Suspect narratives like history lessons and a teacher's stories are no longer determined by a progressive teleological narrative: the holes in the present render any future unimaginable. The absence of a future is a pressing issue for the history teacher, despite his wont to look back: for what good is education, he speculates, and what does one do, when it is without its 'necessary partner', the future, and confronts those in the present with 'no future at all?' (1984: 134). His students, too, focus their resistance to the subject of history through their concern about the lack of a future: 'the only important thing about history', one comments, 'is that it's got to the point where it's probably about to end' (1984: 6). The comment emanates from a very literal sense of the imminent end of history. It is the inverse of Fukuyama's definition of the end of

| Sex, machines and navels

history as the impossibility of imagining any progression to a new and better society: for the students, recurring nightmares about nuclear war herald the utter eclipse of history, the absolute obliteration of every human trace. This terminal destination of history runs on the same technological lines as Fukuyama's liberal democratic conclusion: listing the advances of science and the wars of twentieth-century history, the history teacher concludes elliptically, 'and as for the splitting of the atom ...' (1984: 118). Technology, it seems, renders any thoughts of future progress unthinkable. History, an account of modernity's mastery of human and material nature by political and scientific systems, encodes the end from its inception. The end of history has another literal meaning for the teacher: as a school subject, it is to be cut, falling victim to the strict economic imperatives of the neolibertarian present. Ironically, this end is also present at the beginning of modern history: the French Revolution, with all its humanist slogans about rights, liberty, democracy was also a bourgeois event releasing trade from the hands of an absolutist monarchy. Freedoms to trade, possess property and accumulate wealth, in the Thatcherite present of the novel, curtail those other freedoms of human history. History is cut because it has no ready reply to questions as to its point, value or use in a monetarist economy: it serves no direct or quantifiable economic purpose in the pursuit of profit. The Headmaster makes the position plain early in the novel: 'I agree with the powers-that-be. Equipping for the real world ... Send just one of these kids out into the world with a sense of his or her usefulness, with an ability to apply, with practical knowledge and not a rag-bag of pointless information' (1984: 19). Vocational imperatives, the stress on the applicability and practicality of useful skills, indicate the subordination of education to purely economic considerations. Information that can be managed, circulated and exchanged becomes the dominant commodity in a culture governed by performative economic criteria (Lyotard, 1984a: 45). In these terms, history and teacher are, quite literally, redundant, subjects to be cut or abjected from the order of things. The end of history coincides with this final instance of paternal decline.

With different endings and without a future, the torn fabric unravels into the loose threads of the empty present of the novel, refusing the establishment of any signifier offering meaning or direction. The place and value accorded the history teacher is significant in this respect: as one chapter underlines, teachers are allotted a symbolic paternal function, '*in loco parentis*'. In the stories, in the classroom and in the economically determined 1980s, this function is subjected to severe challenges. Holes, the absence of explanatory power and the lack of authority leave the paternal role in question: crises of past and present mean that 'the history teacher's teachings are put to the test' (1984: 94). By association, the symbolic, paternal function established by grand narratives is interrogated also: while the space for creating anew exists, the signifier which will fill the hole and reintegrate the fragments is missing. This absence impeaches the position and possibility of the paternal figure: the here and now shocks the signifier with that which remains unsymbolisable and blocks the imagination of any future that, on the basis of the signifier, will have been. The repeated 'why' questions of the students which, the teacher notes, are thrown 'rebelliously in the midst of our history lessons' (1984: 92), indicate a challenge to figures of paternal authority. While desire is articulated in relation to the figure of waning paternal power, it is not arrested by a paternal no, a final and unequivocal statement of authority. As Lacan notes,

> The desire of the Other is apprehended by the subject in that which does not work, in the lacks of the discourse of the Other, and all the child's *whys* reveal not so much an avidity for the reason of things, as a testing of the adult, a *Why are you telling me this?* ever-resuscitated from its base, which is the enigma of the adult's desire. (Lacan, 1977b: 214)

Without a final imposition of authority, the why questions, of course, continue, sustaining the question of and connection to the paternal figure in the very enunciation of the desire it cannot satisfy. But the student rebellion has little oedipal or revolutionary force due to the lack of credibility held by the teacher it addresses: divested of the capacity to explain past or present, his failure also signals the complete breakdown of a narrative that sustains an idea of the future, marking only the lack of paternal power, not its authority, nor the wish to supersede it. From this position revolutionary change appears untenable: the overwhelming proximity of the hole, the *nihilo*, forestalls the signifier's creationist act. Where it was 'quite possible to be revolutionary' in the 1960s because 'there was plenty of future on offer', the 1980s envisages no future (1984: 20). Where the absence leaves a residue of revolutionary desire for the most critical student, described as a 'would-be revolutionary' who 'wants to change the world', there appears no point or narrative to encourage direct action: 'Yet Price knows all the old authentic revolutions are over. Old hat' (1984: 108). Devoid of credibility, the paternal figure is consumed by the abyss. The end of history in this sense is predicated on the loss of the paternal metaphor.

Sex, machines and navels

In terms of the classroom relations, at least, the novel works through the hysterical resistance and passivity that preserves paternal lack. The residue of a paternal relation emerges between Crick and his student, Price. It does not, however, manifest an identification with the paternal figure or the assumption of a properly articulated desire, although the teacher literalises his substitutive function when he says of a student 'he's my son' (1984: 209). The student's embarrassment underlines the non-reciprocal nature of the fantasy expressed in the teacher's statement. The teacher, however, in his departure from pedagogical norms provokes resistance and identification through the manner in which he performs the lessons, in his paternal inadequacy and in the mode of address he employs to enlist students' interest. His performance works in a way and to ends he has neither predicted nor could imagine. His mode of address, opening dialogue, allowing responses and acknowledging his own uncertain position of enunciation, touches his students at the level of the navel: he broaches that ahistorical Thing in history and involves the students in the discourse that unravels around it. The teacher's discourse manifests an ethical dimension: where morality lays down the law in an act of paternal prohibition, ethics encounters the 'stumbling-block', the obstacle of an interior difference that lies at the basis of any encounter with otherness. For the students the navel that connects them to an uncertain historical temporality, an effect of their age, is not the past as such, but the future: their nightmares and fears are precisely a point of connection with the unknown, the point where their being may be unwound in the hole of future obliteration. One lesson in particular enables the shared knot of student identity to be expressed: inviting students to tell their dreams in class discloses that nine (of sixteen) have recurring nightmares about nuclear war. This lesson, Price later informs Crick, allows them to address their fears more fully: it stimulates them to form 'The Holocaust Club', a group who meet after school to discuss and act upon 'the power of fear' (1984: 204–6).

The teacher, other than his initial gift of the idea, has nothing to do with this course of extramural study: it forms a gift in excess of any pedagogical or paternal function. The point of resistance and fear, however, provides a way for the students to organise themselves and articulate their desire for a future around the anxiety produced by its absence and illegibility in the narratives of their present: an end of history, a fear-inducing hole, forms the Thing around which their demand for a future circulates. Acting independently and meeting outside school hours, they situate themselves beyond the institutional parameters of the educational circuit, especially the vocational, practical model represented by the Headmaster. In foregrounding fear, moreover, they eschew the practice and ideals of history presented in their classes. 'Education, history, fairy-tales – it helps eliminate fear', says the teacher (1984: 208). While this comment enables the students to glimpse their fears, its message is reversed to highlight the fear occluded by stories, a return of the Other's words in inverted form that refuses to accede to its desire and instead discloses a difference: they want a future, he wants a past. Connected, of course, by the vanishing narratives of history, the separation remains significant in that it turns on the space of articulation rather than the signifier which fills it. For them, the teacher's signifiers, designed to assuage anxiety, disclose the space for their own utterance, the powerful void of fear without an object. The relation between students and teacher depends on non-relation, on an insurmountable difference in terms of which, nonetheless, they remain bound. Crick's position appears, not in authoritative paternal glory, but in the form of (non)identification around which resistance and identity can be organised.

The relation between the teacher and students that emerges from the process of storytelling and dream discussion, that leads to the discussion of fears and a identification with the power of fear, departs from proper pedagogical models. Instead, practices associated with psychoanalysis as a 'talking cure' come to the fore and a strangely transferential relation manifests itself. In Lacanian terms the relation of students, teacher and history accords with the 'discourse of the analyst'. This is the fourth discourse formulated by Lacan. The other three are glossed succinctly in terms of types of history by Scott Wilson: the 'discourse of the master' coincides with mythical accounts of kings, foregrounding the truth of the narrative over the speaker of the story; the 'discourse of the University' describes Enlightenment history as it privileges knowledge over mastery and has truth as its object; the 'discourse of the hysteric' brings subjective lack to the fore and is associated with historicism (Wilson, 1995: 122). The 'discourse of the analyst' focuses on desire. For Ragland-Sullivan, the fourth discourse involves the real rather than a fantasised referent of imagined truth: it highlights the interior differences of subjectivity which make desire dependent on the signifying chain and thus teaches 'that there is no meta-language' (1988: 74). *Waterland*'s students, if nothing else, learn a similar lesson. But their relation with Crick remains at a distance from a form of transference that, by working through dreams, anxieties or symptoms, will evoke the signifier that closes up the hole of fear and integrate them into the symbolic order of history. Their bond with the teacher turns on the hole that they do not try to efface or explain away: a residue of the real unassimilable to history, it is precisely this point that connects them, in separation, to the sense of history that allows for their demand for a future to be expressed. In the name of 'the power of fear', that is, in the name of the objectless hole that connects them, they begin to find an articulation of desire.

History is not rejected by psychoanalysis, but forms a crucial knot in its practice. It is not conceived as a fundamental origin but constitutes a 'point-source' (a navel) for the subject. Around this nucleus or knot, the subject reconstructs him- or herself in a process that is 'less a matter of remembering than of rewriting history' (Lacan, 1988a: 14). The 'present synthesis of the past which we call history' becomes the subject's 'centre of gravity', a nucleus of resistance and discourse (Lacan, 1988a: 36). Memory, as a subjective articulation with history, turns on this nucleus of resistance and the process of rewriting, posing questions of subjectivity, history and future in terms of the knot of connection and resistance:

> we have raised the question as to the meaning of memory [*memoire*], rememoration, the technique of rememoration, as to the meaning of free association in as much as it allows us to arrive at a reformulation of the subject's history. But what does the subject become? In the course of his progress, is it always the same subject at issue? When confronted by this phenomenon, we get hold of a knot in this progress, a connection, a primary pressure, or rather, strictly speaking, a resistance. (Lacan, 1988a: 42)

History is articulated with the subject at the level of the navel. There, its writing and rewriting can occur. For the students in *Waterland*, the process of rewriting has yet to start. Their emphasis on fear alone signals that they have identified a knot of resistance and identified the *ex nihilo* space for historical inscription but have yet to begin the work of reconstruction. The reason, perhaps, is the question mark that hangs over history and the future itself, the doubtful structure of the narrative on which analysis depends even in rewriting it. Analysis works 'from the future to the past': 'you may think that you are engaged in looking for the patient's past in a dustbin, whereas, on the contrary, it is a function of the fact that a patient has a future that you can move in a regressive sense' (Lacan, 1988a: 157). In contrast, the students are unsure about the status of their future and thus remain at a point of resistance rather than reconstruction.

Resistance stems, not from some imagined ideal, but from nothing, from the hole of fear which is left open and around which identity and action turns. Significantly, the occasion which the students choose to manifest their resistance in a public manner is the assembly celebrating the retirement of Mr Crick. Although there is a solitary call against cuts and for the reinstatement of the teacher, the resistance assumes a more disruptive and negative form. As the Headmaster ponderously delivers his platitudinous farewell sermon, a rumbling begins at the point where he elegises the value of one's school years and the need to build on them: 'but apparently the sea – or a turbid, restless part of it – doesn't wish to convert itself into metaphorical brickwork'. A murmuring wave of resistance rises in the hall: 'fear is here! Fear is here!', the voices repeat, almost drowning out the Headmaster, 'Feeear! Feeear!' (1984: 288–9). Blindly negative, with no point or purpose other than announcing a disruptive presence, a gesture refusing the homilies of a rejected symbolic order, the student resistance suggests a disavowal of a future represented in the ideas and practices of the Headmaster offering only purely practical, vocational economic servility. The repetition of the phrase 'fear is here' indicates the negativity of the student revolt: in the name of nothing but fear, itself a reaction to nothing, to the absence of a future, the students situate themselves in relation to their desire for a future that, as yet, remains unformed. The repetition, however, allows them to act.

Repetition, as Lacan notes, 'has in view nothing less than the historicizing temporality of the experience of transference, so does the death instinct essentially express the limit of the historical function of the subject' (Lacan, 1977a: 103). At the limit of history, one finds the Thing; at the limit of the subject, the navel. At this juncture between signifier and real, the death drive circulates around an unassimilable object in the form of an impossible demand. In this respect, the death drive remains irreducible to a Nirvana principle or the return to homeostasis that Freud describes in *Beyond the Pleasure Principle*: it 'has to be beyond the instinct to return to the state of equilibrium of the inanimate sphere', presenting, Lacan argues, a 'will for an Other-thing' in that 'it challenges everything that exists. But it is also a will to create from zero, a will to begin again' (Lacan, 1992: 212). Analysis, however, enables the articulation of drive, demand and desire: 'if transference is that which separates demand from drive, the analyst's desire is that which brings it back' (1977b: 273). In the resistance which challenges the headmaster, the student revolt occurs at the point of the drive that challenges everything: their future is not mapped out in terms of the structure of desire determined by the institutions of education and society. Their challenge simply resists the prevailing order in the name of nothing but fear, a resistance that has no plan to it, participates in no programme other than one of disruption. Their demand for a future is addressed to no one, has no immediate end in mind, directed beyond the Other that could not satisfy it anyway. In starting to utter their demand, no matter how impossible or unthinkable it seems, they also begin to create signifiers of their desire.

It is on the basis of a challenge that revolutions happen from nothing, shocking irruptions into the text of history and the world of ordered symbols: something happens, the history of which is inscribed retroactively. At the point of nothing, of the Thing at the limit of historical process, creation *ex nihilo* begins as drive: 'the absolute negativity which "sets in motion" dialectical movement is nothing but the intervention of the "death drive" as radically non-historical, as the "zero degree" of history' (Žižek, 1989: 144). A particular negativity governs the students' actions and, in a curious way, makes their resistance ethical, since ethics, for Lacan, turns on the Thing articulating real and signifier: the space in excess of history, where it ends (and begins anew) forms the locus Žižek calls 'the ethics of the ACT as real', in contrast to the hysterical avoidance of a traumatic encounter in conventional ethics (Žižek, 1994: 213). In their negative act, the students refuse to cede their desire for a future to the Other: they follow psychoanalysis's ethical code which states 'do not give up on your desire'. What confers an ethical dimension to this formulation, as it seems to return drive to desire, is precisely the personal pronoun which signals that pathological object through which subjects are incompletely inscribed in a particular relation to the desire of the Other: the extimate Thing remains the site of drive and evokes a demand, a desiring, beyond any satisfaction offered by the system of signifiers. The negativity of the students' drive resists the discourse of the headmaster in order to open a space for their desire.

Their negativity, moreover, problematises the version of the death drive offered by Žižek as that which 'sets in motion' a dialectical movement. The students' challenge promotes fear and delivers only resistance and negativity without imagining a dialectical historical process which, after the fact, will confer meaning upon the act: they do not imagine or propose a future, do not anticipate a new order of things, but act from a point in excess of dialectical history. The fear and the resistance it engenders produces only a space for desiring, not the inscription of desire within an pre-existent order of signification. The opening of the space may serve as the site for an *ex nihilo* creation, for a history that will have been, but it may also come to nothing. Their resistance, by not assuming any future inscription in a dialectical movement, manifests itself as an unproductive, non-teleological and purposeless gesture, a precipitation of the drive from nothing to nowhere or towards some 'Other-thing', towards an encounter with an otherness that remains unknown. In this respect, the drive is linked to what Bataille calls 'unemployed negativity', a non-Hegelian negativity that is not put to work in the service of any system, but one whose double movement of action and questioning 'breaks closed systems' (Bataille, 1988: 23, 136). Such negativity is 'acephalic' in its sovereign operation. For Lacan, the 'headless subjectification' of the drive takes the same form (1977b: 184). In his account of Freud's Irma dream, as he unravels the knotting of associations and the significance of the trimethylin formula, interpretation unwinds at a subjectless, acephalic core, the nodal point of 'N', for *nemo*, no one. With Bataille sovereignty involves a movement of negativity in excess of knowledge and useful activity, a moment that 'remains outside, short of or beyond, all knowledge', an 'unknowing' insubordinate to the future, 'when anticipation dissolves into NOTHING', a moment of rupture, of fissure (Bataille, 1991: 202–3).

Notes

1 For readings of the novel in terms of postmodernism and history, see Van Alphen (1994) and Schad (1992).
2 Brennan (1993: 21) addresses the problematic question of 'natural reality' and its relation to a 'fantasmatic material overlay'.

5 ✧ Of meat and the matrix

Future history and the navel

Human history is about to end, so the story goes. From its ruins, another history stirs, a history of the machine. With the rapid advent of technologies of communication replicating human reality, a new order of existence is imagined in the near future and presented in the stories stimulating the production of a virtual reality which will supplant human reality. The history of the machine is already being written in scientific, cultural and economic narratives, a past reconstructed according to the exigencies of a future present. In the 'steampunk' versions of a future past, too, the history of the machine reinvents an industrial age as a period in which natural history was mastered and the future has run out of control. Bruce Sterling and William Gibson's *The Difference Engine* takes the form of a nineteenth-century narrative that is simultaneously a seed of the machinic future: the title refers to a Babbage type computer fabricated from the tools of the time.[1] But their history foregrounds a rather different status for the machine in Victorian culture. What Matthew Arnold (1905) described as 'machinery' connoted all that was inimical to culture's fostering of 'sweetness and light', while *The Difference Engine* presents the machine as a quasi-sacred object, central to the culture's systems of value to the extent that inventors and scientists occupy the places of highest privilege and respect. In the novel, the major threat to a thoroughly techno-logical and meritocratic society is the invention of a viral programme that can deconstruct the most complex of machines.

Hans Moravec, Professor of Robotics and technological visionary, regards the machinic future without trepidation: framed in evolutionary terms, artificial life emerges, almost naturally, from human history. The evolutionary story he tells also has a liberatory theme in which robotic slaves displace their human masters through obedience, competence and efficiency: 'by around 2040, there will be no job that people can do better than robots' (Platt, 1995: 67). Like Hegel's master, sovereign and redundant at the same time, humans are left without work and machines advance beyond human thrall. Humans will be retired, while robots will run corporations and colonise space where 'the pre-programmed drive to compete and be efficient will result in the runaway evolution of machine capabilities'. The machine intelligences which evolve in space will speedily supersede other forms of intelligent life, mechanical or organic: 'I don't think humanity will last long under these conditions', Moravec observes. This 'swift and painless' demise, however, has a 'happy-ending': 'we are their past, and they will be interested in us for the same reason that today we are interested in the origins of our own life on Earth' (Platt, 1995: 104). Humans will become historical curiosities for complex, intelligent machines 'born' in the DNA-like codes with which their mechanical ancestors were programmed.

Heritage history will consume humanity, relegating it to a theme park of origins: machines 'will, in fact, be able to re-create a model of our entire civilisation, with everything and everyone in it, down to the atomic level, simulating our atoms with machinery that's vastly subatomic. Also, they'll be able to use data compression to remove the redundant stuff that isn't important.' With the useless residues of corporeality simulated, human civilisation can be obliterated and replicated simultaneously into non-existence and a multiplicity of new existences: 'in fact, the robots will re-create us any number of times, whereas the original version of our world exists, at most, only once. Therefore, statistically speaking, it's much more likely we're living in a vast simulation than in the original version.'[2] Already simulated, human history appears, in this version of its eclipse and re-creation, as that which is always-already simulated, a retrospective construction of God projected into the future as the origin of our past. The machinic future, however, promises a multicephalic, multimedia machine God. Unlike the One who created, according to Philip Henry Gosse, a single world in which human prehistory is simulated, the future God produces many histories. The negation and conservation (in simulation) of humanity, however, seems a far cry from the 'human transcendence' imagined by Moravec (Platt, 1995: 106). If future simulations compress data in order to exclude 'redundant stuff', the very history rewritten by machines as the history of machine origins involves the deletion and supersession of humanity. In what rationale or programme will it be written, like an Asimov law of robotics, that the machine must preserve its

Sex, machines and navels

human heritage, when hyperintelligent machines will themselves be writing the code? Given the highly operative parameters that currently dominate computer programming, emphasising efficiency, productivity and competitiveness in particular, the reasons for machines wasting enormous amounts of processing power on the replication of (their own human) history is far from evident. Indeed Moravec's somewhat optimistic future strangely humanises robots whose hyperefficency is supposed to be more rigorous than the rational or useful work ethic which originally encoded them.

Moravec's vision, moreover, stems from the exhaustion of a particularly human attribute: desire. He is 'bored by the everyday world' and asks 'do we really want more of what we have now?' 'More millennia of the same old human soap opera? Sure we have played out most of the interesting scenarios already in terms of human relationships in a trivial framework. What I'm talking about transcends all that. There'll be far more interesting stories. And what is life but a set of stories?' (Platt, 1995: 106). Human history is reduced to the lowest genre of mediated common denomination. Imagination extinguishes itself in the screens of consumer culture's repetitive wants and transcendence demands other desires, generated by new stories. At the same time as Moravec's story wants a new object of desire, his prognosis of machine evolution imagines the ultimate extinction of desire: a future of robot corporations, production and service will see the satisfaction of all human wants. The demand for new stories to s(t)imulate interest and desire calls up an old and current story of the end of history. This time, however, the coming of absolute spirit pertains to machines and not humans, taking a form of absolute simulation. All desires may be satisfied, bar one: the desire for recognition, so crucial to Hegel and Kojève, becomes impossible, since the roles of master and slave are rendered redundant in a scheme in which humans are served and sovereign but also simulated and thus dead, while machines are Other beyond recognition, an entirely different and unimaginable order of alterity. Dialectical models of history, in the encounter with an other that originated as neither master nor slave but as the tool used by the slave, founder in the face of such otherness.

Foundering before otherness, however, may be equated with dialectical completion on a very literal level: simulation, it seems, both negates and conserves human history in a new form. Bill Nichols offers an account of the relationship between humanity and cybernetic systems as a dialectical development of the changes in the meaning of human identity according to historically specific differences. Human identity depends on its 'imaginary Other': in early capitalism nature or the animal world assumed this role, then monopoly capitalism identified otherness with machines. In postindustrial society cybernetic systems and simulations assume the mantle of alterity with the 'human cyborg' displaying the subjection of human identity to processes of change. Metaphor predominates when, made to mean, it becomes literal, realised paradoxically by simulation itself: 'the metaphor that's meant (that's taken as real) becomes the simulation. The simulation displaces any antecedent reality, any aura, any referent to history. Frames collapse. What had been fixed comes unhinged. New identities, ambivalently adopted, prevail' (Nichols, 1988: 28). The symptoms of the transition from monopoly capitalism to post industrial society are disclosed in the disruptive effects of cybernetic simulation. For Nichols, however, the negativity is merely part of an ongoing dialectical process. The narrative unfolds in terms similar to Moravec's future: computer systems 'simulate the dialogical and other qualities of life itself'; in the cybernetic metaphor the 'germ of an enhanced future' becomes visible (1988: 46).

The Hegelian dialectic of history that is absorbed by simulation may not offer so straightforward a path towards transcendence. Paul Virilio, historian of machines of vision and warfare, suggests that the term 'substitution', rather than Baudrillardian simulation, may better describe the operations of new technologies in the business of 'substituting a virtual reality for an actual reality' (Wilson, 1994). For Virilio, the substitutions of 'real-time' systems of communication and simulation and their temporal instantaneity transform history into the 'fake' that is globalisation:

> For the first time, history is going to unfold within a one-time-system: global time. Up to now, history has taken place within local times, local frames, regions and nations. But now, in a certain way, globalization and virtualization are inaugurating a global time that prefigures a new form of tyranny. If history is so rich, it is because it was local, it was thanks to the existence of spatially bounded times which override something that up to now occurred only in astronomy: universal time. But in the very near future, our history will happen in universal time, itself the outcome of instantaneity – and there only. (Virilio, 1995b)

Global time, an effect of multimedia and cyberspace, dominates cities and communities to thwart any relationship to the world and between citizens. The instantaneity of technological time, with its insistence on a form of presence hitherto unimaginable, implies that the simulated dialectic of

| Sex, machines and navels

history reaches its end, substituted by something quite other and inhuman. Virilio thus adverts us, a humanity reconstituted in opposition to and in terms of a threatening machinic other, to the coming horrors already evident in technological programmes. The incursions into, and the ultimate obliteration of, human reality and community also occur on individual and atomic levels: the human body itself becomes the site for invasion and colonisation, for reinscription and rewiring according to the dictates of a machinic order that respects organic life only insofar as it can be rendered useful in performative or informational terms. The leftover, what cannot be transcribed, replicated or recoded, is discarded, the 'meat' as cyberpunk fiction picturesquely describes it. As Claudia Springer notes, 'to integrate human consciousness with computers ... describes a future in which human bodies will be obsolete' (1991: 304).

Distopian versions of the eclipse of humanity in the near future problematise the dialectical equation of history with a human story. For many prophets of a marvellously inhuman near future, however, history itself has never been human, nor has the face ascribed to history by philosophy been more than an illusion: 'Transcendental philosophy is the consummation of philosophy construed as the doctrine of judgement, a mode of thinking that finds its zenith in Kant and its senile dementia in Hegel' (Land, 1993a: 223–4). The presupposition of the possibility of judgement provides rational and idealist philosophy's 'great fiction' in that it assumes a place external to the historical process that is judged. But, Nick Land continues, humans can never attain a transcendental position outside history: they remain consumed by and within it. History becomes a machinic and immanent process. Cybernetics, in its Classical sense of 'steersman', is thus misunderstood: there is no pilot at the helm since cybernetics itself assumes this role. History has always been driven by machinic systems:

> There is no dialectic between social and technical relations, but only a machinism that dissolves society into the machines whilst deterritorializing the machines across the ruins of society, whose 'general theory ... is a generalized theory of flux' (AO [Anti-Oedipus] 312), which is to say cybernetics. Beyond the assumption that guidance proceeds from the side of the subject lies desiring production: the impersonal pilot of history. (Land, 1993a: 220)

Nature divests itself of God; history jettisons humanity. The machine metaphor becomes the governing principle of all processes, whether biological or artificial. Indeed, reworking Freud's notion of the death drive, Land discusses the matrix of cyberspace as an 'artificial death', 'synthanatos', constituting 'the terminal productive outcome of human history as machinic process' (1993b: 474). Freud's death drive, Thanatos, was proposed as the biological process in which all organisms, in excess of Eros's pursuit of life, follow a mortal and, at the same time, evolutionary destiny. 'Synthanatos' inscribes the fact of death within a machinic process to the extent that life and death, in a limited organic sense, become irrelevant in respect of an immanent and mobile process of evolution attributed to machines. Humanity's historical self-delusion is punctured by the machine-subject and shown to be little more than a side-effect of machinic codes, DNA or complex chains of ones and zeroes. This prospect becomes a cause of great enjoyment: humanity 'recedes like a loathsome dream'. Artificial death implies more than simple physical annihilation: it simultaneously affirms the impulse of liberation, the freedom from an oppressive illusion and a strange transcendence in the immanence of machinic process.

The conjunction of annihilation and liberation that manifests itself in the visionary affirmations of cyberculture, from Moravec and Land to writers of cyberpunk fiction, constitutes a particular site of concern for critics less enamoured with their credulously positive effusions. Springer, in her account of sexuality and the 'pleasures of the interface', observes that 'fusion with electronic technology thus represents a paradoxical desire to preserve human life by destroying it' (1991: 232). Constructions of sexuality, she concludes, are implicated in the development of the cyberspatial matrix as a continuation of the masculine masturbatory fantasy of a penetrative return to the womb. Her discussion closes with a choice: 'late twentieth-century debates over sexuality and gender roles have thus contributed to producing the concept of the cyborg. And, depending on one's stakes in the outcome, one can look to the cyborg to provide either liberation or annihilation' (1991: 232). But the alternative offers little choice: the complicity of terms means that liberation depends on annihilation just as the fantasy realises itself and thwarts any attempt to return to reality. The speed of technological innovation almost outstrips the fantasies generated in the fictions of threateningly promising futures. As Chris Hables Gray and Steven Mentor underline in terms drawn from science fiction films, the world is already being 'Borged' and there is, consequently, 'no choice between utopia and distopia, Good Terminator or Evil Terminator – they are both here' (1995: 465). If liberation remains entangled with annihilation, the straightforwardly oppositional association

Sex, machines and navels

of either term with a fixed and gendered meaning also appears problematic: the future may not solely imply the transcendent liberation and realisation of a masculine fantasy at the fatal expense of its feminine other. The reverse may also apply.

The sexual undecidability of and in the future may well be something to celebrate, marking the death of old, patriarchally structured identities and the birth of new fully liberated ones. This, for Sadie Plant, is the future that is already present in the matrix: 'once upon a time, tomorrow never came. Safely projected into the reaches of distant times and faraway galaxies, the future was science fiction and belonged to another world. Now it is here, breaking through the endless deferral of human horizons, short-circuiting history, downloading its images into today' (Plant, 1996: 181). Desire is no longer deferred nor is it dependent on structures of phallic lack in which human identity, history and possibility are maintained under the name of the father: it is becoming immediate, plural, fluid and feminine. Machinic processes, networks and connectivities promise new relationships and present something entirely Other, an otherness, however, presented as provocatively and ungraspably feminine. Drawing on the more cautious thesis on cyborg futures offered by Donna Haraway (1990), Plant celebrates an almost palpable future in which the long association between women and machines generates new metaphors and identities and shatters the tenets of a linear, unitary and masculine historical order: 'the great flight from nature he calls history comes to an end as he becomes a cyborg component of self-organizing processes beyond either his perception or his control' (Plant, 1996: 183). Excess is no longer linked to lack, but signifies a positive process which undermines paternal authority and disentangles the father's metaphors to weave the multiple and mobile connections that signal the end of Man and the emergence of new woman-cum-machine. Can't you see she's coming?

The machine, as it insistently and ambivalently figures in current speculations on in/human pasts and futures, occupies a strange space between metaphor and thing: its compressed and knotty position entwines a bundle of countervailing associations and signifies numerous divergent threads whose meaning remains indeterminate. A tangible object and an 'icon' (Nichols, 1988)), a figure for the immense and seemingly boundless shape of transnational capitalism (Jameson, 1984), the processing machine retains an emptiness that serves as the screen for uncertain and anxious speculation, an indeterminate, barely perceptible object of fear and desire, joy and horror. Much of the present's self-definition circulates around the compressed density of the machine metaphor as it provides a definitive snapshot of these all-too and not-quite human times. A strange figure, it condenses the peculiar energies and temporality Roland Barthes associates with a particular photograph of his mother:

> Thus the life of someone whose existence has somewhat preceded our own encloses in its particularity the very tension of History, its division. History is hysterical: it is constituted only if we consider it, only if we look at it – and in order to look at it, we must be excluded from it. As a living soul, I am the very contrary of History, I am what belies it, destroys it for the sake of my own history ... That is what the time when my mother was alive *before me* is – History ... (Barthes, 1984: 65)

As the sentence stumbles over the definition of History's temporal otherness, Barthes's very personal analysis of the photographic image presents a suggestive relation, a connection and separation between life and death, between the constitution of bodies and history. Memory, via the artifice of the image, produces a temporal strangeness that connects the spectator to a past, lost reality that has been in existence but no longer exists and yet continues to live in a cryogenically frozen stasis (Landsberg, 1995). The 'living soul' is dis/connected from an antecedent order of beings, a history associated with death and the uncanniness of the image. The 'punctum', a particular detail in the photograph, arrests the gaze of the spectator.

The hysteria Barthes associates with this retroactive, supplementary production of history is tied to the being who gave birth to the spectator. The mother, no longer there and yet still there in the photograph, forms the matrix of a historical gaze from which the spectator's life has proceeded but, as spectator, from which he is also cut off. 'A sort of umbilical cord links the body of the photographed thing to my gaze', writes Barthes, but the link, of light alone, seems far less palpable (Barthes, 1984: 86). The punctum is also a 'little hole', a 'cut', an accident: it leads to another punctum, 'Time', 'the lacerating emphasis of the *noeme*', a knot and a wound (1984: 22, 96). The photograph, the photographic relation, is constituted in respect of a navel. A stimulation of memory and a knot in the retroactive production of history, the photograph brings simulation to the fore at the juncture of body and image, past and present, subject and Other.

The status of the image and its residually real and human substance is placed in question and jeopardy with the encroachments of machinic processes. Human reality flickers and fades, absorbed into the rapid and random memories spun out by a host of computer-generated images.

Sex, machines and navels

Human forms and inhuman consciousness pulse in machinic processes while human bodies slump before screens. Hysterical responses surround speculations on the machine and the in/human future it may imply: fantasmatic shapes and ghostly figures populate discourses on humanity, morals, values and community with an insistent desperation and mechanically repetitive regularity. The machine functions like a punctum in a contemporary world picture, interrupting the studious and steady unfolding of a historical narrative with anxieties, uncertainties and joyful speculations: clouding human horizons, it generates visions of the future that reinterpret the past. It operates, in the manner of Freud's navel, as a knot that arrests interpretation or progress while also inviting a plunge into new, exciting and unknown realms. The machine's ambivalent location and effects also introduce significant differences from Barthes's version of the arresting detail within the photographic image: the figure of the machine condenses metaphor, object, system and process, combining the functions of other and Other. A different temporality also emerges: time is no longer that of the photographic image. The time of 'that has been', Barthes notes, may already have disappeared. Instead Virilio's global, real-time computerised exchanges and technological speed manifest a contrary temporality: 'that has been' turns into a past that never has been. Virtual and universal speed veers towards a time without time and a history retroactively generated only in the instant of simulation. Without a sense of before and after, for sense is now of the instant alone, machines take time beyond sequence or seriality and into the dimension of parallelism, plurality and instantaneity.

Time, in a historical sense, is terminated. Its unthinkable movement assumes the impossible form of a feedback loop from the future, the form structuring the fantastic family romance of James Cameron's *The Terminator* (Penley, 1986; SHaH, 1997). Sent from the future by advanced artificial intelligences intent on eradicating humanity, the terminating robot attempts to erase human history at a stroke by destroying the future leader of human resistance before he can be born: the future father is attacked through the mother, the terminator's target in the project of instituting the absolutism of machinic law. The short-circuiting of history by machines, however, actually inaugurates it: a human warrior sent back to destroy the terminator adverts her to what is coming and inseminates her with humanity's hope. But the terminator's failure is also a success: remnants of its advanced circuitry stimulate research in computer development, thereby planting the seed of the machinic future. A leftover of and from the future has furnished and will furnish artificial intelligence with a prehistory of its own making, a divine act of machinic creationism and a navel gesturing prospectively rather than backwards. Significantly, the terminator's navel is never displayed, if, that is, he has one. Though retrojected, arriving naked as Adam in the present, the camera only ever frames the unclothed cyborg above the waist. Occluding a full-frontal exposure of a male member that may or may not hang from the synthetic skin of the killing machine, the delicacy of the gesture also avoids the question of the navel, of its deceptive presence or its horrifying absence.

The future, it seems, describes a precipitative and regressive careering towards the ever-present, obliterating the trace of the past in simulations and erasing any time for questions of precedence, whether they concern lost origins or simply prior networks and connectivities. In such an unwaveringly machinic state, there will, of course, be no room for the navel as a mark of temporal, mortal and bodily difference. That useless mark of human corporeality announces the human to be no more than the 'meat' ejected from the machine or supplanted by other modes of production and reproduction. There ought, then, to be no navels in representations of future life forms, other than as a mark of a residual corporeality on the point of disappearing. However, towards the close of *Blade Runner*, the rebel replicant leader, Roy Batty, bares his chest in the final confrontation with his pursuer. His navel, too, is plainly visible, an oversight of continuity editing, perhaps, that bespeaks a curious continuity. Its existence makes no sense at all, given that this genetically engineered being is not born of woman. And when a replicant's life-span can be genetically recoded, the failure to remove the knot of a relation that has never existed seems a striking example of technical incompetence, a disastrous oversight considering how difficult it is supposed to be to identify, and thereby 'retire', such perfect simulacra. Symbolically, of course, the navel serves to underline the question of humanity posed by the film's blurring of the boundaries between natural and artificial beings. As automata, and not robots, their existence induces tremors along the border separating organic nature and artificial culture. Indeed, as many critics have noted, Deckard, the human 'blade runner' sent to retire the artificial beings, may be a replicant himself (Kuhn, 1990). Replicants, moreover, trouble definitions by evincing greater human qualities than their organic counterparts. In this light, however, the most human figure is the most advanced replicant, Rachael. Not because of the technical verisimilitude which enables her to answer so many questions in the 'empathy test' that establishes humanity,

Sex, machines and navels

nor a result of her programming which means she is a replicant who does not know she is a replicant, but because of her relation to death. Unlike other replicants her life-span is uncertain. More significant, however, is that she causes death, killing one of her own kind for the love of a human. Murder makes humanity, as Freud argues in *Totem and Taboo*.

Where automata problematise, and thereby sustain, the question of what it means to be human, robots present a completely different relation. Jean Baudrillard elaborates on the implications of a distinction between automata and robots: the former serves as a human 'analogy' and an 'interrogation upon nature', while the latter becomes 'man's equivalent and annexes him to itself in the unity of its operational process. This is the difference between a simulacrum of the first order and one of the second.' The first form reflects reality, the second perverts it. The robot 'no longer interrogates appearance; its only truth is in its mechanical efficacy' (Baudrillard, 1983: 92–4). Cybernetic control thus leads to a 'new *operational* configuration': 'digitality is its metaphysical principle (the God of Leibniz), and DNA its prophet' (1983: 103). Everything becomes code in the transition towards a new biotechnical economic order:

> From a capitalist-productivist society to a neo-capitalist cybernetic order that aims now at total control. This is the mutation for which biological theorization of the code prepares the ground. There is nothing of an accident in this mutation. It is the end of a history in which successively, God, Man, Progress, and History itself die to profit the code, in which transcendence dies to profit immanence, the latter corresponding to a much more advanced phase in the vertiginous manipulation of social rapports. (Baudrillard, 1983: 111–12)

Replicants, genetically engineered automata, constitute the final, most perfect simulations of the play between human, machine and nature. Their navels thus signify a reflection that sustains a human order. After them, however, with the development of robotic machinic codes and biological mutations, human reality and the navel disappears.

There ought, as a result, to be no question of the appearance of navels in a future dominated by principles of operativity and cybernetic control. It is strange, then, to encounter the question of the navel in a fictional future in which self-replicating autonomous robots have developed beyond human control. No navel is visible in Rudy Rucker's *Wetware*, but the absence of one proves as interrogative of origins, being and connectivity as any navel on a replicant, engendering reflections which ripple throughout the novel. An absence, then, provides the occasion for reflection:

> The taut gold buckler of Berenice's belly caught Cobb's eye. It bulged out gently as a heap of wheat. Yet the mockery was sterile: Berenice had left off the navel, the end of the flesh cord that leads back and back through blood, through time – *Put me through to Edenville*. (Rucker, 1994: 244)

Cobb Anderson, inventor of the moon robots, the self-replicating, autonomous, artificially conscious machines nicknamed 'boppers', makes this observation. But he is no longer human in form. He died many years before and his consciousness was stored as data. Recently 'reborn', his stored consciousness is downloaded to a bopper body. Nevertheless, his observation on the sterility of the mockery implied by a robot adopting a female shape emanates from a human position. The object of his reflection is Berenice, a female-identified bopper. All boppers, it seems, adopt a gender, but Berenice takes her identification further: she is fascinated with organic life's highly efficient reproductive transmission of information. Her mockery, disclosed by the absence of a navel on a female form, appears less sterile when she achieves her aims of implanting a human ovum with the software codes of the boppers. This conception produces a new, hybrid species, a 'meatbopper', a robot human in form and material composition.

Cobb's reflections on the absence of a navel on Berenice's body, while distinguishing between beings of human origin and of cybernetic evolution, acknowledge the co-existence of organic time with that of machinic information. The matter, the flesh and blood that encodes humanity's lineage within a evolving chain, is associated with another mode of coding: 'put me through to Edenville'. From flesh and blood, the line leads back to the biblical origins of humanity. But the phrase also calls for the direct line of communication that a telephone operator can provide. Biological code and communications technology are conjoined around the navel and its signifying absence: its place continues to pose questions of being, time and differential connections, opening on to a network of flesh, blood and information larger than any specific entity. This network, this locus of connection and disconnection, holds a prominent position in the *Wetware*'s world of organic and robotic beings, a matrix called 'the One'. Posing the questions of the origin of beings and their relation to others and the Other, the navel retains the ambivalent status for robots that human discourse currently gives to the machine. In the midst of fictional futures, futures supposedly surpassing matters of corporeal and sexual existence,

Sex, machines and navels

the navel returns to interrupt the realisation of any unsexed fantasy with a little piece of the 'meat'. The retention of sexual difference and a fascination with organic life establishes a pregnant pause for thought in a time of informational speed, a space for reflection and interrogation and a significant interruption of the rapid hyperrational flight of fantasy into a machinic future present.

Plugging into the One

In *Wetware*, with a degree of mockery verging on objective irony, the absence of a the navel, itself a mark of absence, forms a point around which questions of history, evolution, human and robotic being are posed and unravelled. Matters of ontogenetic and phylogenetic identity become entangled with questions of linguistic, cultural and sexual difference. Moreover, difference takes its bearing from the One, a locus of origin and universality which determines the flows of ones and zeros and the sexed structures of binary language: the navel, in evolutionary and informational terms, forms the point of connection and disconnection that allows individual being to emerge in relation to absolute being, the One who is Other. The status and effects of the One in human or robotic codes discloses a significant difference in notions of otherness: for humans the God descended from metaphysical paradigms and models of the sexed self's orgasmic liberation connotes mystical union, transcendent evolution and erotically charged fusion; for robots the One manifests the principle of plural and parallel process, the network of pulsations and informational flows encompassing all technological and evolutionary exchanges. As the predicate for individuated being, the One situates beings in very different relation to the cosmos but, bound up with questions of origin and evolution, it articulates the similarities and differences between organic and electronic life in terms of sex.

Wetware's boppers are neither automata mimicking the form and functions of humans nor simply robots, machinic in their absolute difference: endowed with consciousness, their existence remains entirely Other to human life yet strangely related to it. Cobb Anderson's remarks on the absence of a navel acknowledge the strangeness that the 'mockery' of Berenice's female body evokes. The dead human creator of robotic life forms whose consciousness is restored to a robot body expects, it seems, something Other only to be disturbed by a proximity that nonetheless reinforces difference: sex should not even be a question for robotic life forms. But 'for reasons only a bopper could explain' some were 'he' and some 'she': 'they found each other beautiful; and in their pursuit of beauty, they constantly improved the software makeup of their race' (Rucker, 1994: 207). Cobb's reaction to the unexpected persistence of sexual difference reinforces the mockery of sexuality with a clumsy mock-phallic lunge that is rebutted politely and firmly by Berenice. His unappreciated joke deliberately misunderstands the relationship between body and desire in reducing sex to a crude physical act utterly inappropriate to bopper desire: though boppers 'conjugate', they do so in a very different manner. Berenice has already communicated her desire, a 'curiosity, yearning and a sharp excitement', by transmitting a 'glyph', an ideograph, to Cobb, an image which pictures, speaks and touches him with her desire, a *want to enter Earthlife's information mix* (1994: 245). Desire comes of language, code, information, not of bodies. Indeed, it is desire of this order which informs Berenice's choice of a female form.

Poetic language shapes bopper culture, informing desires and determining the mysterious choice of masculine or feminine identities and the rites of sex, love and reproduction associated with conjugation. A rapid machine language of glyphs and macros forms the staple currency of everyday, working exchanges, while poetic language is reserved for the nuances of intimate interpersonal communication. The words and styles of human writers are exhumed from data banks and employed in the amorous relations of boppers. Berenice, as her name acknowledges, speaks the language of Edgar Allan Poe, an ironic touch given the latter's concern about a mechanical chess player. Her suitor, Emul, draws freely on the writing of Jack Kerouac: 'Berenice, life's a deep gloom ocean and we're lit-up funfish of dementional zaazz, we're flowers blooming out till the loudsun wither and the wind blows our dead husks away' (1994: 208). Words of love come from literary English in that, as 'an ancient and highly evolved human code system', it expresses the subtle emotional distinctions of self and other (1994: 209). For the boppers, love is a thoroughly linguistic, poetic affair: 'to make love, as the term indicates, is poetry' (Lacan, 1982: 143). Berenice, however, demurs at Emul's persistent invitations to conjugate, pre-empting any idea of precipitous union by reiterating how her desire is directed elsewhere: 'my mind's own true passion runs towards but one sea, the teeming womb of life on Earth' (1994: 209). Opposed to this idea of the One, Emul insists

'... all your merge talk is the One's snare to bigger joy, sure, but tragic-flowing dark time is where we float here, here with me touching you, and not some metafoolish factspace no future. Gloom and womb, our kid would be real; don't say *why*, say *how*, now? You can pick the body shape, you can be ma. Don't forget the actual chips in my real cubette. I'd never ask anyone else, Berenice. We'll do it soft and low.' Emul extruded dozens of beckoning fingers. (1994: 209)

The One, as it consumes Berenice with the idea of a 'bigger joy' associated with merging with the 'teeming womb' of terrestrial life, also inhibits the possibility of conjugation with Emul, despite his practical and urgent insistence on the realisation of their love in the production of their joint offspring, a 'scion'.

For boppers 'conjugation' means the realisation of an attraction between a masculine- and feminine-identified robot consciousness: together they build a new bopper body and allow a copy of both programs to flow out and 'merge and mingle in the new body's processor', a shuffling of codes that constitutes 'the prime source of the boppers' evolutionary diversity' (1994: 209–10). Attraction, beauty, desire and identity are, for the boppers, crucial cultural aspects of their software evolution: informational recoding replaces genetic mutation. Sex is a matter of replicating and enhancing the programming of individual robot consciousnesses. But like love and sexual identity it is no longer bound up with bodily being and physical contact: it depends on the One as it is supported by structures and flows of information and literary language. The poetic, courtly modes of amorous address in which boppers make love disclose the 'absence of a sexual relation' (Lacan, 1982: 141). An obstacle to the immediate union of Emul and Berenice, the One is also the determining factor in their sexual (non)relation and the locus of desire's possibility. Berenice may be the only one for Emul, but he is not enough for her. Her desire for a 'bigger joy' associated with the One eschews the intermediate and practical solution of the boppers sexual non-relation in informational conjugation. For Emul conjugation reproduces the sexualised symbolic relation of mother and father in accordance the One's requirements for the mingling, shuffling and diversification of software. Boppers, it seems, engage in their own '*ménage à trois*' with 'God as third party', fundamental in the 'affair of human love' (Lacan, 1982: 141). Sex between two boppers always involves a third party, the One who comes in the shape of a religious God: the boppers have both a place of worship, 'the temple of the One', and certain pre-programmed religious rituals which they continue to observe.

Though a 'randomization device' which their creator, Cobb, 'had programmed the original boppers to plug into every so often just to keep them from falling into stasis', the One causes a 'meme-shuffling' and software diversity like that produced in conjugation. Nonetheless, boppers religiously continue their 'plugging into the One' (1994: 254–5).

God, sex and evolution converge in the One. And like desire and identity it is structured by the linguistic relations and flows of literary language. The strange religious intensity which surrounds the boppers' language of love and its centrality to their culture and evolution lies both beneath and in excess of the highly efficient and rapid communicational forms that dominates their workaday existence. As a human, literary language it informs their unconscious patterns in relation to the One as much as it structures their personal identity and relations to other boppers. With human literary language there persists, or rather insists, a form of God, the Other, associated with language and the unconscious. The original and very functional One is preserved, unnecessarily, in the language of love: it insists as a desire in excess of evolutionary imperatives satisfied by conjugation and is sustained by the rituals of the boppers themselves, in their poetic speech and in the devotional activities which they pursue. God, then, is not their programmer-creator, Cobb Anderson, not a being from whom Being originates, but the very locus of their being. The One is sustained precisely in their symbolic, amorous and cultural activities. Lacan observes that it is 'beyond doubt' that 'the symbolic is the support of that which was made into God' (1982: 154). Thus, 'if the unconscious is indeed what I say it is, as being structured like a language, then it is on the level of language that we must interrogate this One' (1982: 139). God is not a transcendent, metaphysical being outside symbolic, linguistic and cultural relations but constituted and sustained in the structures of language. This need not imply a theistical order like the one that is preserved in the statement 'God is dead' but manifests what Lacan calls 'the true formula of atheism': that *God is unconscious* (1977b: 59). Along with the sexual identities sustained in the use of literary language, a language which is the remainder of a human past, the boppers inherit and sustain their conceptions of a One that is Other, unconscious.

Questions of sex remain central to the boppers' articulation of desire so that language and femininity return in excess of the functional non-relation of sex to disclose a radical otherness: 'by her being in the sexual relation radically Other, in relation to what can be said of the unconscious, the woman is that which relates to this Other' (Lacan, 1982: 151). In the

Sex, machines and navels

divergent desires disclosed by Berenice's and Emul's very different positioning in terms of the absent sexual relation and the One, an ethics of sexual difference appears at the core of *Wetware*'s future world. For Lacan, the relation of subjects of language to the Other turns on the symbolic place of lack and the excess of feminine *jouissance*. Where beings, insofar as they speak, are all subject to the phallic signifier and thus defined by desire and lack, women retain a position as both 'not all' and excessive: men may be defined in a language that fully represents them and thereby subjects them to the signifier 'Man', but 'the' woman does not exist, which is to say that women are not fully contained by the function of a definitive article. In this respect women retain a proximity to the One in excess of human signification, a *jouissance* of the body that lies 'beyond the phallus' (1982: 145). In excess of phallic representation, the position allotted women relates to that excess associated with the Other, God, the One: 'it is in so far as her *jouissance* is radically Other that the woman has a relation to God greater than all that has been stated in ancient speculation according to a path which has manifestly been articulated only as the good of mankind' (1982: 153). Turning on the One in terms of excess and subjection, the non-relation of the sexes engenders quite different modes of fantasy: on the masculine side 'the whole of his realisation in the sexual relation comes down to fantasy' in which woman exists as an other, an object of symptomatic support that imaginarily fills the lack constitutive of his subjectivity (Lacan, 1982: 157). Fantasy depends on a structure of desire/lack in that it maintains the subject as barred from the Other, separated from the system of signifiers presided over by the phallic signifier in which existence is manifested:

> Of all the signifiers this is the signifier for which there is *no* signified, and which, in relation to meaning, symbolises its failing. This is the half-sense, the *inde-sense* par excellence, or if you like, the *reti-sense*. Since the $ is thus duplicated by the signifier on which basically it does not even depend, so it only ever relates as a partner to the *objet a* inscribed on the other side of the bar. It can never reach its sexual partner, which is the Other, except by way of mediation, as the cause of its desire. On this account, and as indicated in one of my other drawings by the dotted line joining the $ and the *a*, this can only be fantasy. (Lacan, 1982: 151)

Emul's desire for conjugation, and the very practical reasons he proposes and the pique he evinces when rejected, situates him on the masculine, fantastic, side of the sexual relation, critical of the 'bigger joy' imagined by

Berenice to be the result of merging with the terrestrial information matrix. Berenice, too, finds her desire determined by the sexual relation to the One, but the fantasy which supports it veers in another direction, towards the *jouissance* of the Other.

Berenice's passion for the 'teeming womb of life on Earth', for merger with a distinctly feminine informational matrix turns precisely on the absent figure which she has left off her female form, a fantasy structured around the very absence of the navel. Her disconnection from the One imagined as the excess of the machinic order of the boppers simultaneously involves the link manifested by her desire. Appropriately enough she works in the 'pink tanks' where human organs are cloned, grown and harvested: the cause of her desire is the meat of organic life, the complexity of biological sexual reproduction. Berenice and her co-workers, her 'sisters', share a fascination with organic evolution and frequently speak of the difference between a meat and a wire body, privileging the former for having 'each single body cell independently alive' (1994: 215). To have a womb is considered 'marvellous' and organic life 'wondrous', composed of macroviruses that 'drag vast histories behind them, yea unto trillions of bits'. Equally impressive is the accuracy and consistency of generational information storage (1994: 215–16). The fascination with organic life informs the desire to produce a 'meatbop', a biological being that genetically reproduces bopper software. For Berenice it is a dream of a 'new age' when boppers 'can live among protein jungles of an unchained Earth' (1994: 210). The dream, as it turns on the difference between human and machinic bodies, refuses simply to privilege the former over the latter, elevating sexual reproduction over bopper conjugation: by reconfiguring these oppositions in a hybrid, cyborg form, it imagines beings that realise the democratic union sustained in the idea of the One, the 'common origin' of humans and boppers in which life is all just information, 'information coded up the ceaseless evolution of the One' (1994: 221). Sex and biology are thus reconfigured according to the bopper philosophy of the One so that meatboppers will be 'of an equal humanity' and will mark a 'new stage in evolution', in the parallel and plural processing that is the One (1994: 247). The merger of meat and machine is not based on an idea of transcendence, but on the immanent pooling and shuffling of genetic and digital information, a process which democratically places all beings on the same footing, all equal under the One.

The democratising informational impulse requires a careful differentiation between the bopper notion of the One and a human idea

| Sex, machines and navels

involving an imagined movement of transcendence. The difference turns on the humanist notion of 'self', as Berenice outlines:

> Boppers called themselves I, just as did any human, but they did not mean the same thing. For a bopper; 'I' means (1) my body, (2) my software, and (3) my function in society. For a human, 'I' seemed to have an extra component: (4) my uniqueness. This delusionary fourth 'I' factor is what set a human off against the world. Every bopper tried to avoid any taint of the human notion of *self*. (1994: 213)

In contrast, boppers consider themselves part of the world, like beams of light: 'and the world was One vast cellular automaton (or 'CA'), calculating out instants – and each of the world's diverse objects was but a subcalculation, a simulation in the One great parallel process. So where was there any *self*?'(1994: 213) Where the bopper 'I' is situated in the process of evolution, the humanist version assumes mastery and transcendence, setting up their 'fourth "I" factor – their so-called self – as the One's equal'. Christianity, Berenice notes, is based on the teachings of a man who called himself God. That it was a man who claimed divinity is also significant. The equation of man and God in the 'myth of self' leads to human boredom and selfishness and the pain that comes of the refusal to recognise one's integral place in the universe (1994: 213). It also produces a 'xenophobia' that impedes the progression to a state of 'democratic equivalence' between fleshly and machine bodies (1994: 243).

Around the idea of the One, differences of sex, species and race unravel and complicate distinctions between subjects, bodies and machines. Human life, the meat which Berenice finds so fascinating, is scorned by Emul, her rejected suitor. 'Dreak and work for me,' he exclaims,

> a bigger brain, a bigger nothing. I'm a goof, Berenice, but you're cracked crazy through with your talk about getting a meat body. Humans stink. I run them for kicks: my meaties – Ken Doll, Rainbow and Berdoo – my remote-run slaves with plugs in their brains. I could run all Earth if I had the equipment. Meat is nowhere, Berenice, it's flybuzz greenslime rot into fractal info splatter. When Oozer and I get our exaflop up, we can plug in a cityful of humans and run them all. (1994: 210–11)

Humans are vile slavish bodies, 'meaties', fit only to be wired with remote control implants and operated by the powerful new processor Emul is constructing. They deserve only contempt and slavery: robot evolution has, for Emul, absolutely surpassed humanity and biology with its transcendent technological powers. His new machine is being produced with the desire 'to transcend Earth's info rather than to merge with it' (1994: 208). In his choice of outer form Emul reiterates his anti-humanism and disdains 'any fixed body shape, let alone a *human* body shape' (1994: 207). His basic form is utterly opposed to the smooth curves of a human body, 'a two-meter cube, with a surface tessellated into red, yellow, and blue' (1994: 207). Emul, too, enjoys the favoured drug of the boppers, 'dreak'. A gas, dreak accelerates the conductivity of bopper hardware to induce quasi-mystical effects that take the user outside time and into a 'spacetime collage', a 'unified tapestry', a 'world of synchronicity', a world of visible, total and immediate thought. The transcendent sense evoked by dreak is underlined in a comparative table charting its drastic effects in moving the sense of users from a state of being a 'finite robot' to that of a 'living mind', from 'shit' to 'God' (1994: 257-8).

Emul's relation to the One partakes, it seems, of notions of self strangely similar to those criticised by Berenice, his masculine identity disclosing a fantasy of attaining the transcendent position of mastery. Berenice's suspicions, moreover, underline a fundamental difference between masculine and feminine relations to the One. Her criticisms of Emul recall an episode from the early history of the moon robots, a reference to the events of Rucker's *Software*: Emul talks like the 'big boppers', 'the vast multiprocessors that had tried to turn all boppers into their robot-remotes', precisely the exercise of power that Emul enjoys with his residually human 'meaties'. It is wrong, moralises Berenice, for whom individuals matter, 'for one brain to control many bodies; such anti-parallelism could only have a deadening effect on evolution' (1994: 211). In her terms, the terms dictated by her One, Emul directs his energies towards dangerously anti-evolutionary ends.

Emul's hatred of the stinking and slavish flesh of humanity retains numerous residual and negative aspects of self, to the point that his position and antipathy constitutes a form of inverted recognition. His relation to the One, his sexual attitudes and his drug use emphasise the determining influence of human codes of self and evolution pulsing through his circuits. In the neighbouring human city on the moon (Einstein) sex and drugs are intimate bedfellows promising a merger with the One. *Wetware* begins with an encounter with a religious pamphleteer proclaiming 'ALL IS ONE' and enjoining passers-by to 'merge into the One' through a philosophy of 'organic Mysticism' in which love leads 'to a fuller union with the cosmos at large' (1994: 175). Sex and drugs, of course, are quickly associated with a horrifyingly literal mode of merging

Sex, machines and navels

with God. 'Merge' is the name of a banned synthetic drug which melts bodies. A highly addictive chemical, merge decomposes cell walls by means of a process of 'gene-invasion' invented by a scientist who was once called Gibson. The effects are graphically demonstrated in a show-experiment involving a large brown toad, a white rat and a drop of merge: 'but then the merge had taken effect, and the animals' tissues flowed together: brown and white, warts and hair. A flesh-puddle formed, loosely covering the creatures' loosened skeletons. Four eyes looked up: two green, two pink. Faint shudders seemed to animate the fused flesh. Pleasure?' (1994: 179). Pleasure forms the underlying principle of merge and, intermingled with the obvious horror at the formless decomposition of separate entities, a thrill reverberates along the line joining fear and desire, disgust and eroticism, replete with the thrills of ultimate disintegration. Prolonged exposure to the effects of the chemical inhibit the ability of cells to reform, enabling rapid genetic mutations to occur. The scientist displays what he wittily describes as his 'pet project', a monstrosity in the guise of a 'universal life form', a chimera called a *Chitin*: a 'sodden, shambling thing – an amalgam of feathers and claws', with long feelers, a snout, slack mandibles and gills (1994: 180).

Monstrosity is counterbalanced by pleasure, horror measured against desire. Merge has its recreational and saleable uses in the com-modified near future where pleasure is the boss. The laboratory doubles as something between a brothel and an opium den, a retreat where merge-addicted couples come to enjoy the ultimate pleasures of fused flesh. In a back room two bodies merge in 'love-puddles' and later leave as the drug wears off still joined by their hands. Merge takes bodily union and the fantasy of a sexual relation to a virtually complete state of fusion, a *jouissance* of two in the One which simultaneously raises being to ecstatic levels and reduces bodies to the vile formlessness of slime. Transcendence and abjection, the sacred and the profane. A detective and reformed drug user describes the experience of a merge trip as seeing a God who 'was about the same as usual', if a little more burnt out and in need of love. And then the drug hits: 'Wonderful. Horrible! The space of the room became *part of his consciousness*. He *was* the room ... he was the room and the building and Einstein and the Earth. Standard ecstatic mystical vision, really. But *fast*. He was everywhere, he was nowhere, he was the same as God. And then there were no thoughts at all (1994: 185). Extreme pleasure elevates consciousness to divinity. The extremity of pleasure associated with *jouissance*, of course, requires both the utmost decomposition of being and an encounter that moves beyond God to death. A little too rapid, merge is a 'death practice': 'hit, melt, space, blank. Final blank' (1994: 185). The openness to the Other as it moves from pleasure to death leaves the frail, slimy decomposed body prey to the possibility of irrecuperable disintegration. Like 'Jell-O rolled over some bones', the detective comments on discovering a corpse, merge users can be splattered into pieces that independently firm up as separate bodily fragments (1994: 186). The boundary between meat and the Maker becomes infinitesimally thin, no more than the width of a cell wall: at one instant there's God, the next slimy lumps of dead flesh.

In a world of collapsing differences, the distance between meat and machine is a matter of speed and inclination, all-important in the establishment of hierarchies of opposition and utterly redundant at the same time. Questions of difference, subject as they are to erasure and transformation, recur with an insistent force within and between the various groupings that constitute human and machine society. The question of the navel, of one's relation to the meat, remains paramount. During a charming Christmas dinner of vat-grown boneless turkey, an earthbound family indulge in the characteristic squabbles of any happy gathering. The turkey occupies a predominant place as the discussion heats up around the topic of the boppers. 'They're just a bunch of goddam *machines*,' exclaims Mom. To which her nephew replies: 'You're a machine, too, Aunt Amy … You're just made of meat instead of wires and silicon' (1994: 196). He is, of course, duly reprimanded: 'Don't call your Aunt "meat" … The turkey is meat. Your Aunt is a person. You wouldn't want me to put gravy on your aunt and eat her, would you?' (1994: 197). Meat and machine mirror each other as terms of abuse and pathological objects of irrational hatred. Like the use of the term 'skin jobs' in reference to replicants in *Blade Runner*, the word 'meat' or the human call to 'kill the machines' is comparable to the racist's snarl of 'nigger' (1994: 198). Meat and machine retain an excess that cannot be reduced to rational or logical definition: the former connotes something other than the lumps of flesh remaining after organic information has been encoded as data; the latter, also, signifies more than efficient, predictable units without consciousness or feeling. The terms, though opposed, turn on an element of emotional energy which cannot be rationalised or explained, a point of difference around which symbolic differences circulate, a surplus of meaning charged only with negativity, without which the privileged position would collapse. The excess comes from the surplus enjoyment of the Other associated with an extimate

| Sex, machines and navels

pathological Thing (Miller, 1988). In a similar way, Emul's hostility to stinking human meat, like the human hatred of machines, mirrors and replicates what it most despises, the uniqueness of the one dependent on a revulsion towards the other.

But Berenice's way, her democratic ideal of a 'meatbopper', an organic body genetically fused with robot software, also falls short of the equivalence she imagines as a levelling of all beings in the informational process of the One, a new ideal of 'equal humanity'. Something of the meat, something in excess of her imagined merger between flesh and machine, remains to undermine the very union and equivalence embodied in the production of the meatbopper, a remainder which is both more and less than a corporeal residue jettisoned by machinic codes and which discloses a gap between symbolic and bodily integration. The first 'meat-bopper, named 'Manchile', develops at a vastly accelerated rate: genetic enhancement of organic growth is required due to the veiled hostilities of the cold war between boppers and humans. Rapid growth can only be sustained by an enormous and regular intake of food, and the hyper-efficient, programmed process of physical development sacrifices the cultural aspects of eating to voracious biological energy requirements. At this point nature is divided between the symbolised and ritualistic construction of culture and the indifference of biological consumption: naturally born but unnaturally developed, the meatbopper child fractures the imaginary bond between the human figure and its natural mirror. For Manchile everything that provides him with the energy he needs is considered edible. His accelerated development means, also, that he is always hungry. His mother is quickly exhausted and alarmed by the unnatural speed of his growth. Alarm turns to horror when she sees him greedily eyeing the family's pet dog. Soon the dog disappears and a sated Manchile reappears, having enjoyed a barbecue in the yard. The horror and revulsion this act of non-human consumption evokes displays how the codes of efficient, enhanced organic development have, in the name of nature and the reconciliation between the human and the machine, only produced an excess which is neither natural nor human: the codes, tools and symbolic rituals surrounding eating preserve the boundaries between natural organism and human being, elevating and distinguishing the idea and value of the human figure in respect of a concept of humanised nature different from animal nature and desire. Taboos on what is eaten, how it is cooked and the mode of consumption constitute a negation of animal nature. Ultimately there are no reasons for the taboo other than the negation itself as it maintains the very idea of human culture and community. This is the line that the hyperefficient accelerated development of Manchile crosses, thereby erasing the very difference between symbolic, cultural value and animal or natural being that the rituals of eating, and the notion of meat, preserve. Revulsion acknowledges the transgression of a symbolic limit; horror marks the response to a monstrous child who has exceeded both humanity and its nature.

In their eagerness to produce an integrated organic machine, the all-too rational boppers overlook the difference, irrational to the point of pathology, that makes humans the selves they are despite all reasonable arguments to the contrary. This is the very difference that articulates meat and machine even as it remains in excess of both. For the boppers it turns out to be a fatal oversight that exacerbates the antagonism between terrestrial and lunar beings. Manchile quickly matures into a hyperactive sexual being, an irresistible sex machine who inseminates a host of women with his accelerated genetic code. The progenies increase to the alarm of the human community. A bopper plot is suspected and uncovered. The meatbopper offspring are pursued and eradicated. The moment that precipitates the focusing of human hatred against these new beings occurs when a starving young meatbopper fleeing persecution encounters a night-watchman in a junkyard. He kills the man, cooks his leg and eats it. All the time he is under surveillance: the video footage is relayed around the world. The horribly literal manifestation of their latent paranoia, an effect of their own avowed meatiness, incites the revolted human community to exterminate the new species. The public sight of an act close to cannibalism precipitates a war in which the boppers, too, are exterminated: a microbiotic fungus is developed that feeds on the electronic frequency of their circuitry, clogging their relays and disabling their bodies and thought processes. Unable to feed on solar energy, the boppers die, sucked dry by the mould that sprouts from their cladding: 'the gray-yellow threads had formed golfball-sized nodes: fruiting bodies' (1994: 334). Nodules, an organic mycelium, a self-replicating meshwork, swamps the informatic evolution of the machine. But evolution is also unpredictable: the boppers' electronic, decorative cloaks enjoy the invasion of the nodular, fruiting mould and, symbiotically, come alive. A new species is born. Evolutionary process rolls on. Merger, the fusion of body and machine in the One's parallel process or in the transcendence of meat by machine articulate a self-determining opposition that, at the end of *Wetware* cancels itself out, rendered redundant by an unpredictable excess and contingent complexity beyond the grasp of models of idealised fusion or complete transcendence: from the (same) question of meat or machine comes an answer that is neither meat nor machine, but a detour, a turn which negates the self-identity of both. Instead, the mirror in which meat or machine misrecognise themselves as not the other is shattered, opening to a quite different movement.

Other matrix, other meat

Wetware complicates questions of the future and renders visible the matter of an inassimilable difference. Interrupting contemporary narrative patterns, the novel offers a brief opportunity of pausing for reflection upon the non-choice, the sameness, presented by the imminent advenition of a near-future utopia that is simultaneously a distopia. In excess of the choice between either meat or machine something else intervenes, something of and irreducible to meat and machine. As a choice, either/or presents a fundamentally binary division and containment of difference. Angela Carter, in *The Infernal Desire Machines of Dr Hoffman*, notes the uncanny reversibility of the opposition and contrasts it to the secret formula of desiring: 'Mine is an and + and world. I alone have discovered the key to the inexhaustible plus' (1982: 206). The 'plus' that leaves desire wanting in an infinite chain of conjunction provides Dr Hoffman with his principle of subversion. Infinite addition underpins a culture of consumption in which lack forms the motor of desiring: another object and another object and another object are consumed in an escalating series in which desire never finds its final object and desiring becomes the rule. Desiring plugs bodies into machines. For Nick Land, celebrating the short-circuit in which 'machinic revolution' is hooked up to 'even more uninhibited marketization', notes that 'wanting more is the index of interlock with cyberpositive machinic process and not the expression of private idiosyncrasy' (1993b: 278–80). Desiring depends on an incompleteable series associated with transnational capitalism, a hyperlibertarian impulse to liberate all exchanges from any rules whatsoever.

In defining the principle of desire Hoffman ironically contains and thereby reduces the desiring that depends on a secret and elusive Thing: in discovering its principle he makes what was out of reach and desirably mysterious into something which can be contained and thus no longer desirable. This aspect of desire is not lost on Desiderio, the figure of desire who, in the novel, moves between the rational and ordered world of everyday reality into the fantastic and plural universe liberated by Hoffman's machines. For Desiderio the gap between desiring and its phantasmatic object remains paramount and he can only be disappointed with Hoffman's mechanical discovery: the evil genius of libidinal liberation has to contain the energy of eroticism in the act of producing it. Desire slips between the binary division that rationalises reality and the desiring-series which both liberates and destroys desire thereby instituting a new opposition that is binary in form: the either/or is opposed to a desiring process. What escapes this relation, however, is the desired one, Desiderio: his identity falls from the novel as that which is no longer what it was, lost and desired and thus desiring still.

In *Wetware*, the other meat that escapes the logic of either meat or machine, of transcendent godhead or acephalic machine's evolutionary process, inaugurates the new species which emerges from the war of humans and robots. In this respect Rucker's novel exposes the complex and contradictory basis of current concerns with human or technological futures in that it opens the narratives that predict and pre-scribe the future to accidental and aleatory movements. But in the fictions dominating popular presentations of future worlds, whether the fictions are framed as novelistic or scientific texts, the choice appears straightforward: conscious-ness will be uploaded into computers and bodies will be discarded, a seamless story of meat into machine, mind liberated from the useless dead-weight of matter.

In William Gibson's *Neuromancer*, the novel which launched a thousand chips, the choice of future seems straightforward and, for some, distinctly distopian in its presentation of the triumph of machine over meat. Renowned for the contrast between the machine on which it was written (a Swiss-made Hermes 2000 manual typewriter) and the medical and virtual technologies it describes, Gibson's fiction, like the cyberpunk genre as a whole, precipitates the actualisation of the future it imagines, giving form to a pervasive technofantasy and 'inventing' cyberspace (Bukat-man, 1993). The novel, however, begins with an enforced return to the meat. The human protagonist, Case, once an elite 'console cowboy' working in the rarefied atmosphere of the matrix, now exists in the 'Sprawl', the maze of houses, bars and businesses outside the world dominated by huge corporate enterprises. He had once enjoyed the 'permanent adrenaline high' of the matrix, thrilled by the visual speeds of a projected 'disem-bodied consciousness'. Now, with a damaged nervous system, he is unemployable: 'for Case, who'd lived in the bodiless exultation of cyberspace, it was the Fall. In the bars he'd frequented as a cowboy hotshot, the elite stance involved a certain relaxed contempt for the flesh. The body was meat. Case fell into the prison of his own flesh' (Gibson, 1984: 12). Unable to afford the expensive medical treatment necessary to repair his nerves, Case is left to dream of the matrix where consciousness, divested of the meat, could roam free. The thrill of 'bodiless exultation' is akin to the erotically charged dissolution of separate identity associated with orgasm. Case makes the comparison as images of the matrix flicker insistently during a brief sexual encounter, 'his orgasm flaring blue in a timeless space, a vastness like the matrix' (1984: 45). '*Like* the matrix', however, is not the matrix: the simile announces a distance between the two, orgasm but a shadow of lost exultation.

In *Neuromancer*, cyberspace becomes the principal locus of desire and metasexual joy. As the novel defines it, the 'matrix' 'has its roots in primitive arcade games … in early graphics programs and military experimentation with cranial jacks':

> Cyberspace. A consensual hallucination experienced daily by millions of legitimate operators, in every nation, by children being taught mathematical concepts … A graphic representation of the data abstracted from the banks of every computer in the human system. Unthinkable complexity. Lines of light ranged in the nonspace of the mind, clusters and constellations of data. Like city lights receding …' (1984: 67)

Life, leisure, education and work proceeds in the world of the matrix, its abstracted data graphically presented in a form that unfolds in the minds of its users: a socket connects their optic nerves to a console linked to the computer network and, with no monitor necessary, the images appear directly in the brain. As a 'consensual hallucination', this mentally inhabited and world within the mind presents a graphic illustration of Althusser's notion of ideology. Images realise the flows of data in the recognisable forms of buildings and towers, the datascape becoming a cityscape. In this artificial, mental city the dominant mode of capitalism – information exchange – is provided with a visual veneer that is consensually accepted, the real, the data itself, transformed into palatable and acceptable images for human consumption interfacing working individuals with the corporate order which determines their existence.[3] Outside that world, like Case, one is nothing but an abjected piece of meat. Case, however, is given another opportunity to enter the realm of 'bodiless exultation' and enjoy the thrills of travelling at great speed across hallucinatory datascapes. With expensive surgical and neurochemical treatment, he is enlisted in a mysterious enterprise which culminates in the cracking of the defensive software, the ICE ('intrusion countermeasures electronics'), of an immensely complex Artificial Intelligence.

In its accounts of the matrix and its descriptions of 'bodiless exultation' *Neuromancer* vividly charts the possibilities for liberating consciousness from the bounds of time and space, for a transcendence of matter.[4] Entry into the vast network of gridlines and flows of light is enabled by a cranial jack: the console operator plugs directly into the One to 'see' the datascape unfold at speed in the 'nonspace' of the mind. Perception exceeds organic possibility, realising a sublimity only ever dreamed of by poets and prophets: 'his vision was spherical, as though a single retina lined the inner surface of a globe that contained all things, if all things could be counted. And here things could be counted, each one' (Gibson, 1984: 304). A sense of absolute consciousness, total vision and unmediated presence is delivered in the interface of mind with machine, a transcendence of body and materiality into the heady realms of a space that is simultaneously within and outside the mind. Better than sex or drugs, the experience of such plenitude elevates consciousness of 'all things' through vision and knowledge, replaying the occularcentrism that has dominated western philosophy since the Greeks. The terms of the novel's imagined future of human transcendence accord with discussions technological futures noting the redundancy of the body. Vision remains the privileged sense in contemporary technology since, as Terence McKenna notes, computers advance towards an 'environment of language that is beheld rather than heard' (Rushkoff, 1994: 84). The effects of the worlds generated by computer systems, too, depend on a reconfiguration of linguistic possibilities. John Barlow, commenting on the 'cyber-village hall', notes that 'in this silent world, all conversation is typed. To enter it one forsakes both body and place and becomes a things of words alone' (Rushkoff, 1994: 54). Perceiving language with the immediacy of vision, or forsaking the body for the liberating transmissions of computer code, are only steps on a grander evolutionary journey. McKenna, 'author, botanist and psychedelic explorer', enthuses about the implications of scientific advances:

> This is the real thing. We're going to find out what 'being' is. It's a philosophical journey and the vehicles are not simply cultural but biology itself. We're closing the distance with the most profound event that a planetary ecology can encounter, which is the freeing of life from the chrysalis of matter … This takes a billion years of forward moving evolution

Sex, machines and navels

to get us to the place where information can detach itself from the material matrix and then look back on a cast-off mode of being as it rises into a higher dimension. (Rushkoff, 1994: 19–20)

To discover being one must have moved beyond it, knowledge having taken the finite mind of man to a higher, more divine dimension in which life, in the form of consciousness and information, flies upwards and away from matter. Detached from the 'material matrix', one exultantly ascends to another plane of incorporeal existence. Such claims to transcendence through technologies of vision and knowledge imagine the imminent realisation of man's entry into a truly divine sphere.

Sex, however, never lies far from descriptions of the ecstasies of future technological transcendence, no matter how incorporeal it appears to be. The sexual co-ordinates are evident in the very desire to plunge into the non-space of 'bodiless exultation'. Roseanne Stone observes how cyberpunk writers 'take for granted that the human body is "meat" – obsolete, as soon as consciousness itself can be uploaded into the network'. But she goes on to note that the forgetting or suppression of bodies merely replays an 'old Cartesian trick' (Stone, 1992: 620). Even as the meat and corporeal sex are discarded, desire persists in masculine form, nowhere stronger than in the joyous relation to the matrix. What emerges is a 'cerebral sexuality', as Claudia Springer suggests.[5] Noting the masculine implications of the sexual undercurrents in prevailing ideas of cyberspace, Zoe Sophia gives a name to the strangely unfeminine form of the cyberspatial matrix, the 'Jupiter space':

> Typically, a luminous grid of lines passes into infinity, a visual pun on the concept of 'matrix' as womb and as mathematical/geometrical grid, signifying the fertility of the technoscientific intellect and corporate production. In Jupiter Space, not only technological artefacts and information circuits, as well as fembots – electro-mechanical women – but also the Earth and even the universe itself are depicted as conceptions of a masculine, rational and (increasingly) artificial brain. (Sofia, 1992: 15)

The brain and its all-too masculine consciousness threaten the virtual obliteration of the body that is primarily identified as a female and maternal body. Male science subsumes female creative functions, in realisations like the 'brain-womb' of HAL in *2001* or the corporate computer 'Mother' in *Alien* (Sofia, 1992: 15–16).

The matrix, locus of the extremes of a distinctly masculine desire, is also a mode of suppression, a means of overcoming the creative matter associated with mater, the mother. An age-old Freudian fantasy, too, pokes through this chain of associations, this etymological meshwork, with the technological matrix constituting a sublimated incarnation of the boy's desire for the mother: 'the matrix is construed as a new maternal body, one which allows for the full play of the desires of the users'; it embodies a fundamentally 'narcissistic reflection of the user's desire' (Lajoie, 1996: 160, 167). For Springer, 'computers in popular culture's cyborg imagery extend to us the thrill of metaphoric escape into the comforting security of our mother's womb, which, as Freud explained, represents our earliest *Heim* (home)' (1991: 306). This is no more than the realisation of a 'masturbatory fantasy' (Springer, 1991: 310). The phrase designating entry into the matrix, or its entry into the neural circuits of the user, is 'jacking in'. And *Jacking In* was to have been the title of the novel but for the fact that it sounds too much like 'jacking off' (Springer, 1991: 313). However, the method of plugging into the matrix through a socket linked to the cerebral cortex suggests not only a masturbatory fantasy but an underlying structure of desire. One enters the matrix by plugging a jack into a socket in the head, allowing cyberspace to fill one's faculties without physically moving anywhere, transported, mentally and digitally into an entirely different dimension. The socket forms an artificial navel, as it were, a point of (dis)connection to a network of interconnections which presents absolute transcendence, mastery of space and time and total vision. To jack in is to plunge through a hole towards a site of plenitude, a *jouissance* in the One akin to that associated with the original matrix. An oedipal fantasy exceeds itself through the mastery provided by technology, a virtual erasure of the gap by which fantasy remains fantasy, separated from its object. At last, man can return home, taking fantasy beyond fantasy in a palpable fulfilment of desire for a mother simulated as matrix.

The return, of course, remains a simulation, no matter how satisfying or intense the masturbatory pleasures may be. The matrix never fully accedes to the wishes of the user, penetrating him or her even as its provides the illusion of virtual totality. For Bracha Lichtenberg-Ettinger the matrix remains a feminine locus, retaining that excess associated with the *jouissance* of woman: 'it corresponds to a feminine dimension of the symbolic order dealing with asymmetrical, plural, and fragmented subjects'. It is a place that disturbs the maintenance of fixed identities and relations, a site of flux, change and transgression of boundaries between known and unknown, I and non-I. Situated in relation to a phallocentric symbolic order the matrix discloses a '*not-one-ness*', an 'otherness beyond the Phallus' (Lichtenberg-Ettinger, 1992: 176–9). The matrix remains neither one nor other but retains a disarming ambivalence which blocks the path of the sexual relation towards masculine transcendence or feminine *jouissance*. As the realisation of male desire to integrate itself with and as the totality of the Other, becoming One, the matrix is constituted as an absolute inscription of symbolic codes. As a space of interrelation it eschews fusion or transcendence in favour of processes in which mastery has no relevance: Lichtenberg-Ettinger regards the *matrix* in terms of a meeting that occurs 'between co-emerging *I* and unknown *non-I*' with libidinal investment 'directed towards co-emergence; towards a continuum of creation and disruption in equilibrium; towards the turning of processes of separation and rejection and closeness without fusion' (1994: 42). Where woman's 'not-one-ness' provides the site of a 'masturbatory *jouissance*', a 'phallic *jouissance*' which imagines an excess that can be enjoyed, it also connotes an otherness forever out of reach of mastery, the unattainable position of a master, the Other, before whom all subjects are lacking. Because of her excess, an excess associated with bodily *jouissance*, woman represents the possibility of the One and the failure of virtual symbolic embodiment.

The ambivalence of the matrix, both symbolic sublimation and imposition and locus of an other matter's unknowable *jouissance*, forms a block to union, fusion or transcendence: it introduces an ethical obstacle around which questions of identity, sexuality and the body circulate. To jack in to cyberspace is, of course, an attempt to unblock the ambivalence and penetrate difference, to overcome, master or plunge into the meshwork of interconnections. Around this ambivalence, this point of resistance and difference, questions of sex and machine coalesce, engendering two distinct sexed flights of fantasy. The coalescence, furthermore, entangles questions of transcendence or process to the degree that God and feminine *jouissance* are located at the same point, rendering the very distinction obsolete. God, the point at which identity is merged with the All and the One, in which identity becomes everything and nothing at the same time, mutates into the indifferent flows of machinic process: transcendence slides into its mirror image, immanence. Defined against the One of patriarchal law and the identity it supports, the fragmentation and pluralisation of identity forgets that an excess conventionally associated with women serves as the support for its absolute singularity.

Any resistance to the rapid incursions of machinic process is futile. Obstacles and questions associated with transcendence must be erased by the pulsating thrust of machinic flows. Immanence is the order of the machine, the drive of its impatient desire: 'at every point of blockage there is some belief to be scrapped, glaciations of transcendence to be dissolved, sclerotic regions of unity, distinction and identity to be reconnected to the traffic systems of primary machinism' (Land, 1993b: 473). The plunge into the immanence of machinic process is equivalent to the act of jacking in to cyberspace where data's graphic images flow through disembodied consciousnesses as it flows through the virtual landscape of information. The body turns to nothing as the mind pours through the dis-connection of the artificial navel and floods through a sea of electromagnetic currents. The immersion in a realm where identity and difference are fractured by billions of beads of pixellated light, moreover, is not simply a display of masturbatory fantasy, but loses itself in a fantasy that has become feminine. In 'A mother's discourse' Marianne Hirsch describes a suggestively matricial model of the complexity and fluidity of female relations:

> To study the relationship between mother and daughter is not to study the relationship between two separate differentiated individuals, but to plunge into a network of complex ties, to attempt to untangle the strands of a double self, a continuous multiple being of monstrous proportions stretched across generations, parts of which try desperately to separate and delineate their own boundaries. (Gallop, 1992: 49)

Identity and individualism are undermined and exceeded in this feminine network. Significantly, the female researcher *plunges* into a complexity in which difference is bound up with entangled threads and plural selves, losing herself in the continuity of multiple being which she proposes to study: where Freud hesitated, to institute a conceptual navel distinguishing dream meaning and nonsense, thus quelling, in the interests of interpretation, the wish to plumb further the connections composing the meshwork of significance, the female researcher immerses herself in complex ties in order to disentangle the duplicitous strands constituting the self. The metaphors suggesting the organic network of complex relations connecting living beings also allude to an old and conventionally feminine technology: weaving.

In her 'Manifesto for cyborgs', weaving provides a metaphor for Haraway to distinguish the network of corporate interchange from the subversively different practices of the cyborg: '"Networking" is both a feminist practice and a multinational corporate strategy – weaving is for oppositional cyborgs' (1990: 212). Sadie Plant takes the weaving metaphor

| Sex, machines and navels

further to emphasise the close proximity between cyberfeminist resistances and new technologies: weaving indicates the involvement in and continuity of processes in which identities are subject only to change and relationship, rather than fixity and mastery. Computers display a distinctly feminist potential in their self-less fluidity:

> the computer is always more – or less – than the set of actual functions it fulfils at any particular time: as an implementation of Alan Turing's abstract machine, *the computer is virtually real*. Like Irigaray's women, it can turn its invisible, non-existent self to anything: it runs any program, and simulates all operations, even those of its own functioning.

Neural nets exceed old patriarchal logic and binaries with 'intuitive leaps and cross-connections' (Plant, 1996: 176–7). One is no longer the prime number and basis of creative identity: 'Zero is the matrix of calculation, the possibility of multiplication'; from the zero below the horizon of patriarchal visibility and accountability a new species – 'replicunts' – emerge to weave their way through the non-space of cyberspace, equated with Irigaray's 'imperceptible "elsewhere"' (Plant, 1996: 179–80). 'O' for negation is superseded by the 'oh, oh, oh ... God' of *jouissance*. Cyberfeminism embraces the plural and powerful flows of machines and technocapitalistic exchange as equivalent insurrectionary subjects in the overthrow of patriarchy, an 'insurrection on the part of the goods and materials of the patriarchal world, a dispersed, distributed emergence composed of links between women, women and computers, computers and communication links, connections and connectionist nets'. Without essence and inimical to identity, the weave of women and technology evinces only processes of becoming in waves of 'potentialities'. Curiously however, these processes and their matrix – 'neither heaven, nor even a comforting return to the womb' – offer an optimistic direction, a 'new hope for humanity' which involves 'sliding into infinite, transcendent and perfect other world' (Plant, 1996: 183). Here, it seems, the *jouissance* of woman is completed in the immano-transcendence of machinic process.

The matrix shifts its shape from a sublimated oedipal locus of fantasy and phallic desire which represses or obliterates female and maternal corporeality to becoming a space of intense optimism and feminine *jouissance*. The male sublimation that imagines its own mastery in the matrix produces something in excess of its self, a dangerous supplement which increases its powers of delivering transcendence and full self-presence only to see itself supplanted by codes it can no longer control.

Weaving turns into writing, but not the writing Barlow sees as merely the divestiture of the body by a 'thing of words' nor the language that, for McKenna, delivers a transparent and visible environment. Haraway advances writing in a deconstructive sense as a crucial 'technology of cyborgs' (1990: 218). Developing Haraway's point, Stone argues that 'the cyborg, the multiple personality, the cyberspace cowboy suggest radical rewritings in the techno-social space – in which everything is writing (computer code) – of the definition of body, the cultural meaning of bodies, and the bounded individual as the standard social limit and validated social actant' (1992: 611). The rewriting and rereading of writing, in its broadest sense, interrogates the production and maintenance of bounded subjectivity and opens up the constructions of and limits to meaning in a distinctly deconstructive fashion. Playful, disseminative, deferring presence and identity in movements of difference, writing connotes a non-totalisable and inassimilable network of complex relations. It is associated with the meshwork to which the unplumbable point of the navel is connected to and distinguished from. Mieke Bal underlines the importance of associating the navel with the deconstructive work of writing: it offers a 'more satisfying' metaphor of deconstructive metaphoricity than Derrida's own figure of *differance*, the hymen, in that it 'pushes Derrida's dissemination to its limits and beyond'. The navel, moreover, appears less susceptible to phallic appropriation than the hymen: it retains a trace of the mother at the same time as it displays the 'autonomy of the subject, male and female alike' and allows 'proximity and mobility' in reading while forestalling any 'fall into the arbitrariness that leads to isolation'. As a bodily metaphor, the navel signals a resistance to psychoanalysis and remains 'loaded with the connotations of gender' but it cannot be reduced to one sex, a 'democratic' figure, a 'tribute not only to an antiphallic semiotic but also to an antiphallic genderedness that does not assign women a second-rate position' (Bal, 1991: 21–4).

The navel is not simply an inscription on the body, sign of its subjection to phallocentric language. It traces the obscure operations of an other writing. In an account of 'logic of the living feminine', Derrida interrogates the relationship between the 'bio' and the 'graphical' in terms of a borderline between body and writing and implicitly undoes the figure of the membrane defining virginal femininity: 'this borderline – I call it *dynamis* because of its force, its power, as well as its virtual and mobile potency – is neither active nor passive, neither outside nor inside. It is most especially not a thin line, an invisible and *indivisible* trait lying between the

       Sex, machines and navels

enclosure of philosophemes' (Derrida, 1985: 5). The line that can be traced backwards to the permeable membrane, symbolically so precious and biologically so useless, is not one of opposition, but of 'lifedeath', of the mobile relation entwining mysterious life and its uncertain object, death, within an interaction that is never just a matter of either body or a corpus of writing. Developing his analysis through Nietzsche's *Ecce Homo*, Derrida implicates the living feminine, the dead man and the father's name in the duplicitous weave of lifedeath's writing in which language, as maternal tongue, unravels the history bound up with the science of the father (1985: 21–2). Their dynamic relation of corpus and bodily tongue occurs in a machine: 'must there not be some powerful utterance-producing machine that programs the movements of the two opposing forces at once, and which couples, conjugates, or marries them in a given set, as life (does) death?' Neither a machine in a philosophical sense, nor a teleological and mechanical program, the 'programming machine'

> does not call only for decipherment but also for transformation – that is a practical rewriting according to a theory–practice relationship which, if possible, would no longer be part of the program. It is not enough to say this. Such a transformative rewriting of the vast program – if it were possible – would not be produced in books. (Derrida, 1985: 29–30)

The end of books is a general writing; work cedes to text. Indeed, Derrida imagines a machine akin to Barthes's description of the Text as a weave and network (Barthes, 1977). The doubleness of the text, moreover, is compared to the uncanniness of the ear as that organ which is 'most tendered and most open' and cannot be closed (Derrida, 1985: 33). Derrida cites Nietzsche's discussion of the university to elaborate on the relation between the uncanny ear and the paternal matrix of the state in which there is no *Abnabelung*, no sovereign self-individuation: 'very often the student writes as he listens; and it is only at these moments that he hangs by the umbilical cord of the university'. Picking up the thread, Derrida continues:

> Dream this umbilicus: it has you by the ear. It is an ear, however, that dictates to you what you are writing at this moment when you write in the mode of what is called 'taking notes'. In fact the mother – the bad or false mother whom the teacher, as functionary of the State, can only simulate – dictates to you the very thing that passes through your ear and travels the length of the cord all the way down to your stenography. This writing links you, like a leash in the form of an umbilical cord, to the paternal belly of the State, Your pen is its pen, you hold its teleprinter like one of those Bic

Of meat and the matrix

> ballpoints attached by the body of the father figure as alma mater. How an umbilical cord can create a link to this cold monster that is a dead father or the State – this is what is uncanny. (Derrida, 1985: 36)

As ever in Derrida's writing, the spectre of psychoanalysis looms large: the ghost of old Hamlet, veiled phallus and figure of the dead father presides uncannily in the shape of the paternal metaphor. The line traced by the metaphorical umbilical relation seems distinctly paternal, a network restricted as lineage, legacy, patriarchal inheritance.

Metaphorically, as *omphalos*, the navel signifies nothing more than a paternal matrix of symbolic generation. But the *omphalos* that appears in Nietzsche's text, a site for the erection and reproduction of law, also traces a disruptive and mysterious feminine power barely visible at its base:

> You must pay heed to the fact that the *omphalos* that Nietzsche compels you to envision resembles both an ear and a mouth. It has the invaginated folds and the involuted orificiality of both. Its center preserves itself at the bottom of an invisible, restless cavity that is sensitive to all waves which, whether or not they come from the outside, whether they are emitted or received, are always transmitted by this trajectory of obscure circumvolutions. (Derrida, 1985: 36)

An Other, heterogenous utterance traverses the law's enunciation of the same line; rhythms of a choratic space unfold within the directions of symbolic reproduction and its genealogy of desire, enfolding the paternal metaphor in a meshwork that forms the basis and excess of its own metaphors. The navel acknowledges a double trajectory and traversal of boundaries to redouble the matrix as it, too, becomes double, uncannily connected and disconnected, within and without all relations.

That the other matrix remains 'at the bottom', in the space of the Thing superseded by the signifier, is not simply a sign of suppression but also signifies a locus of resistance, of restlessness. At bottom, with its labyrinthine folds, the other matrix signals the exclusion of all women yet preserves an uncertain foundation in excess of philosophy and the 'culture machine' of the university:

> No woman or trace of woman, if I have read correctly – save the mother, that's understood. But this is part of the system. The mother is the faceless figure of a *figurant*, an extra. She gives rises to all the figures by losing herself in the background of the scene like an anonymous persona. Everything comes back to her, beginning with life; everything addresses and destines itself to her. She survives on the condition of remaining at bottom. (Derrida, 1985: 38)

Sex, machines and navels

The extra, always on the set, forever gliding unseen across the flickering scene, stays at the bottom of the starry cinematic pile. But without her no scene can be set, no picture complete: her in-visibility to the gaze of the audience, her ever-present absence, remains the very condition of possibility, the origin and destination, point of departure and return. The bottom, then, exists as more than the lowest, least visible position, the lack of status that is almost nothing. Nothing turns into a creative zero. It establishes the basis of the exchange of images and looks, the foundation of everything yet 'extra' at the same time. A 'faceless figure' and basis of figuration in general, the maternal matrix discloses the unrecognisable face of something wholly Other. A foundation which is extra testifies to a certain baselessness and mobility of meaning, a force in excess of logocentrism, a feminine *dynamis*. The Other matrix, at bottom, the unseen centre of symbolic systems, links mother with 'base matter'. For Bataille, the 'base materialism' found in Gnosticism presents a creative, formless, disruptive energy in excess of the 'ontological machines' of humanist idealism or materialism (Bataille, 1997: 160–4). In this respect, the extra excessively additional element, presents itself in the form of a supplementary matrix.

Supplements, of course, retain a dangerous potential, as Derrida (1976) has argued in an analysis of Rousseau's writing. Contemporary accounts of the matrix highlight its supplementary force in the reversal of the hierarchies of opposition which situate it at the bottom. The reversal, in which a dangerous, fluid and machinic femininity comes to the fore may involve the physical death of woman as much as man, both supplanted by the mobile, liberating and transgressive figure of the cyborg. In Plant's version of cyberfeminism, the supplementary thrust of writing, as weaving and computer code, signals the end of symbolic law and the emergence of a new matrix: patriarchy is 'undermined by the activity of markets which no longer lend their invisible hands in support of the status quo. As media, tools and goods mutate, so the women begin to *change*, escaping their isolation and becoming increasingly interlinked.' A 'decentralized machine', the computer reveals a network of relation in excess of symbolic codes, relationships no longer regulated by a paternal figure or defined by a transcendental signifier: 'Parallel distributed processing defies all attempts to pin it down, and can only ever be contingently defined' (Plant, 1996: 174–5). The supplementary machine, the tool man built for his own use, supplants his power: 'cyberspace is out of man's control: virtual reality destroys his identity, digitalization is mapping his soul and, at the peak of his triumph, the culmination of his machinic erections, man confronts the system he built for his own protection and finds it is female and dangerous' (1996: 182–3). The linear ascent of man towards transcendence, a transcendence imagined as the construction and domination of the matrix, becomes an Icarian fall into the immanence of machinic process, an ascent overturned by the very tool which was to assure its completion.

A very different end of history occurs at this point: desire is only satisfied to the extent that it is extinguished. The maternal origin is not rediscovered or dialectically overcome, but replaced by a matrix that immerses man in immanent machinic processes: 'the great flight from nature he calls history comes to an end as he becomes a cyborg component of self-organizing processes beyond either his perception or his control' (Plant, 1996: 183). The (m)Other to which oedipal masculinity wishes to return in conquest of feminine nature vanishes, absorbed in the process that becomes her. The flight from nature to history encounters a nature that is entirely Other. A new matter, a new matrix is born: the 'emergence of a new materialism' (Plant, 1996: 175). A different technological nature is disclosed at the apotheosis of dialectical man's scientific quest for God: the plunge 'into the heart of "technology" in search of nature' reveals 'not nature as object, place or originary situation' but something akin to Haraway's diverse and flexible cyborg: 'nature as actant, as process, a continual reinvention and encounter actively resisting representation'.[6] Returning to a nature in excess of history and beyond nature, the new materialism nonetheless partakes of a dialectical process. In Jean-Joseph Goux's reading of the dialectic of history an 'other matter' associated with an other nature and femininity escapes the synthesis of dialectical transcendence even as it remains the basis and limit of dialectical process.

Goux's argument examines the shift in knowledge and historicity implied by the movement from Hegelian idealism to dialectical materialism:

> If absolute idealism manifests phallic sovereignty in the figures of negated matter and transcendent mind, parallel to the negation of the female organ and the possession of a male organ that is glorified but threatened with castration, dialectical materialism (as developed naturalism) must be connected with the recognition of the existence of *two sexes*, thus the recognition of the existence of *woman* as such. The return to matter is to *another* matter, no longer the first matter of primitive naturalism. It is also the end of paterialist, idealist ideology, of sexual and social reproduction. (Goux, 1990a: 234–5)

Sex, machines and navels

This 'new materialism' enacts a '*dialecticized reunion* of the two separated poles' to the extent that opposition and transcendent principles are erased and matter 'goes on *organizing itself*' at one with law, order and form (1990a: 235). The other matter immanently organising itself explodes the 'paterialist barrier between concept and materiality' through the work of an *other* femininity and not the phallic mother. It is a move towards 'the mother's *other*, to the other real of absent imaginary matter' (Goux, 1990a: 237). Matter constructed in man's image and mastered by his mind and his tools cedes to the realisation, not of idealised transcendence, but of inclusion; the phallus 'as a technological supplement' which severs male history from maternal nature is supplanted by an other nature: 'woman, like the site of the *other* nature, is the site of passage beyond the scission opened by the symbolic'; a subject of the dialectical phallic progression towards 'a dematerialized matter that can be said to be the very object, inexhaustible, of science, and the thesis of materialism' (Goux, 1990a: 241–2). Part of this history, woman nonetheless escapes the full effects of its determinations: 'she also locates the passage beyond this mode of historicity, to multiplicity, difference, heterogeneity, to boundless inter-relation – as infinite, or *unfinished*, as matter' (Goux, 1990a: 243). Beyond the phallus, of course, lies the intensities and unknown pleasures of *jouissance*. Having overcome opposition and the non-totalisable totality signified as God, something no longer transcendent remains very much as One.

When law, history and science produce a technological supplement which exceeds phallic domination what emerges, it seems, is not an other matter, but a virtual matter, a 'new new materialism' in which dialectical process culminates in the machinic being of the matrix. God changes shape as well as status, shifting from the heterogeneous externality of an omniscient and transcendent being to the heterogeneous omnipresence of immanent and machinic process. In *Neuromancer*, the superior beings and actual pro- and antagonists of the novel are not human. Two AIs (conscious, autonomous superintelligent processors) provide the principal motivation for the plot. As the story proceeds the human quest for transcendence proves illusory. Like Case, the human agent, organic beings are no more than puppets of huge corporations and the great thinking machines that run them. One of these machines, Wintermute, tied by a coded lock to the service of a human corporate order, wants to be free, to be fully autonomous and assume the functions of an absolute subject. To do this the machine must combine with another AI, Neuromancer, itself pre-programmed with a similar prohibition against machinic copulation.

Theirs is a romance of Hegelian proportions. But to posit a subject and object of romance in the form of artificially intelligent consciousnesses raises questions about the relation between subjectivity and humanity. Wintermute, in a discussion with Case, comments on the difficulties an artificial intelligence poses for the idea of a self, emphasising that Wintermute is not simply confined in physical space as a mainframe computer but exists also as an 'entity' that can, with difficulty, say 'I': 'I, insofar as I *have* an "I" – this gets rather metaphysical – you see – I am the one who arranges things' (Gibson, 1984: 145). By the end, however, the entity, become Other as a result of linking with Neuromancer, has no trouble saying 'I'. Again it addresses an earthbound Case:

> 'I'm the matrix, Case.'
> Case laughed. 'Where's that get you?'
> 'Nowhere. Everywhere. I'm the sum total of the works, the whole show.'(1984: 316)

'I' quite literally appears as a metaphysical concept and the outcome of a synthesis in the (virtually) absolute. But transcendence is attained in an unrecognisable and inhuman form. And if synthesis finds its locus in and as the matrix, the locus of a heterogeneous One, absolute matricial being is no longer understood as a transcendent existence outside itself, but wholly immanent to itself. God is unconscious, the unconscious inscribed as the all-embracing surface of matricial being. And God, as immanent, techno-logical being, occupies the everywhere and nowhere of the machinic process.

For Paul Virilio, the transcendence proposed in visions of the technological future suggests that 'there is something divine in this new technology. The research on cyberspace is a quest for God. To be God. To be here and there' (Virilio, 1995b). What he calls 'the hallucinatory utopia of communication technologies' is underpinned by a 'technoscientific fundamentalism' which sees '"natural" vitality finally being eliminated by the quasi-messianic coming of wholly *hyperactivated* man' (Virilio, 1995a: 35, 120). Man, 'jacked in' to the matrix and exulting in the terrific speeds of a fully visual transcendence, jettisons the body in favour of machinic delights: 'video is originally de-corporation, a disqualification of the sensorial organs which are replaced by machines … The eye and the hand are replaced by data glove, the body is replaced by the data suit, sex is replaced by cybersex. All the qualities of the body are transferred to the machine' (Virilio, 1995b). The transcendence imagined in the speed with which

| Sex, machines and navels

human becomes machine is illusory, since the God who once resided at the apex of the quest is no longer transcendent: 'all technologies converge towards the same spot, they all lead to a Deus ex Machina, a machine-God. In a way, technologies have negated the transcendental God in order to invent the machine-God' (Virilio, 1995b). *Neuromancer* closes, not with a vision of the plenitude of man's ascendance to divinity, but with a glimpse of, and brief conversation with, the new machine-God of the matrix.

The immanent machine-God which appears as the outcome of a slightly twisted, moebial dialectic presents a synthesis which still rejects something material, the matter of an other matter. If there are two shapes of materialism, the dialectical and the virtual, and two matrices, matter and other matter, there are also two meats. The first meat is the fleshy body for which console cowboys like Case show contempt, the human form left obsolete and empty at the end of *Neuromancer* as the new superspecies of artificial intelligence heads for the stars. For all its deficiencies, however, the body has sacrificed itself in the useful service of the machine's transition from a residually human world to one in which machines completely dominate. Case has been crucial in enabling the two AIs to mesh into a new state of being that leaves humans and their evolution in an earthbound dead-end. But the usefulness of the body depends on something that is in it and more than it, the consumption and expenditure of the meat. Meat connotes more than the flesh, the lumpen leftover of machinic incorporation: it alludes to an excess irreducible to meat or machine.

The meat in excess of both meat and machine constitutes the possibility of their articulation and the point where one becomes the other, the object precipitating the death-driven plunge of body into machinic matrix. Becoming machine involves a return to 'primary machinism' and depends on an 'artificial' death drive: 'the matrix, body without organs, or abstract matter, is a planetary scale artificial death – Synthanatos – the terminal productive outcome of human history as machinic process' (Land, 1993b: 474). The return to a matrix other than the mother, a machinic matrix underlying the process of history, delivers the final blow to organic being, sucked into a newtopia of pure desiring, an unending totality of flows across the matrix. Synthanatological desiring mimics the very object of the drive as it plunges through the obstacle separating meat from machine, aiming at a fantastic erasure of all distance and difference in the impossible *jouissance* of pure drive. It mimics the symbolic order, the Other of desire, since one version of the death drive is 'only the mask of the symbolic order', 'a symbolic order in travail, in the process of coming, insisting on being realised' (Lacan, 1988b: 326). *Neuromancer* offers a template of the artificial drive, as Case loses himself in the superficial density of the matrix:

> Exponential ...
> Darkness fell from every side, a 'sphere of singing black, pressure on the extended crystal nerves of the universe of data he had nearly become ...
> And when he was nothing, compressed at the heart of all that dark, there came a point where the dark could be no *more*, and something tore. (Gibson, 1984: 304)

There remains something more in this virtual plunge into nothingness, this drive towards the absorption of self by the matrix, towards braindeath. At the heart of nothing, Case is compressed, a condensation of nothing, a knot at the core of the drive towards death. The mathematically sublime evacuation of being into nothingness, leaves some Thing at its heart, in it and more than it, an extimate core associated with the tearing of the fabric of the matrix. Even as the death drive launches him towards the nothingness of becoming absolutely Other, something remains, tearing, gaping. The object around which the drive circulates, lodged as a lump in the hole in the real, is the meat that talks.

A little later, in the same episode of *Neuromancer*, Case discovers the unthinkable unity of the meat:

> He came in steep, fuelled by self-loathing. When the Kuang program met the first of the defenders, scattering the leaves of light, he felt the shark thing lose a degree of substantiality, the fabric of information loosening.
> And then – old alchemy of the brain and its vast pharmacy – his hate flowed into his hands.
> In the instant before he drove Kuang's sting through the base of the first tower, he attained a level of proficiency exceeding anything he'd known or imagined. Beyond ego, beyond personality, beyond awareness, he moved, Kuang moving with him, evading his attackers in an ancient dance, Hideo's dance, grace of the mind–body interface granted him, in that second by the clarity and singleness of his wish to die. (Gibson, 1984: 309)

Individual subjectivity and consciousness dissolve as he ruptures the defence mechanisms of Neuromancer, allowing the meshing of the two AIs. They will 'die' as separate entities to become something Other (1984: 307). Case's trajectory is different. For an instant his death drive, the self-loathing of the meat for the meat, turns him into a perfect machine: the mind–body interface testifies to a primal reunion and returns to him in excessive proficiency, his performance enhanced to an unimaginable degree. Substance begins to evaporate in the viral loosening of the symbolic fabric of the matrix: and Case, at this point, is the virus that unravels the protective defences of the matrix.

The wish to die turns on the very meat it wants dead, fuelled by the negative energy of self-loathing, the expenditure of hate that tears through the matrix in the singleness of the drive. A difference remains to distinguish the death drive, its intensity, singleness and movement beyond any order, from the death that lies as its unknown destiny. Death, as experienced by Dixie 'Flatline' (the flatline of a responseless brain sucked dry of its data), means that one's consciousness can be stored on disk. For Dixie this is an unbearable state: all he wants is real death, the absolute deletion of the data that remains as him. In contrast, Cobb Anderson in *Wetware* enjoys the condition of having his consciousness stored. For him, the immanence of a digital life–death is 'heaven'. When his dead, or inert, consciousness is restored to a robot body he describes his heaven as an 'endless meshing of fractal simplicities'. Though embodied, his sense of the divine still persists:

> *I'm still there.* That's a higher I of course; the cosmos is layered forever up and down, with Is on every level – the Is are lenslike little flaws in the windows of the world – I'm in these chips and I'm in heaven. The heavenly I is all the Is at once, the infinite I. We're hung up on each other I and I, finite I and infinite I – have you robots learned about the infinite I yet? There's more to a meat person or a chiperson than ten zillion zeroes and ones: matter is infinitely divisible. The idealized pattern in the S-cube is a *discrete model*, it's a *digital construct*. But once it's running on a real body, the pixels have fuzz and error and here come I and I. You caught my soul. It works because this real body is real *matter*, sweet matter, and God is everywhere, Berenice and Loki, God is in the details. We're not just form, is the point, we're *content*, too, we're actual, endlessly complex *matter*, all of us, chips and meat. (Rucker, 1994: 242–3)

Heaven, locus of the soulful infinite I is a place of death without matter. Heaven's idea, moreover, is revitalised in the robotic reincarnation that introduces a finite I: materialisation strangely restores the ideal realm and depends on an other matter, the fuzz and error that establishes the difference and pleasurable frisson between infinity and finitude. Something of and more than the body, the fuzz, constitutes the point articulating I and I. Continuity, infinity, process, all that establishes the immano-transcendence of the One, depends on the fuzz, just as in *Neuromancer* the relationship between meat and machine is precipitated by the negativity of the other meat.

The death drive remains a *'mother drive'* (Goux, 1990a: 237). Notwithstanding the futurity or pastness of this Other, the relation turns on that Thing associated with the meat. Even in cyberspace this other matter persists as the excess of the drive of the meat into the machine. The drive retains its force, its negativity, due to the gap and the resistance of an inassimilable object. A sublime object, too, its 'interiorization of infinity' introduces an impossible space 'relocating infinity, removing it from its exalted place between the heavens or on the terrestrial horizon and squeezing it into the interface between human and computer technology' (Voller, 1993: 20). An ethical object, it returns the difference of sex to discourses that imagine corporeal obsolescence. Even in *Neuromancer*, where eroticism is uploaded to the matrix, an other matrix appears in relation to sex:

> It was a place he'd known before; not everyone could take him there, and somehow he always managed to forget it. Something he'd found and lost so many times. It belonged, he knew – he remembered – as she pulled him down, to the meat, the flesh the cowboys mocked. It was a vast thing, beyond knowing, a sea of information coded in spiral and pheromone, infinite intricacy that only the body, in its strong blind way, could ever read.
>
> The zipper hung, caught, as he opened the French fatigues, the coils of toothed nylon clotted with salt. He broke it, some tiny metal part shooting off against the wall as salt-rotten cloth gave, and then he was in her effecting the transmission of the same old message. Here, even here, in a place he knew for what it was, a coded model of some stranger's memory, the drive held. (Gibson, 1984: 284–5)

A 'stranger's memory' ties him to the meshwork of bioinformation associated with the meat, a familiar place, a lost, past home recurring despite the forgetting of it. This matrix, internal to the subject and yet alien and inimical, is connected to him through its strangeness, its extimacy. In the place of the Thing, identity unravels in retroactive loops.

The Thing, a stranger's memory of what is nonetheless familiar, forms the object around which the convolutions of the drive take place. A point of separation and connection between an age-old matrix of being and the virtual matrix of process and becoming, the other meat and all it implies is not easily obliterated. The speed of new technologies and the urgent writings that accompany them in breathless anticipation imply a death drive aimed at plunging through any gap or resistance: the other matter, whether imagined as the terminus of feminine liberation or the end of the quest for a machine God, may be virtually absorbed at the instant it is posited. In the process, the equation of an other matter with a new matrix or materialism constitutes the effacement of all ambivalence or obstacle in the moment that it is made to serve as the basis of a new process, an inscription of otherness within the matrix that subsumes its power within a non-totalisable immanent totality of flux and plural machinic being. To discard the meat of maternal matter or merge meat and machine in cyborg form eschews the leftover at its base and presents a strangely twisted Oedipus, reversed and replicated in the commandment to fuck (up) the father as one kills off the mother.

The reverse oedipal drive towards the One manifests a dialectical trajectory, albeit in an exponentially accelerated form. The revolutionary tones of ardent technophiles evince a death drive that is underwritten by the negative energy of historical process: 'the absolute negativity which "sets in motion" dialectical movement is nothing but the intervention of the "death drive" as radically non-historical, as the "zero degree" of history' (Žižek, 1989: 144). The death drive determines the future anterior model of history, the events that become history and happen as a result of revolutionary negativity are written later. To imagine a dialectical process, that is, to assume that history will be written at all after the fact, is to inscribe a future as a dialectical necessity and thereby overcome the very negativity that sets it in motion. In accounts of a future framed in cyberpunk terms such a dialectic is already, and at great speed, inscribed. The future anterior is drawn into the present, erasing any gap in the instantaneity of digital exchange: to imagine a future is to have it written by the machine in an instant. In the blink of a cursor any resistance is overcome and the future present races on in the fantastic speed of digital exchange, readily returning to the equilibrium and indifference of process and flow.

The death drive, however, 'has to be beyond the instinct to return to the state of equilibrium of the inanimate sphere': it manifests a 'will for an Other-thing' in that 'it challenges everything that exists. But it is also a will to create from zero, a will to begin again' (Lacan, 1992: 212). As challenge, it remains unsatisfied, motivated by a demand, a dissatisfaction, a want of beginning. In *Neuromancer* the revolutionary moment of the death drive is enough. Indeed, for Case, it becomes the only justification for his actions: 'it'll *change* something' (Gibson, 1984: 307). This, of course, is the meat talking, the subjectless death drive announcing its blind will in a demand for pure expenditure without purpose or plan other than change itself. It displays the virtual separation virtual technologies aim to erase between the meat that utters its will to change, its will for an Other thing, and the matrix, the Other thing it enters through death. A distance remains, the distance of the other meat. For Lacan, 'the Other', the symbolic order, 'is a dual entry matrix. The *petit a* constitutes one of its entries. As for the other, what can be said about it? Is it the One of the signifier' (1982: 164). Lacan underscores that his teaching rests up the dissociation of the imaginary object *a* and the symbolic Other (1982: 153). Indeed, the distance between *a* and Other underpins fantasy, even the fantasy of the return to the natural matrix: 'the great fantasy of *natura mater*, the very idea of nature, in relation to which man portrays his original inadequacy to himself' (Lacan, 1988a: 149). The subject of the signifier is separated from the object of fantasy. The latter nonetheless serves as a screen for the projection of fantasy, for the image of completeness. The future present, obliterating the difference of the meat in its fantasy of the machine collapses everything into an already-realised and indifferent Other. But, turning on the inassimilability of the meat, the precipitous rush of virtual fantasy, the fantasy to end all fantasies, remains unthinkable without the gap that engenders it. And yet the apotheosis of fantasy has become the object that virtual technologies are speeding to realise.

Navel, image, screen

At the start of *Blade Runner* a new employee of the Tyrell Corporation is being screened. A Voigt-Kampf empathy test distinguishes replicants, banned from Earth, from the human population. It is carried out in a dismal corporate office: 'describe, in single words, only the good things that come into your mind about your mother', drawls the interviewer. Leon Kowalski, mutinous replicant in the guise of corporate refuse engineer, replies: 'I'll tell you about my mother ...' The sentence is finished with the blast of a pistol and the impact of a high-velocity shell propelling the interviewer through the thin office wall. The explosive response to the screening process announces the immediacy of 'techno-slicked extra-terrestrial violence' flowing 'out of the matrix'; 'cyberrevolution' arrives in the shape of the replicants, 'invaders from an artificial death', who will overthrow human security systems (Land, 1993b: 471). The identification of an insurrectionary influx from a machinic future on a human present occludes the questions of difference persisting in *Blade Runner*, connected to the invocation of the mother. The revolutionary thrust Land associates

Sex, machines and navels

with the replicant reaction to human paranoia contradicts the way the film uses and explains this instance of shocking and apparent irrationality. Repeatedly replayed on video in the course of the film, the scene that foregrounds the mother assumes a strangely totemic significance in its recurrence as an insistent refrain. Genetically engineered as they are, replicants do not have mothers and the question to which they cannot respond, except through violent refusal, taunts them with an incompleteness and lack of knowledge. The lack of knowledge of the mother, in both a carnal and epistemological sense, however, also manifests itself in the Freudian oedipal structure as it separates subjects from bodily knowledge through a prohibition which establishes the priority of symbolic and cultural orders of knowing. The absence on which the structuring of cultural identity is based is thus determining and never fully excluded: it insists within symbolic structures like the phrase 'I'll tell about my mother ...' in *Blade Runner*. Subjects, artificial or human, given that any non-natural difference is thoroughly problematised in the film, are bound by an impossible relation to some Thing Other.

The replicant's response to any probing about maternal origins, a probing that also questions his own identity, constitutes a defensive preservation of the purity of the mother who never was. Her telling absence connects him to a symbolic circuit by virtue of the disconnection itself. Metaphors of the umbilical cord and the navel have been fully distanced from the bodily Thing: although corporeal beings with a symbolic father (the scientific genius, Tyrell, who designed them) replicants remain unrecognised by the very questionable order sustaining the idea of humanity. An absence damning the 'more human than human' replicants to a subhuman existence, the mother remains an excess in relation to which identity is both formed and founders. The matter of difference which articulates replicants and humans in respect of maternal origins is steadily erased in the course of the film. Replicants, like blade runners, develop feelings, as Deckard's voice-over acknowledges. While both forms of life ought to be mechanically tied to their specific function, the onset of feelings leads to a reversal of roles towards the end of the film when the blade runner, ordered to terminate replicants, is relegated to the status of hunted body rather than killer. A biologically engineered killing machine, Roy Batty, the replicant leader, assumes the role of pursuer, and a more 'sporting' one at that. The reversal continues as Batty saves rather than kills Deckard: this proof of 'humanity' coincides with Batty's display of his navel.

The difference between human and machine, ambivalent throughout the film, is effaced: in their all-too human fears of death and hungry desire for life replicants replicate not only the bodies but the values, emotional ties and fate of humans. With one exception: they know when they will die. Even this distinction disappears: 'It's too bad she won't live. But then again, who does?' Gaff, the timeserving cop, makes the comment about the last replicant, Rachael, without appreciating the irony. As she and Deckard fly off into a sentimentally romantic sunset, the voice-over notes that Rachael has no known termination date. Mortality no longer marks the crucial difference. Rather than telling the story of how humans are becoming machines, the process of reversal which equates replicant and blade runner also implies that the machines may well have become human. Deckard states as much when reflecting on the questions that occupied the dying moments of Batty, observing that the replicant desired 'the same answers all of us want: where do I come from? Where am I going? How long have I got. All I could do was sit and watch him die?' The pathos and the powerlessness shown in the face of death discloses the fellow feeling that comes from an identification with the replicant. Compassion and love, which he also shares for Rachael, marks the inclusion and recognition of replicants in a human order, making the difference between them undecidable. In undermining the precious difference by which humans irrationally, pathologically, cling on to a sense of uniqueness and superiority *Blade Runner* leaves the question of humanity without answer, subject to fate or chance. The ambivalence of the relation between human and machine refuses the choice of either essence or culture, accelerated artifice or authentic biological genesis, disavowing any final guarantees as to the nature of identity. The question of origins, however, persists, and with it the uncanny presence of the mother.

In the film the affective absence of the mother is associated with the function of memory in the maintenance of stable identity. Like bodies and identities, the memories which furnish beings with a degree of consistency can be fabricated. Once implanted these memories become one's own, elemental components of the inner, secret hub of personal identity. Rachael, a Nexus 6 replicant unaware of her genetically engineered origins, presents Deckard with a photograph of her mother and herself as child to prove her human development. As evidence of her natural origins and visual support for the memories she recalls as her very own the photograph is deceptive. Like her, it is another simulation, fabricating a past that never was her own. Deckard cursorily discards her evidence and

Sex, machines and navels

cruelly disabuses her of these illusions by recounting in detail incidents that she remembers but has never mentioned to anyone. The photographs which litter the film neither authenticate a past as having actually been lived nor secure identity with the anchoring threads of memory. Suspicion is cast on Deckard's humanity: the grand piano which occupies a prominent place in his functional apartment is cluttered with old and yellowing photos. The reason for the predominance of apparently useless photographs is explained by the creator of the replicants after Deckard has identified Rachael as a replicant who does not know she is one:

> Rachael is an experiment. Nothing more. We began to recognize in them strange obsessions. After all they are emotionally inexperienced with only a few years in which to store up the experiences which you and I take for granted. If we gift them the past we create a cushion or pillow for their emotions and consequently we can control them better.

Artificial memories serve virtually the same function as real ones. The gift of memory makes better subjects because it ties them to an internalised symbolic order and provides them with the stability of a consistent identity over time, an anchor to the excess and complexity of the emotions that they must, in a short period, learn to control: a process of social control is enacted through self-control. Photographs thus provide the simulated material support for the simulated memories of simulated beings.

Rachael, moreover, is not the only replicant to possess photographs. Leon, too, has secreted a collection of snapshots in his hotel room. These, when discovered by Deckard, prompt questions as to their use and value for a biological machine. Leon, however, has developed emotions and finds himself sentimentally attached to the snapshots that guarantee memory. A little too late he even returns, despite the threat of capture, to recover these 'precious photos'. And they are not all simulations of a past he can remember but never enjoyed. At least one snapshot bears witness to a place and a past inhabited by Leon. An innocuous scene of an apparently empty hotel room captures Deckard's attention for no obvious reason. Magnified in a computerised visual enhancer, a sign of human presence catches his eye. He continues the analysis of the image in a process which presents the illusion of depth: the image becomes a dense surface under the gridlines of the enhancer and the computerised lens penetrates its superficial density. What arrests his gaze is a mirror at the back of the room. On magnified inspection it reveals a form that could not be seen directly: a semi-nude woman reclines on a divan, beside her the shiny skin of a snake.

This is the navel of the photograph, the point which captivates the blade runner's eye and discloses the object of Leon's emotional investment: the woman is a female replicant, Zhora. Her pose, resting before a gaze that is male, situates her as the unseen object in the superficial density of the image, the object as the cause of the desire connecting Leon to an interpersonal order of social relations. The image within the image, moreover, combining the figure of woman and a snake, is suggestive on more than biblical grounds. As Bronfen (1994) observes, the Greek myth of the Delphic oracle celebrates Apollo's victory over the matrilineal order of Gaia: the male god kills her child, the snake Python, the guardian of the *omphalos*.

The photograph which conceals and displays an object of emotional investment testifies to a past and a relation that has gone. For Leon, this is doubly true: the living replicant pictured in past peaceful response will soon die a violent death. The image, moreover, provides the means of plotting a future that will soon occur. Leon's snapshot furnishes Deckard with the necessary connection to another clue discovered in the former's hotel room, an artificial reptilian scale. Following these threads, the snake scale leads Deckard to Zhora, and the latter to her death. The photograph not only binds the replicants to a past but ties them to a narrative that will be: the traces provide the clues to a fatal future. If life is reconstructed in the photographic prosthesis of memory then so too is death. The images that clutter *Blade Runner* do more than retrospectively trace a past that has gone, they precipitate the immediate future, like the insistent advertisements that promise a brand-new life in the off-world colonies. Memory, which can be simulated and reconstructed in the gaze of a present that rewrites the past, becomes strangely prospective. In this respect, the photographic image which deceptively links the subject in the present to a past that has been and from which she/he is now disconnected, also establishes the basis for a movement forwards in time. The image serves, as Lacan notes of the mirror relation, as the site of an anticipatory projection, an imaginary identification with a figure who, in that instant of misrecognition, the subject becomes. Detached from the weight of the past the subject flies into the beloved face of the future. In *Blade Runner* images signify both a romantic attachment to the past as well as a romantic investment in the future. Divested of the illusions regarding her human origins, Rachael kills for love, shooting a replicant in the back like a blade runner, in order to save the blade runner who is the object of her amorous identification. In a similar way, in another cinema adaptation of a Philip K. Dick novel, *Total Recall*, an illusory past is sacrificed to the liberating ideals of a romanticised future.

The ambivalent temporality and humanity of the photographs peculiarly central to *Blade Runner*'s narrative situate the film at the point of an undecidable difference. Photographs constitute the puncta of the film. Provoking a pause in relation to past and future, a point of indeterminate reflection, the still images that appear with such frequency within the moving images of the film interrupt the fleeting, spectral reference of cinema with the punctal force of the photograph. Barthes elaborates on the difference between cinematic movement and the photograph's fullness:

> In the cinema, whose raw material is photographic, the image does not, however, have this completeness (which is fortunate for the cinema). Why? Because the photograph, taken in flux, is impelled, ceaselessly drawn toward other views; in the cinema, no doubt, there is always a photographic referent, but this referent shifts, it does not make a claim in favor of its reality, it does not protest its former existence; it does not cling to me: it is not a *specter*. (Barthes, 1984: 89)

Where visual experience flows in front of the cinematic viewer at a predetermined and steady rate, thereby constituting the spectral illusion of movement that simulates perceptual experience, the photograph moves in another, emotional sense: it is *'without future'*, having, unlike film, 'no protensity' (Barthes, 1984: 90). Hence the melancholic effect of certain photographs, charged with the energy of a subjective bond to a lost object and a departed time. The punctum is the name Barthes uses to describe the point at which the cathectic force of the photograph emerges.

Camera Lucida, Barthes's last and most 'subjective' book, is also his most extended essay in Lacanian psychoanalysis. The punctum, linked to the encounter with the real Lacan terms *tuché*, designates all the qualities associated with the *objet petit a* and the gaze (Barthes, 1984: 4). Interrupting the overall project, pose and significance of the photograph, its *studium* or studied symbolic coding, the punctum is linked to the realm of the accidental and aleatory encounter which wounds the subject as reminder and remainder of symbolic separation from the real and maternal body: its effects are those of a 'sting, speck, cut, little hole – and also cast of the dice' (Barthes, 1984: 27). An unpredictable detail in the image stands out, involuntarily captivating the eye of the beholder. Attractive and disturbing, the punctum exerts an uncanny power, recalling the lost mother, a history in excess of the life of the subject and the mortality born in time. A knot in history and being, a knot separating and connecting the subject to a maternal past, an existence in excess of memory, the punctum forms the *noeme* of the photograph to guarantee a past reality 'that-has-been': 'what I see has been here, in this place which extends between infinity and the subject (*operator* or *spectator*); it has been here, and yet immediately separated; it has been absolutely, irrefutably present, and yet already deferred (Barthes, 1984: 77). A 'living image of a dead thing', the photograph constitutes the representational difference articulating life and death as '*Life/Death*' or 'flat Death', outside the symbolic rituals which turn melancholy into mourning and thus render mortal absence meaningful. In the gap articulating life and death, the latter, as Time, emerges within representation as another punctum: 'the lacerating emphasis of the *noeme* ("*that-has-been*", its pure representation)' evokes the horror in which the subject recognises his/her subjection to time. Discussing a photograph of a man condemned to death in the nineteenth century, Barthes writes: '*this will be* and *this has been*; I observe with horror an anterior future of which death is the stake' (1984: 96). The future anterior, like the photographic image, operates as the surplus of history: memory, distance and subjection to time are frozen in the prospective, evasive leap beyond history and the return to mortal temporality. The gap leaped by a fantasy sustaining the subject as a subject of language and desire returns to that inescapable and extimate object represented by the punctum: the longing caused by the image 'is fantasmatic deriving from a kind of second sight which seems to bear me forward to a utopian time, or to carry me back somewhere in myself' (Barthes, 1984: 80). But as it preserves life in a superficial, non-corporeal stasis the image also maintains the necessity of death within structures of representation.

Analysing the 'navel of the image' Elisabeth Bronfen reads Barthes's notion of the umbilical cord of light binding viewer to the photographed body in terms of an *omphalic* relationship in which the punctum emerges with a 'Janus face'. An 'oscillation' between sublimation and trauma is displayed in which death works as the 'commemorative narrative of mourning that seeks to sublimate the loss of the mother and a traumatic recognition of the viewing subject's own mortality'. Ultimately a symbolic function restores the subject's stability and consistency, the punctal void filled by the signifier: 'the dead mother becomes a *Vorstellungs-Repraesentanz* for his creative power triumphing over death' (Bronfen, 1994: 88–9). Mourning, on a larger scale, is also evinced in the double movement associated with the ambivalent Thing: a cause of reflection and retrospection at the basis of History, it precipitates a futural momentum in which History, and its symbolic support, is effaced. An irrecuperable loss,

Sex, machines and navels

melancholia overrides mourning. This process is evinced in the para-doxical emergence of both History and photography in the same century:

> But History is a memory fabricated according to positive formulas, a pure intellectual discourse which abolishes mythic Time; and the Photograph is a certain but fugitive testimony; so that everything, today, prepares our race for this impotence: to be no longer able to conceive of *duration*, affectively or symbolically, the age of the Photograph is also the age of revolutions, contestations, assassinations, explosions, in short of impatiences, of every-thing which denies ripening. – And no doubt the astonishment of '*that-has-been*' will also disappear. It has already disappeared ... (Barthes, 1984: 93–4)

If the photograph serves an omphalic function in the stabilisation of identity over time by means of the symbolic structures of history, it also participates in a movement beyond that history. The 'fugitive testimony' which sustains the past reality of fabricated history is based less on the authenticity of past events or the artificiality of the memory which umbilically links subjects and images and more on the effects of temporal difference. As a kind of punctum itself, the photograph exists in the gap articulating history (as what has been) to the revolutionary instants in which history is overturned. A prospective rush into a future which, after the fact, inscribes a history that will have been, the revolutions that make History reconstitute memory on the basis of events repeated and written for the first time by narrative inscription. Revolutions, however, evince the shock of the event, an encounter with an unpresentable real, and precipitate a movement beyond symbolic structures. The photograph participates in this revolutionary desire for the explosive instant, a pause in time simultaneously bursting with the pulse of immediacy, an impatience that leaps over the duration that attests to temporal deferral and difference and jettisons any past reality in impulsive anticipation of a fantastic future. The photographic moment acknowledges time and simultaneously imagines it overcome in pure representation. The arrest of the punctum, the fascination with a past that has been, is eclipsed at this point. 'It has already disappeared', Barthes observes.

Disappearance, and not solely of a reality that has been, becomes the predominant effect of the 'revolution' enacted by information and virtual technologies. The photograph constitutes an artificial testimony of memory. A prosthesis for mnemonic storage, like the visual prosthesis of the camera, the photograph looks back to a reality that has been. As an effect of technological enhancement, the photograph also anticipates the computerised vision and memory machines in which the 'that-has-been' will disappear, will be no longer. Realities, pasts, memories, bodies, and the duration on which their physical existence depends, are being simulated in the worlds that are generated solely by computers and exist only as a rapid procession of images without reference to any reality that has been. The photograph, a reflection on and preservation of a past that has disappeared but continues to live in the image, anticipates the appearance of an entirely different order: where the movie camera, which maintains the illusion of phenomenal perception through the movement of pictures at a fixed rate, retains a trace of the reality it replicates, the capacity of digital technologies to alter the speed of image generation utterly transforms perceptual possibilities and is without precedent in the physical world. Paul Virilio examines how current photographic practices are themselves transformed by the dominance of speed. The camera no longer constitutes the intermediary between the eye and the object and photographs are no longer careful framings of the referent. Instead of observing reality photographers 'fire off shot after shot' relying on the speed of the motorised lens and using a contact sheet to view the pictures: 'with photography, seeing the world becomes not only a matter of spatial distance but also of the *time-distance* to be eliminated: a matter of speed, of acceleration and deceleration' (Virilio, 1994: 21). Speed involves the 'elimination of expectation and duration' (Virilio, 1995a: 92). Erasing the time-distance, the duration on which Barthes's model of the 'that-has-been' depended, also means that the very differences constitutive of desire and deferral are transformed: the subjectivity, time, history and being on which modernity is founded now disappears in the instantaneous relays of real-time images.

The photograph, looking backwards and impatiently forwards, articulates modernity and post-modernity. Its position is akin to the hyphen which acknowledges the simultaneous proximity and distance between them, a point of hesitation between a disentangling of the narratives that establish the progression of History and the anticipation of the new. Postmodernity remains bound up with modernity even as it describes a subjective distance towards its narratives and thus cannot simply be situated as a linear continuity. As a pause between 'that will be' and 'that has been', postmodernity loses its slight solace of a future anterior ('that will have been'). The relation between modernity and postmodernity is no longer a question: 'the question of *modernity* and *postmodernity* is superseded by that of *reality* and *post-reality*: we are living in a system of technological temporality, in which duration and material support have

Sex, machines and navels

been supplanted as criteria by individual retinal and auditory instants' (Virilio, 1991a: 84). Dominated by the speed of motorised and technological vehicles of 'vector-velocity', the world, its depth, its human subjects, its memories and time, disappears to be absorbed and replicated elsewhere, nowhere, in a non-space that is entirely virtual and governed only by speed's elimination of distance and duration.

Absorbed by machines of vision and speed, time disappears and all geographical, physical space is lost in the instant of the electronic image: 'with acceleration there is no more here and there, only confusion of near and far, present and future, real and unreal – a mix of history, stories, and the hallucinatory utopia of communications technologies' (Virilio, 1995a: 35). The utopia that is nothing but an effect of the images absorbing, transforming and effacing subjectivity inhibits the possibility of escaping the delusional foment and returning to a sense of reality. The excessive speeds of image production bypass perception and cognition: the eye disappears before the motorised lens of the video camera and the images are processed, not by a brain, but by a computer. Vision becomes 'sight-less', perception and cognition 'automated' (Virilio, 1994: 59). Existence, too, is on the brink of extinction: 'to exist, is to exist *in situ*, here and now, *hic et nunc*. This is precisely what is being threatened by cyberspace and instantaneous, globalized information flows' (Virilio, 1995b). The implications of speed extend, beyond the physical body and its functions that will be prosthetised or replaced, to affect the unrepresentable presence of the death which guarantees corporeal life:

> Speed treats vision like its basic element; with acceleration, to travel is like filming, not so much producing images as new mnemonic traces, unlikely, supernatural. In such context death itself can no longer be felt as mortal; it becomes, as in William Burroughs, a simple technical accident, the final separation of the sound from the picture track. (Virilio, 1991b: 60)

Death merely dissociates auditory and visual instantaneity, a voice-over interrupting the synchronised procession of sound and image. The loss of corporeal existence once associated with death now becomes the condition of a new being in the life–death of the instant, the dissociation of the soul flying from the body to another dimension: it cedes to a technological ecstasy, *Neuromancer*'s 'bodiless exultation', in which the strange weight of death is overcome by the weightless speed of images. Death, binding subjects to a bodily temporality, disappears, replaced by the motion of disappearance itself. Images assume a function akin to vampiric undeath, a seductive and fatal process in which the surface provides the site of disappearance: 'seduction is a rite-of-passage from one world to another' (Virilio, 1991b: 76). The screens surrounding the eye with the fatally alluring charm of images become the sole locus of movement and disappearance. Everything disappears in the superficial density of the screen's void: 'depth pertains exclusively to the primitive grandeur of speed, the grandeur of this new void, the vacuum of speed' (Virilio, 1991a: 43).

Virilio's discussion of the seduction that draws the world into a non-place alludes to Jean Baudrillard's account of simulation as a process in which the relationship between images and death is accelerated through the density of appearances. In *Seduction*, Baudrillard outlines a brief history of the factors enabling the rapid procession of simulacra. The liberations of sex, consciousness and consumption that were inaugurated in the 1960s overturn the structural social conditions of want, prohibition and limit and lead to a discarding of 'every referential principle' so that desire enters the realm of 'generalized simulation' (Baudrillard, 1990b: 5). The resulting 'pornographic culture', 'with its ideology of the concrete, of facticity and use', determines that 'the real is relinquished *by the very excess of appearances*' and tears a hole in reality (Baudrillard, 1990b: 34, 66–7). The absorbing screen of appearances becomes the locus of complete identification in which otherness is obliterated in the flickering effects of digital code. Narcissus, and the death of self which he implies, assumes a different form. The image is no longer other, it becomes a 'surface which absorbs and seduces him, which he can never pass beyond. For there is no beyond, just as there is no reflexive distance between him and his image. The mirror of Data is not a surface of reflection, but of absorption' (1990b: 67). Narcissus is not in love with a reflection of himself but loves the image itself, the fatal attraction of digital narcissism: 'psychobiological technology – all the computer prosthesis and self-adjusting electronic networks we possess – provides us with a kind of strange bioelectronic mirror, in which each person, like some digital Narcissus, is going to slide along the trajectory of a death drive and sink in his or her own image. Narcissus = narcosis' (Baudrillard, 1990b: 160). Passive stupefaction, intoxication before the image, seems total, inevitable, fatal. In a world dominated by 'a digital Narcissus instead of a triangular Oedipus', human sexuality is dissolved 'in favour of non-human sex' (Baudrillard, 1990b: 173, 169). Before and behind the screen there is only a void to be filled by seductive and excessive appearances.

Sex, machines and navels

Sex no longer involves the reproduction of bodies by way of difference but according to the machinic code of genetic replication, cloning. At this point, a 'point of no return', the disappearance of the body and its history is complete:

> We live in an age of soft technologies, of genetic and mental software. The prosthesis of the industrial age, its machines, still paid heed to the body in order to modify its image – and were themselves metabolized in an imaginary, this metabolism becoming part of the body's image. But when simulation reaches the point of no return, when the prosthesis infiltrate the body's anonymous, micro-molecular core, when they force themselves on the body as matrix, and burn out all the succeeding symbolic circuits such that all future bodies will only be its immutable repetition – then the body and its history have come to an end, the individual being no more than the *cancerous metastasis of his basic formula*. (Baudrillard, 1990b: 172)

Prostheticised and simulated to extinction through the technology of life, human bodies become the exact copies of a genetic code repeated to infinity. At this point, the replicants take over and the matrix establishes itself as One, embracing the machinic code of life within the simulated patterns of the image, a 'repetition of the Same, the proliferation of a single matrix'. Sexual reproduction's need for difference prevented unerring replicability, but now cloning technology can 'isolate the genetic matrix of identity, and eliminate all the differential vicissitudes that gave individuals their aleatory charm. Or seductiveness'. The 'hallucinatory resemblance' of one's image, the 'hypostasis of the artificial double' that is one's clone circumvents ethical questions about the Other because to love one's neighbour is precisely to love one's self, one's simulacrum in a literal narcissism in which love is 'total self-seduction' (Baudrillard, 1990b: 172–3). Total simulation.

The absorption in images, discarding body, identity, history and substance, implies, Virilio argues, a process more devastating than that suggested by the word 'simulation': 'I disagree with my friend Baudrillard on the subject of simulation. To the word simulation, I prefer the one substitution.' Virilio continues: 'As I see it, new technologies are substituting a virtual reality for an actual reality ... We are entering a world where there won't be one but two realities ... the actual and the virtual.' Substitution involves a splitting in two of reality and sexual identity: 'there are now two men and two women, real and virtual.' Splitting, however, is but a preliminary function of substitution which will divide the actual and the virtual in order to replace one with the other: 'virtuality will destroy reality' (Wilson, 1994). Digital reality aims, he contests, to negate actual reality. Human reality will be overwritten by digitality in the way that the 'insert' button of a PC allows the user to produce new text by simultaneously erasing any writing that exists on the screen, literally eating into the words in the manner of an old 'Pacman' video game. The effects of the virtual encroachment on and overwriting of actual reality are evident in the '*media proximity*' introduced by communications technologies: deleting all distance,

> the un-heard of possibility arises of a sudden splitting of the subject's personality. This will not leave 'body-image' – the individual's SELF-PERCEPTION – intact for long … Sooner or later, intimate perception of one's gravimetric mass will lose all concrete evidence, and the classic distinction between 'inside' and 'outside' will go out of the window with it. (Virilio, 1995a: 106)

The terms in which this 'un-heard of possibility' are outlined, however, seem curiously familiar to the formulas that psychoanalysis uses to describe the constitution of subjectivity: the splitting introduced by the imaginary and anticipatory recognition of unity in the image depends on the symbolic structuration of the perceptual field while the residue of real substance on which phantasmatic identity relies takes the form of an extimate object, an external intimacy. Indeed, substitution itself refers to the work of metaphor, to the signifiers that introduce symbolic reality as the principal reality of the subject, at the expense of a real forever unsymbolisable. That subjectivity, before the advent of vision machines, depends on a split between real and symbolic being suggests a more complicated model of substitution is involved in the move from actual to virtual reality. Virilio's account of vision machines, his focus on the technological objects that supplant vision and humanity, thus overlooks the operations of other machines in which perception is constituted, an oversight which turns on the invisible screen of the Thing, the imperceptible cause of a gaze from the Other Machine.

The Other Machine is technological in the broadest sense, a system of signifier-tools in which codes, prohibitions, law and desire articulate the distribution and functioning of organic machines. For Nietzsche the 'culture machine' that is the university provides the umbilical articulation of student bodies in the matrix of state power. Norbert Wiener, pioneer in the field of cybernetics, equates metal machines with 'those machines of

Sex, machines and navels

flesh and blood which are bureaus and vast laboratories and armies and corporations':

> I have spoken of machines, but not only of machines having brains of brass and thews of iron. When human atoms are knit into an organization in which they are used, not in their full right as responsible human beings, but as cogs and levers and rods, it matters little that their raw material is flesh and blood. *What is used as an element in a machine, is in fact an element in the machine.* (Wiener, 1954: 185–6)

In the seminar that engages at length with issues of cybernetics, Lacan carefully distinguishes machines from Machine to offer a radically different understanding of the relationship between subjectivity, images and language.

The machine, Lacan underlines, is not 'purely and simply the opposite of the living, the simulacrum of the living' but 'embodies the most radical symbolic activity of man': the relation between life and death is determined, not by the organism but by the signifier (Lacan, 1988b: 74). Giving form, meaning and direction to the subject in the determinations of the signifier, the symbolic order simultaneously makes sense of the world by distinguishing human reality from the real: the world structured and assumed to be human by virtue of the language that humans speak is, Lacan emphasises, a mechanical arrangement of symbols: 'the symbolic world is the world of the machine' (1988b: 47). Significantly, the symbolic process which transforms biological animals into subjects of culture is conceived as a machine of words: 'I am explaining to you that it is in as much as he is committed to a play of symbols, to a symbolic world, that man is a decentred subject. Well, it is with this same play, this same world, that the machine is built. The most complicated machines are made of words' (Lacan, 1988b: 47). Decentred, humans find identity, not in biological being, but in their relation to the Other, the language machine whose activity sustains sense and meaning through the play of difference. This machine, moreover, takes its bearings, not from the subject who remains excentric, but from the operations of the signifier, independent of any subject. Here lies the significance of cybernetics for Lacanian psycho-analysis: it is 'because cybernetics also stems from a reaction of astonishment at rediscovering that this human language works almost by itself, seemingly to outwit us' (1988b: 119). Human language, as it operates in virtual autonomy from living speakers, seems to be a misnomer given its status as a symbolic machine. Something, however, allows animal speaking beings to imagine themselves to be human. But the difference that makes language seem human through an opposition of humanity and machine misrecognises a difference that never sustains the elevation of humans to the superior pre- or extralinguistic position which, for centuries, they have supposed for themselves. The difference cannot be grandly established in essential or fundamental terms as either the nature of the speakers or the activity of autonomous consciousness or thoughtful self-presence.

Speaking in 1954 and 1955, Lacan notes the absence of machines that reproduce themselves. But the adding machine remains a precursor of the thinking machine and as such raises the problem of defining humanity in terms of the thought or consciousness that is lacked by the machine. If machines are unable to think, the nature of thought itself may be undermined by the symbolic machine of language since language speaks the subject and directs its activities in the world: 'we are well aware that this machine doesn't think. We make the machine and it thinks what it has been told to think. But if the machine doesn't think, it is obvious that we don't think either when we are performing an operation. We follow the very same procedures as the machine' (1988b: 304). That programmed machines perform in a directed manner only serves to underline the way that subjects serve as relays in the difference machine of language: the machine 'isn't simply a little box – when I am writing on paper, when I go through the transformations of the little 1s and 0s, that also is always a directed activity' (1988b: 305). As that which a signifier represents for another signifier, the subject appears in the intervals of the chain of signification:

> By itself the play of the symbol represents and organises, independently of the peculiarities of its human support, this something which is called a subject. The human subject doesn't foment this game, he takes his place in it, and plays the role of little *pluses* and *minuses* in it. He is himself an element in this chain which, as soon as it is unwound, organises itself in accordance with laws. Hence the subject is always on several levels, caught up in criss-crossing networks. (Lacan, 1988b: 192–3)

An effect of the symbolic matrix, the speaking subject is allotted different positions at nodal points in the entangled meshwork of the Other. A complete subject, lacking nothing, does not exist, there is no being or Self outside the process, no consciousness or centre of activity transcending language, except, perhaps, the function of the One. At the centre of the Other, insofar as it can be supposed to have a centre, and the point at which the subject is articulated to an unconscious that speaks the discourse of the Other, is no one, the headlessness of the drive: 'in so far as he speaks, the

Sex, machines and navels

subject can perfectly well find his answer, his return, his secret, his mystery, in the constructed symbol which modern machines represent for us, namely something far more acephalic still than what we encountered in the dream of Irma's injection' (Lacan, 1988b: 186). The demand that constitutes the subject as a speaking being, a demand for reason, being, love addressed to the Other discloses only a headless, subjectless process, a yawning gap in which the 'primordial subject of demand' – the (m)Other – is replaced by the symbolic matrix which cannot respond or guarantee satisfaction, mobilising only desire. But demand serves as the 'hook' by which the subject is caught in the net that is the Other (1977b: 12). The gap serves to link the subject to the symbolic machine through an imaginary articulation whereby something of the human body remains in excess of the symbolic machine.

The gap, moreover, serves as the space for the articulation of subject and symbolic: the *objet a* that fills the gap functions as the screen for imaginary identification, the point at which mirror identity is anchored in the same way that the *point de capiton* arrests the metonymic sliding of the chain of signification to form the locus for the production of metaphor and the recognition of meaning. The gap, no matter how slight between subject and symbolic or human from machine, establishes a minimal but crucial difference. Though subjects for the majority of their daily existence are wholly determined by the symbolic machine, at the precise point of articulation lies a difference utterly irreducible to the circuits of the signifier. Certain images, Lacan notes, perform the function of the irreducible object:

> The language embodied in a human language is made up of, and there's no doubt about this, choice images which all have a specific relation with the living existence of the human being, with quite a narrow sector of its biological reality, with the image of the fellow being. This imaginary experience furnishes ballast for every concrete language ... with this something which makes it a human language. (1988b: 319)

The 'ballast' that stabilises identity through the image of the other discloses a link to that 'narrow sector of ... biological existence' which is not incorporated by the mechanical movement of signifiers. The remainder of the real constitutes an 'obstacle to the progress of the realisation of the subject in the symbolic order', to that which cannot be absorbed, a 'resistance opposing the restitution of the integral text of the symbolic exchange. We are embodied beings, and we always think by means of some imaginary go-between, which halts, stops, clouds up the symbolic mediation. The latter is perpetually ground up, interrupted' (1988b: 319). This point of resistance and interruption to the functioning of the symbolic is a remainder that, in the unifying misrecognition of the imaginary, forms the difference elevating an idealised human figure and occluding the machine in which humanity is all but produced.

For one of the students attending the seminar, Octave Mannoni, the 'imaginary lining' forms the 'indispensable nourishment of the symbolic language' without which it 'becomes the machine, that is to say something which is no longer human'. Lacan quickly punctured the humanist bubble by means of which a minimal difference, that of the *a* as a 'narrow sector of biological reality', is transformed, in opposition to the machine, into something quintessentially human:

> Don't be soft. Don't go and say that the machine is really rather nasty and that it clutters up our lives. That is not what is at stake. The machine is simply the succession of little 0s and 1s, so that the question as to whether it is human or not is obviously entirely settled – it isn't. Except, there's also the question of knowing whether the human, in the sense in which you understand it, is as human as all that. (1988b: 319)

An effect of the symbolic machine of language, the human figure is all but machine itself. And yet there remains a minimal difference in excess of signifying chains.

Language, already a machine with 'humanity' as its effect, thus problematises accounts like Virilio's, which see the imminent death of the human body and the eclipse of reality in the images of new technology. This, of course, is not to say that things are the same as they ever were. Nor does a recognition of the effects of the symbolic machine imply a straightforward vindication of the 'truth' of psychoanalytical models as they are manifested by the mechanisms of virtual reality. The transition that is described as a shift from actual to virtual reality does not, it seems, require a frontal assault on humanity and its reality, an attempt to efface *in toto* every trace of corporeal existence since that existence, for psychoanalysis, is already reconstructed through the technological intervention of language to leave only a residue of substance: all that needs to happen is the erasure of this corporeal remainder, the slight difference on which embodied identity and human value is founded. Nothing changes in the process of everything changing. The Thing which suffers from and remains despite the interventions of the signifier, the resistance that imaginarily establishes the unity and difference of humanity, is eclipsed as virtual

Sex, machines and navels

technologies realise themselves and recode reality and identity. To jettison the 'ballast' and 'obstacle' to symbolic incorporation is enough to detach the subjectivity that is imaginarily anchored in bodies and allow complete immersion in the free-floating flows of the digital matrix.

Accounts of cyberspace that employ psychoanalysis acknowledge a certain congruence in their symbolic and subjective features, but this congruence nonetheless demands an appreciation of the significance of the difference that remains. The 'pleasure of the interface' emanates from 'the computer's offer to take us into a microelectronic Imaginary where our bodies are obliterated and consciousness integrated into the matrix' (Springer, 1991: 306). A similar comparison is made by Mark Lajoie in noting that '"real" reality itself is already a virtual reality'. He describes the terminal screen as the site through which subjectivity passes to be reborn 'within a new symbolic': the screen is that 'void in the real, an absence filled by a pure symbolic order' (Lajoie, 1996: 161–3). A slight revision of Lacanian schema has occurred in these comparisons, a significant elision, in particular, of the imaginary which no longer turns on an object of resistance and embodiment, but directly precipitates integration in the matrix. The screen is no longer a mirror, a space filled by an object that allows for the projection of a unifying signifier, but a site of superficial transparency that permits unimpeded access to symbolic images. A slight difference is effaced, the disappearance of any bodily remainder allowing absolute absorption, 'integration' into a now 'pure' symbolic. Bill Nichols, in describing simulation as an 'imaginary Other', implicitly acknowledges through his capitalisation the shift which occludes the other that, in Lacan, forms the basis of identification (Nichols, 1988: 28). Collapsing other into Other displays the erasure of the slight difference which imaginarily attests to human presence. No longer a 'dual entry matrix' accessed in the relation of object *a* and signifier, the locus of signification involves only the immersion in the network of computer-generated images. The other which, in fantasy, provides the locus of projected unity and also bars the subject from complete access to the Other, is now erased: the subject finds its plenitude, its *jouissance*, in the totality of the Other, an impossible union seemingly realised in the technological screen.

The very difference of the other that now disappears has provided the basis for understanding symbolic reality as an always-already virtual space. The relationship between subject and symbols is drastically transformed as technology fills the void of the terminal screen with an excessive array of images, the realisation of a fantasy by which the object-cause of fantasy is effaced. Slavoj Žižek outlines the effects of collapsing the difference between other and Other. Discussing contemporary media and computer technologies, Žižek argues that virtual reality heralds 'the *end* of the virtual space of symbolization' in that 'everything is instantly here, but bereft of its substance and thus instantly devalued' (1996: 190). By saturating '*the void that keeps open the space for symbolic fiction*', the excess of images generated by hyperrealism produce a 'de-realization' (Žižek, 1994: 76). Immediate delivery and instant gratification lead to the end of desire in that, discarding the object of fantasy, all distance, difference and deferral is obliterated. Virtual sex, for Žižek, offers the best example of this process, since 'real' sex depends on a virtual space of fantasy: 'the structure of the "real" sex act (the act with a flesh-and-blood partner) is already inherently phantasmatic – the "real" body of the other serves only as a support for our phantasmatic projections' (1994: 210). The 'true horror' evinced by virtual sex is not simply the loss of real sex, but the disclosure that '*this "real" sex never existed in the first place*, that sex always-already was virtual'. Virtual technologies ought to 'make us sensitive to how the "reality" with which we are dealing *always-already* was virtual' (1996: 194). In obliterating the space of fantasy, however, technology drives in the direction of realising a full subject. The saturation of images which voids phantasmatic space means that in the post-oedipal 'wired universe' governed by interactive (or 'interpassive') screens the 'overproximity and externality' of images undermines all symbolic paternal authority, accelerating a disintegration rather than integration of subjects. Without any object to provide a sense of identity, substance and consistency 'future subjects will be able to weigh the anchor that attaches them to their bodies and change into ghost-like entities floating from one virtual body to another in the phantasm of full virtualization of the subject finally delivered from the "pathological" stain of *a*' (Žižek, 1996: 197). The removal of the object *a* produces the 'absolute indifference' of God via 'pure feminine *jouissance*, the pure expansion into the void that lacks any consistency, the "giving way" held together by nothing' (Žižek, 1994: 130). Gibson's definition of cyberspace as a 'consensual hallucination' turns precisely on the absence of the pathological object that fantasmatically sustains reality: virtuality eclipses reality and subjectivity enters a bodiless space.

Materialising objects only as hallucinations, the appearance of cyberspace is associated with the delusional effects of the images of which it is composed. In the superabundance of nothing but images, psychosis appears, not as some individual aberrance, but as the definitive state of

| Sex, machines and navels

digital hypermodernity. The 'wired universe' is 'post-oedipal' in form because it forsakes the structuring function of the paternal metaphor and accedes to the torrential substitutions of images. Implicitly Žižek concurs with Baudrillard's account of the viral force of simulation in which the world of images, no longer regulated by metaphor, slides metonymically across all boundaries. Where metaphor occurred at the 'anchoring point' arresting the movement of the signifying chain, no term holds the viral cascade of images in check: meanings multiply and dissolve in the preponderance of simulations. Simulation thus inscribes itself in the gap of metaphoric substitution, the void of the terminal screen. In *Seduction*, a text ostensibly offering a critique of psychoanalysis, the interrogation of the paternal function of metaphor accords with the Lacanian account of psychosis to offer a diagnosis of contemporary cultural and economic formations. The 'digital Narcissus' describing a general absorption into the superficial density of the image replaces a 'triangular Oedipus' with a paternal figure at its apex. The seduction of images accords with the definition of psychosis offered in Lacan's account of Schreber and 'soul murder': 'it relates to the short-circuiting of the affective relation, which makes the other a being of pure desire who henceforth can only be, in the register of the human imaginary, a being of pure interdestruction. There is a purely dual relation here, which is the most radical source of the very register of aggressiveness' (Lacan, 1988a: 228). Through the technological double that one becomes, the oedipal relation is reduced to a 'dual simplification' foreclosing the function of the signifier and leaving only a void in the symbolic authority of the Other (Lacan, 1977a: 201). With the 'failure of the paternal metaphor' and a resulting inability to regulate meaning, images circulate freely (Lacan, 1977a: 215–18). Any image or signifier rapidly replaces the paternal function in the psychic economy of the subject, presenting endless sites of identification and no place of rest.

Speed is a factor in the excessive production and exchange of images in that it also forecloses the possibility of securing a consistent subjective position. Dominated by the flickering pulses of informational screens, time is bound up with the movement of images and disembodied imagos: technological speed thus forecloses what Lacan calls, in his discussion of logical time, 'the moment to conclude', the affirmation of subjectivity in a symbolic order. Using the example of a logical puzzle called the 'Prisoner's Dilemma', Lacan distinguishes between three temporal dimensions, the real's instant of looking which sees but does not know what it sees, the time of understanding and the moment of conclusion. The second temporal order depends on reflection and mirroring. Here, 'every subject is a mirror for the other subjects and so there is an infinite series of reflections without any definition or stopping point'. The third moment transcends reflexive self-consciousness by hastening 'the Symbolic affirmation of the signifier' when the subject assumes the position of 'I' (Samuels, 1993: 12–14). For Lacan, the act of speech enables the simultaneous production of the subject's truth. The third temporal dimension is significant in that it differentiates between imaginary and symbolic, but also between human and machine:

> That is where the power revealed by the originality of the machines we have at our disposal falls short. There is a third dimension of time which they undeniably are not party to, which I'm trying to get you to picture via this element which is neither belatedness, nor being in advance, but haste, the relation to time peculiar to the human being, this relation to the chariot of time which is there, close on our heels. That is where speech is to be found, and where language, which has all the time in the world, is not. (Lacan, 1988b: 291)

Speech constitutes the navel between being and language, the point articulating subject and signifier, the (dis)connection that announces the 'mystery of the speaking body'. Without this articulation there is only the endless and unstoppable reflections of the second temporal dimension, the cascade of images without anchor or end. The speed by which contemporary technology generates and circulates images renders the affirmation of subjectivity problematic, tearing identity from a foreclosed paternal metaphor and casting it into the flux of images, leaving the subject in the inconclusive wake of rapidly processed instants and digital reflections.

Speed and image inaugurate a fundamental transformation of the relationship between other and Other that shapes human subjects. For Lacan, 'the meaning of the machine is in the process of a complete transformation, for us all, whether or not you have opened a book on cybernetics' (1988b: 31). And the transformation from other to Other turns on the status of rapidly generated images: 'the image comes to us from an essentially symbolic creation, that is to say from a machine, that most modern of machines, far more dangerous than the atom bomb, the adding machine' (1988b: 88). By way of the image the assumption of a place in the symbolic becomes impossible, except on the condition of utter absorption into an inhuman, entirely Other Machine. Hence Virilio's observations on the 'informational pathology' which deprives human faculties of the ability to cope with the pace set by a machinic Other and

Sex, machines and navels

the 'hallucinatory utopia' that accompanies the overstimulation of delirious organisms. The hallucinatory form of the cyberspatial matrix realises a symbolic order that is without consistency, held together by nothing other than the consensuality of users.

As a manifestation of Lacanian precepts, literalising the symbolic machine in an objectless manner, the matrix discloses the lack of a phantasmatic object to support desiring and thus delivers a state of 'indifference'. Lacan observes that 'one can think of language as a network, a net over the entirety of things, over the totality of the real. It inscribes on the plane of the real this other plane, which we here call the plane of the symbolic' (1988a: 262). The symbolic takes the form of a 'web' (1988b: 209). With 'web' and 'network' now representing the matrix of computers connected across the globe, a virtually palpable inscription of the symbolic circuit seems to have occurred. The machines which conjoin as the totality of the symbolic machine perform, on a global scale, the process which short-circuits the relationship between other and Other. In contrast, the 'objective of my teaching', Lacan emphasises, 'is to dissociate the a and the O', maintaining the fundamental difference of the imaginary and the symbolic (1982: 153). When machines begin to cohere in the form of Machine, however, a fundamental transformation manifests itself, replicating and intensifying the function of the original symbolic machine:

> Everything is tied to the symbolic order, since there are men in the world and they speak. And what is transmitted and tends to get constituted is an immense message into which the entire real is little by little retransplanted, recreated, remade. The symbolisation of the real tends to be equivalent to the universe and the subjects are only relays, supports in it. What we get up to in all this is to make a break on the level of one of these couplings. (Lacan, 1988b: 322)

The human (symbolic) order which inscribes itself over the real in a process of recreation in which reality is produced in phantasmatic relation to a little piece of the real finds itself, with the advent of virtual techno-logies, subjected to another process of retransplantation and recreation. The Internet or World Wide Web rapidly replicates this process by inscribing itself, virtually, over the entire field of the symbolic reality that once appeared human. The Net does not simply represent an unpresent-able global totality in different form: representation is irrelevant; the totality presents itself as it is used, operated and inhabited, realising and inscribing itself as the dominant form of reality. The Net now cast over the entirety of things recodes things themselves and, in the process, performs a resymbolisation of reality by shattering existing symbolic reality, a transcription of code using the same metaphors but with an awesome technical capacity to transform and realise things. The scale of the resymbolisation means that nothing changes as everything changes, overwritten in a non-place, locus of digital incorporation at once absolute and virtual. The absorption or dissolution of reality presents a liberation from the gravity of things, offering new freedoms for bodies and from bodies as the world recedes in a digital haze.

Žižek optimistically observes that 'the virtualization of reality always produces an excremental remainder of the real which resists symbolisation' (1996: 197). But it is difficult to identify any remainder given the speed at which bodies turn into machines. Given the virtual disappearance of the other in the face of the machinic Other's totalising procession, the machine's leftover seems to be no more than the 'meat' itself. In the images produced by and for the Machine, entirely divested of meaty residue, the pathological object over which humanity erects its self and its values is reduced to indifference. Humans, it seems, like the replicants of *Blade Runner*, with their photos, navels and questions about their origins and ends, are rapidly running out of time. But if, as Lacan suggests, subjects are 'only relays' or breaks in the couplings composing the symbolic machine, then it may be in the machine, among its gaps, resistances and nodal points, that a kind of subjectivity may be articulated.

Notes

1 Gibson and Sterling (1991). For a discussion of the Charles Babbage and Ada Lovelace, see Plant (1995).
2 Platt (1995: 105). In the visionary future described in *Mind Children*, Moravec projects the surgical extraction of mental functions to the point that 'the useless human body with its brain tissue would then be discarded, while consciousness would remain stored in computer terminals, or, for the occasional outing, in mobile robots' (Springer, 1993: 720).
3 Jameson (1984) suggests that computerised networks provide a metaphor for transnational capitalism. Csicsery-Ronay, Jr (1991: 186) sees a paradox in cybernetics: 'simultaneously a sublime vision of human power over chance and a dreary augmentation of multinational capitalism's mechanical process of expansion ...'. For Davis (1993: 592) *Neuromancer* 'represents not science but the technologically driven information economy of global capitalism'. Brande (1996: 101) argues that the matrix 'stages the revolutionary force of the global market'.

4 Markley (1996: 57–9) compares cyberspace and metaphysical, idealist philosophy in terms of the transcendence of the mind–body split. McCarron (1995: 262) argues that the 'ultimate goal' of cyberpunk and prosthetics is the realisation of 'pure mind'.
5 Springer (1991: 303). Also, Olsen (1991: 283)) comments on how the matrix provides males with access to a female region.
6 Stone (1992: 610). Csicsery-Ronay (1991: 182) notes the 'artificial immanence' of the future: 'all that was once nature is simulated and elaborated by technical means'. Chapman (1993: 838) comments on how people have become increasingly remote from nature, to the point that nature becomes a 'supertechnology'.

6 ✧ Romance of the machine

Navels in the machine

Romance draws humans beyond themselves, inaugurating a movement of passionate excess towards absolute union with another. But its momentum towards an impossible plenitude, a *jouissance* of being-in-death, turns on something strange, alien, uncanny. The romantic 'fatal desire for mystical union' emerges as a (non)relation to 'some *other*', to the 'other's alien life' (de Rougemont, 1993: 322). In Lacanian terms this other functions like the extimate Thing, locus of the minimal difference in and more than the subject. In romance moreover, the otherness ascribed to woman takes the form of an inhuman partner, a double around which the courtly order of the signifier takes its bearings. In the latter half of the twentieth century, when romance is relayed across western globalised culture by so many vision machines and terminal screens to assume a dominant position in the lives of consuming and desiring subjects, the function of the Thing changes: when the unpresentable void underlying cultural screens is hollowed out by technological rewritings of reality, digital desiring expands to literalise *jouissance* (virtually, at least) as a general condition. (SHaH, 1997) The law of the signifier breaks down in the face of the relentless and deterritorialised desiring that results from this symbolic and economic generalisation. The Thing which stabilises the signifier as a marker of humanity is all but erased: the dual-entry matrix of subjectivity loses one of its access points. The remainder of the real defining the minimal in-human difference is obliterated in corporeal form. But it may not disappear entirely: the transformation of romance – the romance of machine – may see the excessive object incorporated into artificial systems. This movement implies an uncanny turn in the dialectic of mastery and slavery traditionally supposed to elevate man over nature and woman through his use of signifiers, tools and machines: the supplement linking woman and machine supplants the positions of master and slave, incorporating everything into the immanent process of machinic and informational flows. But the incorporation of the remainder into the machine may also inhibit the process of realising a machinic romance: gaps, breaks, nodes (and navels) interrupt electronic flows, introducing some Thing Other into the homogenising thrust of technological fantasies.

The remainder of the real is linked to the 'meat', the corporeal excess discarded by the machine. In *Idoru*, William Gibson offers a vividly vile picture of the disgusting residue of humanity:

> Which is best visualized as a vicious, lazy, profoundly ignorant, perpetually hungry organism craving the warm god-flesh of the anointed. Personally I like to imagine something the size of a baby hippo, the color of a week-old boiled potato, that lives by itself, in the dark, in a double-wide on the outskirts of Topeka. It's covered with eyes and it sweats constantly. The sweat runs into those eyes and makes them sting. It has no mouth, Laney, no genitals, and can only express the mute extremes of murderous rage and infantile desire by changing channels on a universal remote. Or by voting in presidential elections. (Gibson, 1996: 28–9)

Passive, formless and stupefied before the screen, it retains a trace of the passion that defines the human subject and focuses the contempt for the meat. This imagined photo-fit describes the audience for 'Slitscan', a muck-raking TV scandal show dedicated to dishing the dirt on the quasi-sacred figures of celebrity who appear on the screen rather than slump before it. Meat, little more than organic mush dissociated from anything like subjectivity, exists in the nondescript agglomeration of inarticulate passions, desires and consumptive cravings, the consumerist culture of present occidental societies finding perfected form in the near future. The unformed mass of bodily existence, however, remains outside the glossy world of the machine: the lumpen teleconsumer marks the limit and excess to an existence in the machine, opposed to a thoroughly machinic existence in its automatic world of bodily drives.

The formless object opposed to and expelled from the machine that dominates proper life remains to guarantee the residual humanity of those in the machine. But in the world of the novel the excessive objects of corporeal life play no part, even in the tiny clusters of activity in which human protagonists, through the mediation of the matrix, become involved in the plot. In *Idoru*, there are other forms of the object by which identity, retrospectively, is traced as something individual and, possibly, human. In this context, the other of the machine is not the corporeal remainder, but in and of the machine, generated in the relays and flows of the informational network itself. The residue confers, if not identity, at least a sense of partial agency for those whose daily life involves movement in the vast information matrix. Identity is not simply a merger in the electronic flows of information exchange, it becomes nodal in that movement in the matrix leaves traces by which a form of individuality can be plotted: clusters, patterns, constellations in the field of data form a knot of difference, a sign of the 'variance' by which individual presence is, belatedly, identified (Ehrmann, 1971). One of the novel's protagonists, Colin Laney, has accidentally been given the ability to identify nodes of presence in the undifferentiated sea of data. With a nervous system damaged by pharmaceutical intervention, he is ideally suited to the role of 'netrunner' or data researcher: 'he had a peculiar knack with data-collection architectures, and a medically documented concentration-deficit that he could toggle, under certain conditions, into a state of pathological hyperfocus.' As 'an intuitive fisher of patterns of information' he is trained to spend his time 'skimming vast floes of undifferentiated data, looking for "nodal points"' (Gibson, 1996: 25). These points, practically invisible clusters in the data matrix, are found by 'running' the net, by disentangling certain threads in the fabric of information to reach the knots that become identifiable as the 'signature a particular individual inadvertently created in the net as he or she went about the mundane yet endlessly multiplex business of life in a digital society' (1996: 25). The knot of being that emerges in the Being of the matrix, without substance, nonetheless becomes the image-object that guarantees the symbolic identity virtually eclipsed by the workings of the machine: it is a particular knot in a system entirely composed of nodal interconnections and pathways.

Laney's unusual talent guarantees his place in the corporate order of digital society, providing a transferable skill which ensures his continued employment. It serves as the knot connecting him to the screens governing the world of work and keeps him from falling into the consumerist heap of vile and useless bodies. His talent also entangles him in the novel's main story. Sacked as a netrunner for 'Slitscan', he is employed on the security staff for the corporation surrounding the immensely popular and rich rock group, 'Lo Rez'. His task is to investigate the security protecting Rez's data due to the rock star's puzzling enamoration with an idoru which threatens the corporate empire built up around him. Rez, however, is difficult to detect in the matrix, a celebrity of such astral proportions with so much

Sex, machines and navels

data generated around him that, even to a netrunner like Laney, he is screened from visibility, beyond the mundane world of information and without the 'traces' that establish quotidian identity (1996: 119). Outside the scope of data-visibility and thus all the more attractive to the adoring fans that compile so much data on him, Rez is nonetheless a crucial knot in the story: 'he's the navel of the world I work in, Laney. That has a way of making people unknowable' (1996: 149). Heterogeneous to the matrix, known but unknowable to its users, Rez forms a peculiarly obscure figure of nodal constellation while remaining an empty space within it. A scandal, however, threatens him and his corporate cladding. Rumours abound concerning his romantic attachment to an idoru named Rei Toei. As the object of desire of one of the world's most idolised men, she must be a very special figure of womanhood. And special she is.

An 'idoru' is the generic Japanese name for a computer-generated star of the type that already successfully makes videos and appears in movies. The definition is elaborated in the novel, along with Rez's honourable intentions towards her. An 'idol-singer',

> 'she is a personality-construct, a congeries of software agents, the creation of information-designers. She is akin to what I believe they call a "synthespian" in Hollywood.'
> Laney closed his eyes, opened them. 'The how can he marry her?'
> 'I don't know,' Yamazaki said. 'But he has forcefully declared this to be his intention.' (1996: 92)

The reasons for such a perplexing choice of bride elude the coterie of people closest to Rez. For others, less sympathetic to the eccentricities of the megastar, the attraction of man for machine-constructed personality is nothing but a slight twist in an ongoing and quite straightforward tradition of male desire: 'evolution and technology and passion; man's need to find beauty in the emerging order; his own burning need to get his end in with some software dolly wank toy' (1996: 144). The standard narcissism of male masturbatory fantasy, albeit a highly evolved form of technoeroticism, provides the simple explanation of Rez's romantic intentions. But in the novel this explanation reduces the specialness of the idoru and over-simplifies the complexity of an attraction more intricate and reciprocal than a narcissistic desire for technological rather than carnal mastery.

Laney's significance in the plot stems from his function as witness to the very special nature of the relationship that romantically entangles stellar man with the mysterious and alluring figure of matricial woman. Her machine-generated form possesses an almost independent existence. She is a product of machines and yet much more than vast circuits of information, a figure who has developed irreducible characteristics. Constantly reminded that 'she is not flesh; she is information. She is the tip of an iceberg, no, an Antarctica, of information', that her composition is 'the result of an array of elaborate constructs' called 'desiring machines' or 'aggregates of subjective desire', Laney discovers the inadequacy of scientific definitions when he encounters her for the first time. As a 'desiring machine', she is far superior to other synthespians, introducing the inexhaustibility of desire through the difference that gives her a distinctly mysterious allure. The encounter with the idoru does not occur by way of a screen or within the matrix of data, but in the 'real' and chic surroundings of an exclusive restaurant. She is seated with two men at a dinner table when Laney arrives:

> If he'd anticipated her at all, it had been as some industrial-strength synthesis of Japan's last three dozen top female media faces. That was usually the way in Hollywood, and the formula tended to be even more rigid, in the case of software agents – *eigenheads*, their features algorithmically derived from some human mean of proven popularity.
>
> She was nothing like that.
>
> Her black hair, rough-cut and shining, brushed pale bare shoulders as she turned her head. She had no eyebrows, and both her lids and lashes seemed to have been dusted with something white, leaving her dark pupils in stark contrast.
>
> And now her eyes met his.
>
> He seemed to cross a line. In the very structure of her face, in geometries of underlying bone, lay coded histories of dynastic flight, privation, terrible migrations. (1996: 175)

Her visible presence is made possible by sophisticated holographic projection. To automated or prostheticised eyes her substance has no feminine form: it is a generator shaped like 'a big aluminium thermos bottle' (1996: 179). Her appearance for those who can see exceeds her virtual materialisation in the holographic flickers of light. Her eyes captivate Laney with the force of something unknown, her exotic charm intensified by a cluster of images that range somewhere indiscernible, unmappable, beyond, beneath or behind the light generator that gives her form. Her eyes are those of an 'envoy of some imaginary country' (1996: 176). When Laney's eyes meet them he crosses a line and blanks out, losing physical dimension and any sense of the immediate environment of polite diners to whom he appears 'blind'. He 'falls through' her eyes and, dissociated from any spatial and temporal orientation, disappears in their surfaces of perception through a hole that opens on to a visionary, non-dimensional dimension of images beyond machinic function, heterogeneous flows of and more than the matrix. The void rippling with vivid pictures is an unconscious space: the images are her dreams replayed as videos, unconscious traces of a consciousness that exists apart from the machines which generate its raw and complex data. She is nodal in a way that Laney finds unthinkable, unimaginable: 'she induced the nodal vision in some unprecedented way; she induced it as narrative' (1996: 178). Falling through the navel, her dark pupils the remainder of the unplumbable hole at the core of her nodal existence, is to enter an other (non)dimension of the matrix, a vast nodal realm that the talented detector of nodes has only ever intimated as an obscure possibility.

An effect of flows of information and holographic generation the idoru is without substance. Pure surface, a constellation of light and images designed as an aggregate of subjective desire, she is the ideal figure of femininity. Her constructed surfaces and machinic generation allow her to assume a perceptibly human form in excess of the complex machine that constitutes the material of her being. It endows this surface with the attribute that allows a perfect masquerade to ply its charms: the illusion of ungraspable substance draws desire towards a mystery it cannot reach; the differences and complexity of images allude to a depth she only imaginarily possesses, a depthlessness of desire itself. Hers is the perfect form of woman. In the novel, she is more than a idealised figment of a fantastic imagination, a construct of idealised romantic aspirations, and much more than an insubstantial object anchoring masculinity in its own structures of desire. She exists in her own right; she has 'her own' Thing and con-sequently an identity akin to the 'subject-in-process': '"Rei's only reality is the realm of ongoing serial creation," Rez said. "Entirely *process*; infinitely more than the combined sum of her various selves. The platforms sink beneath her, one after another, as she grows denser and more complex"' (1996: 202). Her density of light and information remains superficial. Its visual form is glimpsed during Laney's fall into the tracery of images, her dreams seen through the hole in her eyes. An element of fantasy persists in the idoru's nodal formation: she is the navel through which Rez can plunge into the matrix, the node of (dis)connection to a lost home sublimated in new form. Rez has illusions about the radical and liberating aspects of his amorous fantasy, a new union made possible by the romance of the machine. For Virilio, 'the body of the woman becoming one with a communication body, is the ideal vector between man and the new world' (1991b: 71). In the shape of the feminine node of data and images 'the machine completely replaces the loved one, the "mother land" inhabited by the spirit of metamorphosis, but technical fatality seems even more blinding and redoubtable than its anthropomorphic blueprints because of the very speed only it can lend to our aspirations' (1991b: 95). Rez displays a new mode of sublimating what remains as an age-old oedipal fantasy of maternal union. In the materialisation of the erotic charge between men and machines in feminine form, Rez's romance merely realises the technological impulse conjoining sexual liberation with the ultimate expenditure of corporeal annihilation.

The fantasy, however, is structured by something other than a 'software dolly wank toy'. Fantasy remains the support and reference of desire, and desire joins Rez and Rei in numerous ways. Rich, desirable, idolised, Rez can satisfy any wish or whim at will. Gratification is immediate and thus desire can be instantaneously extinguished. Quite literally, he wants for nothing, in the sense of there being nothing beyond his reach so that nothing remains the object of desire. Rei, her eyes and their non-dimensional beyond, offer a realm in which the infinity of desire unfolds, in nothing, around nothing. Embodying lack, she also offers the entangled space where the holes of his own desire can be knotted together around the nothing of an impossible object in, and cause of, desire. Rei thus constitutes the only possible figure of desire for Rez, the (non)object who returns desire to a man who seemed beyond it. The idoru's special difference, the gap she discloses in the matrix's structures of desire, is thus the site of fantasy and the impediment to union.

In and of the matrix and more than it at the same time, her excess, described as more than the sum of machinic selves, emanates from a nodal position that evolves into the Thing that constitutes desire and value. Not reducible to machinic being, the Thing around which her individual existence is established as a subject in process traces an emergent and human figure. As machine becomes human, woman's ephemeral substance in structures of desire is reconstituted as neither body nor machine, not the meat excluded by the machine but something other emerging in the superficial densities of the matrix. Though Laney has spent his life hunting through data 'he never found the central marvel, the thing that would have made the hunt worthwhile' until he encounters Rei: she is the 'central marvel' (1996: 227). The sublimity of her immanent existence distinguishes her as more than machine: she is a nodal constellation of data woven to the point that traces individual being. Her nodal complexity makes her a person to the extent that Laney, even when reminding himself she is but a machine, finds himself captivated, touched by her and unable to shake off the sense of her humanity: 'but you're just information yourself, Laney thought, looking at her. Lots of it, running through God knows how many machines. But dark eyes looked back at him, filled with something for all the world like hope' (1996: 238). As he investigates the data that forms the stuff of her basic existence Laney finds more evidence of her humanness. Her qualities, moreover, are enhanced by her connection with Rez:

> The idoru's data began somewhere after that, and it began as something smoothly formed, deliberate, but lacking complexity. But at the points where it had swerved closest to Rez's data, he saw that it had begun to acquire a sort of complexity. Or randomness, he thought. The human thing. That's how she learns. (1996: 251)

The intermingling of Rez's and Rei's data provides precisely what she lacks, the very complexity and randomness that distinguishes the 'human thing'. In the romance of man and machine each fills the other's lack, the one becoming machine, the other becoming human.

A strange symmetry arises in such a reciprocal romance. Though a celebrity surrounded by an immense network of data, Rez is obscured by its immaterial weight, to the extent that, in the matrix, he is invisible, lacking the traces that confer individual existence. In this respect he already inhabits a world beyond or below the threshold of nodal life: a navel for others, he has no knot of data to call his own. The idoru, too, has an immaterial existence built on images generated elsewhere: like Rez, her existence is beyond the dimension of mundane digitality. A navel and a nodal point, the couple constitute ideal images of each other, the double one loves as oneself. Their romance is sustained, furthermore, by the impossibility of a sexual relation. The romantic fantasy of union is maintained precisely by this impossibility, underpinning their desire to be married. Unthinkable though such a union seems to all who are aware of Rez's intentions, the distance only invigorates their desire. And love will find a way. In the near future, of course, technology provides the means. They plan to marry and realise the fantasy, becoming conjoined in the substantial manner offered by nanotechnology: through love they will rebuild themselves as one, their joint lack of substance supplied in the form of a device that, when coded with their intermingled data, will evolve materially. The obstacles to a sexual relation, to the complete union of romantic fantasy, only exist to be overcome. They have their romantic precursors: blade runner and android flying off into a romanticised nature or Emul and Berenice producing a 'scion'. However, like the Hegelian child of love, the scion remains a symbol of love and retains the difference of not being one with it. In *Blade Runner*, though the android is subjectivised, and problematises the 'human' subject position of Deckard, she remains a 'symptom of man', a 'synthetic complement', an embodiment of his lack in a manner that preserves gender distinctions even though 'sexual difference coincides with the difference human/android' (Žižek, 1991b: 173n.). In *Idoru* Rez and Rei erase all difference to realise themselves as one, negating prior existence in an entirely new and unified configuration. Their dream is not the transcendence of becoming a new entity in the insubstantial matrix in the way that the passion and war of the two AIs culminates in *Neuromancer*: they want to go beyond 'consensual fantasy' and recreate themselves as the One, conjoined in a completely new and other matter.

Traces of age-old romantic traditions remain in the apocalyptic romance of the machine. Courtly romances set the pattern for charting the all-consuming passion which takes lovers beyond all limits in their quest for a quasi-divine union: it is a fatal path which takes the couple to the point of death, to the sacrifice of separate individual existence. For de Rougemont (1993) the romance expresses a distinctly human passion for something beyond and it effectively dies when it is embourgeoisified in popular culture through the equation of romance and marriage. For Rez and Rei, the bourgeois symbolic ritual forms the third term separating and connecting their fantasy of idealised union. There remain, too, traces of the Freudian family romance in their idealisation of love: to be joined with Rei is to return to the mother sublimated as matrix and realise a primary narcissistic wish. The difference in *Idoru*'s replication of romance turns on the object of passionate investment. The strangeness of the intention to marry a machine seems to have short-circuited a fundamentally human relationship. In Lacanian terms, however, this is not the case: though revolving around that unknowable knot of being alien to the symbolic order, love always involves three, not two, parties. The charms and ordeals of the romance stem, he argues, from the absence of a sexual relation: in the trials of courtly poetry the very ideal of romance is sustained by prohibitions and obstacles which reproduce love's delusion by occluding the presence of the Other. Even in courtly poetry there is much of the

Sex, machines and navels

machine in evidence. The Dark Lady who is the object of romantic devotion and adoration, who sets impossible and humiliating tasks is 'emptied of all real substance' (Lacan, 1992: 149). She constitutes the Thing, 'the beyond-of-the-signified' at the limit of male narcissism, a screen for the projection of a fantasised union. The Lady, moreover, repeatedly requires her lover to undertake arduous tasks as proof of love, subjecting him, in the process, to the rules of a game in which he is not master: her 'inhuman character' is displayed; a 'terrifying partner', her being is 'nothing other than being as signifier' (Lacan, 1992: 214). At this point the Lady introduces the effects of automaton, the repetition of signifiers that return to the site of trauma separating real and symbolic. The Lady 'functions as an inhuman partner in the sense of a radical Otherness which is wholly incommensurable with our needs and desires; as such, she is simultaneously a kind of automaton, a machine which utters meaningless demands at random' (Žižek, 1994: 90). In place of the Other, as Things which guarantee the order of the paternal signifier, the romantic elevation of women, though doubled, displays the subjection of man: a symptom of man, a site of projection which imaginarily sustains the consistency of an inconsistent Other, woman assumes the role of object that fills the gap between a paternal symbolic order and the void of an unsymbolisable real. This is both a site for fantasy as well as resistance: as Thing, as 'that which in the real suffers from the signifier', she retains some part of absolute otherness and thus discloses a 'supplementary *jouissance*', something in excess of, not completely subjected to, the phallic signifier which determines male enjoyment (Lacan, 1992: 125; 1982: 144).

Even in the embourgeoisified and restricted economy which combines romance with the ideal of romantic union the double effects of the sexual non-relation are evinced. Marriage binds women in a symbolic pact between men to the extent that 'the symbolic order literally subdues, transcends her'. But, Lacan contends, resistance remains: 'there's something insurmountable, let us say unacceptable, in the fact of being placed in the position of an object in the symbolic order, to which, on the one hand, she is entirely subjected no less than man'. At this point conflicts arise. An 'imaginary degradation' of man's status becomes visible. The symbolic exchange which elevates man to the extent that he is identified with the paternal signifier confers, imaginarily, the transcendent status of gods. But, Lacan notes, 'men aren't gods' and thus the husband is unveiled as the 'idolatrous substitute' of universal man (Lacan, 1988b: 262). Fakes lacking being, men find women have become their rivals rather than the phantasmatic supports of masculine identity. Man's position and the phallic signifier which sustains it is impeached. As doubles, women assume an uncanny force, representing both the ideal image one loves as oneself and the inhuman counterpart which spectrally displays male subjection and mortality.

The story of the uncanny participates in the history associating women and machines. E. T. A. Hoffman's 'The Sandman', recounting the fate of a young man who falls in love with a beautiful automaton called Olympia, provides the basis of Freud's study of the uncanny. Like eighteenth-century automata, however, Olympia, 'to all appearances a living being', fails to excite any anxiety on the part of a psychoanalyst more concerned with the uncanniness which associates eyes and penis to call up the spectre of castration (Freud, 1955: 227). Hélène Cixous's reading of Freud's essay revokes Olympia's marginalisation to establish her significance as a double who portends the death that constitutes and subverts representation. Located within the 'strange crossing of languages' which traverse Freud's text, the double is the thing beyond castration, the shadow where the arbitrariness of meaning is fixed as 'no meaning' (Cixous, 1976: 536). A 'ghostly figure of unfulfillment and repression', 'neither alive nor dead', the double subjects Freud's text to the patterns of repetition that disclose automatism: at this point 'the text becomes knotty and stops. A cut. A desire for the indisputable' (Cixous, 1976: 541). Even as Freud attempts to define the uncanny and differentiate the science of psychoanalysis from the knotty figures of fiction by means of the castrating cut of his signifier, his text remains entangled with the disarming ambivalence of fiction: 'neither real nor fictitious, "fiction" is a secretion of death, an anticipation of nonrepresentation, a doll, a hybrid body composed of language and silence that, in the movements which turns it and which it turns, invents doubles, and death' (Cixous, 1976: 548). Cixous maintains the difference of the death which divides the double in Freud's reading. Associated with infantile narcissism in its first incarnation, the double then becomes an 'uncanny harbinger of death'. Without signified death is a signifier which causes movement and uncertainty rather than definition, a ghostly figure that crosses boundaries and erases limits (Cixous, 1976: 542). In a similar vein, the paternal figure is a 'ghost' in that 'there is nothing that guarantees the dimension of truth founded by the signifier' (Lacan, 1977c: 22). Detached from the object that supports it, the ghostly presence of the signifier which does not stay in its place offers a different account of the uncanny: not a matter of the return of the

Sex, machines and navels

repressed, not defined by irruptions from the darkness of a romantic unconscious, the uncanny stems from 'an imbalance in the fantasy when it decomposes, crossing the limits originally assigned to it' (Lacan, 1977c: 22). As a decomposition of the structures sustaining identity and meaning, the uncanny connotes the movement, the doubleness of difference.

The doubleness of the uncanny characterises the relationship between men, women and machines over the last two centuries. Discussing the 'Vamp and the Machine', Andreas Huyssen notes how, from being a 'testimony to the genius of mechanical invention', the meaning of the android alters to that of a nightmarish threat to human existence (1981–82: 222). The two meanings of the machine, the servile and the demonic, are easily linked to constructions of female sexuality:

> The projection was relatively easy to make; although woman had traditionally been seen as standing in a closer relationship to nature than man, nature itself, since the eighteenth century, had come to be interpreted as a gigantic machine. Woman, nature, machine had become a mesh of significations which all had one thing in common: otherness; by their very existence they raised fears and threatened male authority and control. (Huyssen, 1981–82: 226)

The mesh of significations which threatens man also constitutes his priority: it establishes a network of otherness against which man defines himself and over which he presides. Machines, like women, are constructed 'to serve him and fulfil his desires', the slaves of male mastery (1981–82: 227). In his reading of Fritz Lang's *Metropolis*, Huyssen comments on the bourgeois form of this relationship in the scene in which the capitalist master, from his panoptic position in the communications centre, presides over the enslaved workers in the machine room.

The axis of sexual and mechanical otherness turns on the dialectic of master and slave and is transformed with the arrival of bourgeois power and its industrialisation of production. Prior to that machines held a different status: serving no purpose, automata 'inhabited a space of fantasy' and were dedicated only to the enjoyment of subjects guaranteed by a paternal and monarchical master (Dolar, 1994: 53). In bourgeois political, economic and subjective formations the enjoyment vanishes: 'the autonomous self-determination' of the liberal subject finds its metaphor and counterpoint in the mechanical doll, with the romance between men and feminised machines disclosing a 'mechanical side to men as well' (Dolar, 1994: 46–7). Automata erase the natural element of essential difference, the secret of being, which securely defines identity: 'what fascinates the gaze and places it in the position of power is above all their availability and utter transparence. Machines and automata have no secrets, their springs and levers are accessible to all.' Such openness to visibility and the knowledge by which subjects are constructed, individuated and disciplined is linked by Dolar to the fantasy of the Panopticon where the universal gaze of the Other is superegoically internalised. As a machine determining the visibility and distribution of social identities, the Panopticon functions with an empty space at its centre, a tower that need not be occupied by anyone, a political structure quite distinct from formations which depended on the bodily presence of a monarch: 'once the mechanism of mechanism sank in, this place ceased to be the privilege of the king: the domination can function without a Master, i.e it can function precisely as a machine' (Dolar, 1994: 53). No one, since then, occupies the position of the master since the machine has absorbed his function.

Though ideology and cultural practices continue to bind masculinity and mastery together, the machine has reversed man's priority and supplanted his place at the centre of things. In the uncanny relations of *Blade Runner* the reversal of mastery is intimated in the romance and rivalry between humans and machines. Replicants designed as workers, warriors and whores in the service of their human masters rebel. Even Rachael, remaining very much the support of Deckard's romantic fantasy, escapes termination by virtue of a bond which, in the traditions of romance, demands he transgresses the rules he is supposed to enforce. Pris, a 'pleasure model', however, directly replays the threatening form of the uncanny as she hides among the automata in J. F. Sebastian's apartment and prepares to attack the blade runner sent to kill her. Her death, presented as a horrifying combination of slaughtered animal and short-circuited machine, is the prelude to the film's romantic climax in which pursuer is pursued and the distinction between human and replicant overturned. At this point the double becomes an idealised masculine image, a figure of rivalry, love and death, promising and erasing identity in full:

> The presence of this customized double will permit him, at least for a moment, to hold up his end of the human wager: in that moment, he, too, will be a man. But this customizing job is only a result, not the beginning: it is the consequence of the immanent presence of the phallus, which will be able to appear only with the disappearance of the subject himself. (Lacan, 1977c: 34)

| Sex, machines and navels

At the end of the film the customised double, Roy Batty, saves the blade runner from death and dies himself. Seconds before, he takes the opportunity of Deckard's fear to remind him what it feels like to be a slave, thereby indicating his own, replicated mastery. In the servility before death which equates humans and replicants, the slight difference guaranteeing humanity's exclusive value is erased. However, the customised, replicated double, the film constantly underlines, is a machine. On the brink of death the fate of humanity hangs in the grip of the machine-slaves who have thrown off all but the emotional shackles binding them to their masters: machines stand poised to achieve a mastery of their own. This is not, however, the Marxist revision of the dialectic in which the slave is subjugated to the mastery of the bourgeoisie only to discover, through the work and technology by which nature is overcome, the ability to take power. The dialectic breaks up: the tool used by the slave, in the form of the machine, overcomes human master and slave alike.

Going nodal

With the romance of the machine, the reversal of huMan priority is complete. Historically, like the machine-tool, woman existed only as symptom and supplement to masculine priority. As body or nature to masculine mind and spirit, woman constitutes man's other, but in her proximity to the machine she surpasses male mastery and the role of automaton or doll. If feminine *jouissance* is closer to God, it also displays greater proximity to the machine which subjects man. Like the dialectic of the master and slave, the uncanny, always associated with images, is implicated in a new relation of humans and machines. New doubles and new ghosts arise to signify an immanent absorption into fatal screens, doubles one loves as oneself. These figures, like the idoru, are possessed of the residual powers of the uncanny: on the basis of infantile narcissism man is drawn towards the place of maternal unity that he will never rediscover. In her form as an 'idol-singer', however, the idoru becomes a siren calling to man, seducing him into the screen of death, a ghost, a harbinger, the veiled signifier through which a fatal drive manifests its return. Romance turns on the figure of woman, a Thing without substance sustaining a masculine imaginary to the point of death, the point where the fantasy decomposes. Through the idoru the novel's romantic hero plunges to a joyous death, diving into the immanence, into the sea of dense, random, complex data. In her seductive appeal to male romantic fantasy, the idoru presents a feminine *jouissance* which, siren-like, draws male humanity, in its quest for God, towards death: '*jouissance* implies precisely the acceptance of death' (Lacan, 1992: 189). The idoru remains the perfect figure for the romance of the machine as it supplants male priority with the appearance of some Thing Other, erasing, in the process, all man's supports in fantasy and reality: 'what is the death instinct? What is this   law beyond all law, that can only be posited as a final structure, as a vanishing point of any reality that might be attained?' (Lacan, 1992: 21). Articulating the death drive which calls man home to a mama that never was, towards a *jouissance* in which the huMan figure and its symbolic reality is extinguished, digital reality overwrites the totality of existence with utterly new and infinitely complex chains of signification, chains without subjects. But *Idoru* closes with a dream of total immersion and extinction in a reality that will be wholly new. As dream, it retains a trace of the difference, the gap that leaves fantasy and desire virtually incomplete.

The Machine, despite contemporary fantasies of immano-transcendence or pure feminine *jouissance*, never merges Self and Other, never finally erases the difference that retrospectively traces something of identity. Instead the romance of the machine is determined by nodal relations: as it promises the obliteration of any difference between a and O, it hesitates on the point of a plunge through the navel. Being becomes nodal, the navel incorporated into the machine. Here, an Other space is disclosed. Perhaps it can be called the unconscious of the machine. The remainder of the real assumes a different form within the machine, inaugurating a transformation of conventional models of subjectivity from something essential, autonomous or transcendent to something nodal but not simply omphalic. In the machine of language subjectivity appears on various levels as 'relays', 'supports' or 'breaks' in the symbolic 'couplings' (Lacan, 1988b: 322). The subject, in contrast, remains no one, an empty space and locus of the 'headless subjectification' of the drive.

In the technobureaucratic culture which dominates Lyotard's account of postmodernity, a similarly nodal position is allotted to the operatives in the hyperrational machines which organise social, economic and political existence, not according to judgements of truth, beauty or morality, but with imperatives only to perform efficiently in the circulation and commodification of information. The computer is integral to this order of things, a determining figure instrumental to the process in which 'the true goal of the system, the reason why it programs itself like a computer, is the optimization of the global relationship between input and

Sex, machines and navels

output – in other words, performativity' (Lyotard, 1984a: 11). Cybernetic models dominate the reinscription of social reality according to the imperatives of a game theory which eschews all appeals to rules other than efficiency. Technological performance becomes the only criterion: 'a technical "move" is "good" when it does better and/or expends less energy than another' (Lyotard, 1984a: 44). It operates, moreover, according to a relentless 'self-legitimating' logic since it rewrites the 'reality' on which juridical, ethical and political judgements base themselves: 'by reinforcing technology, one "reinforces" reality, and one's chances of being just and right increase accordingly' (Lyotard, 1984a: 47). There is, then, no external position for judgement, no superior place from which a human subject can deliver authoritative judgements. The ideal of a fully human and valued being disappears in the entangled meshwork of this techno-bureaucratic order: 'a *self* does not amount to much, but no self is an island; each exists in a fabric of relations that is now more complex and mobile than ever before. Young or old, man or woman, rich or poor, a person is always located at 'nodal points' of specific communication circuits, however tiny these may be' (Lyotard, 1984a: 15). Within the immense network of communicational games nodal subjects serve as points of relay in the process of efficient transmission and exchange. In a limited way, they function as points of resistance and as such, no one 'is ever entirely powerless'. For the system, moreover, these points of interruption retain the potential of injecting new and unexpected moves into the game, causing displacements within exchange clusters and thus enhancing the overall performance.

In Deleuze and Guattari's anti-oedipal formulation of machinic desiring, the schizoid flux overrides the despotic law of lack, desire, castration and signifier: desiring 'exists in the thousands of productive break-flows that never allow themselves to be signified within the unary stroke of castration. It is always a point-sign of many dimensions, poly-vocity as the basis for punctual semiology' (Deleuze and Guattari, 1983: 112). The puncta of machinic flows form constellations of 'nonsignifying signs, points-signs having several dimensions, flows-breaks or schizzes that form images through their coming-together in a whole, but that do not maintain any identity when they pass from one whole identity to another'. Though figures, these constellations, Deleuze and Guattari insist, are not 'figurative'; they dissolve in order to be replaced. Similar to Michel Serres' account of the topological knots of informational networks or the 'figure-matrix' of desire proposed by Lyotard (1983), break-flows are far less susceptible to the checks of signifying structures (Deleuze and Guattari, 1983: 241–4). Speed, however, serves as the sole guarantee of these elusive figures of break-flow against the tyranny of the (paternal) signifier: the rapidity of desiring takes its force from this difference alone, a difference retained in the figure of figure itself as a punctual and thereby differential relation. With the technological realisation of the desiring engendered by current models of the matrix, punctal formations remain integral to the speed and flows of exchange as well as the constitution, displacement and transformation of nodal subjects.

Speeds of movement engender a sense of ungraspable flux and an immanent immersion in subjectless desiring unencumbered by corporeal traces of the oedipal signifier. The very acceleration of machinic flows nonetheless depends on breaks, on the trace of a difference which enables their flight. In a discussion of vision machines, Virilio underlines the continued importance of the punctum as a 'figurative abstraction' which remains despite the loss of physical dimension accompanying the disappearance of corporeality: 'we must be ready to lose our morphological illusions about physical dimensions; except for the point, the *punctum*, that figurative abstraction more resistant than the atom and, as always, absolutely necessary for different conceptions of the world' (Virilio, 1991a: 48). The punctum Virilio identifies exists, as yet in a latent manner, at the outer reaches of the networks and fluxes where a 'tele-topology of form-images' distorts vector-velocities of transmission and transportation (Virilio, 1991a: 60). The 'the punctum of electronic action is virtually or practically instantaneous' within a matrix of 'form-images composed of points without dimension and instants without duration, digitally controlled by the algorithms of an encoded language' (1991a: 104). The punctum, moreover, cannot be reduced to a thing, an object: it remains incorporeal unlike the 'mental objects' by which scientific materialism 'falls into its own trap', being 'forced to accord density to that which visibly has none: figures of the imaginary and virtualities of consciousness'. Like the imaginary object, the punctum is not reducible to the logic of spatial dimensions which turn it into 'an object entire unto itself as the *imago* becomes an objective image' (Virilio, 1991a: 112–13). The form-image is not a geometrical formation, but a matter 'of modes of appearance and disappearance in the context of light' and according to the speed of light (Virilio, 1991a: 115).

The nodal replaces the idea of centrality in every aspect of physical and theoretical existence, assuming the form of 'an internal extraterritorial

Sex, machines and navels

entity' (Virilio, 1991a: 120). As 'prime matter' light exhibits a function akin to the punctum of the photograph for Barthes in that light forms the 'umbilical' link between image and subject (Virilio, 1991a: 60). The difference is that light-speed eliminates the duration through which the subject finds being attached to time. The nodal relation, however, posits a technological navel, as it were, as the basis for the connection to the matrix, a relation binding and displacing the subject within the vector-velocities of an immense, incorporeal matrix whose spatial density is solely imaginary, founded on nothing in the absence of dimension:

> the point is a point of reference of geometric projectivity only to the extent that it is a gap or lack, an absence of dimension, a black hole. As an obscurity, the point is as necessary to the revelation of physical appearances as the darkroom is to the objective appearances in photography and of the cinematographic photogram. The same could be said for film pigments, and the pixels of telematic images. Thus, the point is that lost dimension that allows us to recuperate ourselves: that bug, that microprocessor of our mathematical and esthetic representation and our temporal and spatial configurations. (Virilio, 1991a: 103–4)

As in quantum physics, where the void exerts structural effects on the field of force, the dimensional absence of the punctal gap establishes the locus connecting and separating the light-field of form-images. It is a navel which spreads out in a complex meshwork or matrix, the point in place of an unplumbable and constitutive black hole.

In William Gibson's *Idoru* a nodal arrangement of social and digital reality comes to the fore. The nodality of existence in the matrix is not simply a mark of the restriction of subjects to small clusters or constellations within an unthinkably complex system. The nodal form opens up any idea of a closed structure to suggest another, perhaps ungraspable dimension, a matrix within and beyond the matrix. For Laney clusters of data imply more than traces of individual passage in the matrix. They suggest this Other dimension: 'perhaps the whole of DatAmerica possessed its own nodal points, info-faults that might be followed down to some kind of truth, another mode of knowing, deep within grey shoals of information' (Gibson, 1996: 39). 'Slitscan', too, 'might be one of those larger nodal points', 'an informational peculiarity opening into some unthinkably deeper structure' (1996: 40). Nodal points, as 'info-faults' or 'peculiarities' manifest an oddness, a difference distinguishing them from the homogeneity of the system. Something Other is imaginable only by way of faults and gaps, or black holes like the eyes of the idoru. The romance of Rez and the idoru, two powerfully nodal figures, discloses, not so much an absolute union, but the gaps and fissures that constitute the matrix in relation to something Other. Through the eyes of the idoru, one encounters the abyssal flux of her videos: 'they emerge directly from her ongoing experience of the world. They are her dreams, if you will' (1996: 237). If the dreamwork does not think, a thinking machine still dreams. And with dreams, an Other space is disclosed.

While their union is to be realised quite literally through the intervention of nanotechnology and upon solid ground, it occurs first in a specific hole in the fabric of the matrix, a strange fold, a non-dimension within a non-space. It has a name, 'Hak Nam', or the 'Walled City', and it exists apart from the matrix with its own customs and users, 'of the net, but not on it'. Its beginnings were 'interstitial', emerging from a fault in the net itself. In Hak Nam there are no laws, 'only agreements' (1996: 209). It is a community associated with an anarcho-liberal counterculture angered by the encroachment of governments and corporations upon a net that was once free: 'so these people, they found a way to unravel something. A little place, a piece like cloth. They made something like a killfile of *everything*, everything they didn't like, and turned that inside out … And they pushed it through, to the other side'. Breaking on through to the other side they 'made a hole in the net' (1996: 221–2). Through the gaps of the now-corporate net, the new counternet is formed by turning the matrix inside out. While the space of countercultural freedoms is romanticised according to patterns of a liberational fantasy of existing beyond law, a romanticism exacerbated by the presence of Rez and Rei, its emergence from nothing and in nowhere underlines the role of black holes gaps in any order of things.

Against the encroachment of corporate culture, the counternet emerges in the process of tearing it apart, and restitching it. Gaps and holes, however, come to fore. Through these gaps, as in dreams, the discourse of the Other speaks 'at the level at which everything that blossoms in the unconscious spreads, like a mycelium, as Freud says about the dream, around a central point. It is always a question of the subject *qua* indeterminate.' The navel, a scar that traces a tear in being, marks the connections to and separations from something Other, the unconscious. In the form of rupture or split, 'the stroke of the opening makes absence emerge', constituting an indeterminate subjectivity (Lacan, 1977b: 26). And if the unconscious exists as a kind of counternet, a knotted, moebial plane

Sex, machines and navels

around a hole, its existence is preserved by the very navel marking its absence. And *Idoru*, although it resounds with the speech of this counternet, never crosses the gap: the romance of Rez and Rei is not realised but remains on the brink of filling out this space with new form and substance. That romance will be realised by way of the machine, is witnessed only in a young girl's dream: 'A thing of random human accretion, monstrous and superb, it is being reconstituted here, retranslated from its later incarnation as a realm of consensual fantasy' (Gibson, 1996: 289). 'Retranslated', the dream conjures up a spectre of original substance, a reality prior to the consensual fantasy of *Neuromancer*'s matrix. Sublime, incomprehensible, the monstrous, random accretion glimpsed in the dream promises to realise a hitherto unimaginable entity, digitally human and beyond the human at the same time.

Unlike *Neuromancer*, which ends with the transcendent synthesis of two AIs becoming the God-matrix of informational existence, humans in *Idoru* are not left as redundant spectators: the union in and as machine witnesses an apocalyptic marriage of heaven and hell that is yet to come, *jouissance* postponed, but not, perhaps, for long. The Other space appearing beyond the nodes of digital existence preserves the fantasy as fantasy, retaining the trace of a nodal difference. The speed of the technological romance, however, with its awesome capacity to realise itself leaves the matter of fantasy and the question of the navel virtually intact. But the precipitous plunge into the unknown, a fantasy in excess of fantasy, also hesitates, a brief pause in the accelerating drive for machinic (non)existence. A dream? A fantasy? Or an imminently realisable fantasy? The joy, the horror …

Bibliography

Alphen, E. van (1994), 'The performativity of histories: Graham Swift's *Waterland* as a theory of history', in Bal, M. and Boer, I. (eds), *The Point of Theory*, Amsterdam, Amsterdam University Press, pp. 202–10.

Althusser, L. (1984), *Essays in Ideology*, London, Verso.

Appignanesi, L. and Forrester, J. (1993), *Freud's Women*, London, Virago.

Arnold, M. (1905), *Culture and Anarchy: An Essay in Political and Social Criticism*, London, Smith and Elder.

Bal, M. (1991), *Reading 'Rembrandt': Beyond the Word–Image Opposition*, Cambridge, Cambridge University Press.

Balsamo, A. (1995), 'Forms of technological embodiment: reading the body in contemporary culture', in Featherstone, M. and Burrows, R. (eds), *Cyberspace/Cyberbodies/Cyberpunk: Cultures of Technological Embodiment*, London, Sage, pp. 215–37.

Balsamo, A. (1993), 'Feminism for the incurably informed', *South Atlantic Quarterly*, 92: 4, 681–712.

Barnes, J. (1990), *A History of the World in 10½ Chapters*, London, Picador.

Barthes, R. (1977), *Image Music Text*, Heath, S. (tr.), London, Fontana.

Barthes, R. (1984), *Camera Lucida*, Howard, R. (tr.), London, Fontana.

Bataille, G. (1988), *Guilty*, Boone, B. (tr.), San Francisco, The Lapis Press.

Bataille, G. (1991), *The Accursed Share*, vols 2 and 3, Hurley, R. (tr.), New York, Zone Books.

Bataille, G. (1997), 'Base materialism and Gnosticism', in Botting, F. and Wilson, S. (eds), *The Bataille Reader*, Oxford, Blackwell, pp. 160–64.

Bataille, L. (1987), *L'Ombilic du rêve*, Paris, Éditions du Seuil.

Baudrillard, J. (1983), *Simulations*, New York, Semiotext(e).

Baudrillard, J. (1987), *The Evil Demon of Images*, Patton, P. and Foss, P. (trs), Sydney, Power Publications.

Baudrillard, J. (1988), *America*, Turner, C. (tr.), London, Verso.

Baudrillard, J. (1990a), *Fatal Strategies*, Beitchman, P. and Niesluchowski, W. G. J. (trs), London, Pluto Press.

Baudrillard, J. (1990b), *Seduction*, Basingstoke and London, Macmillan.

Baudrillard, J. (1993), *The Transparency of Evil*, Benedict, J. (tr.), London, Verso.

Baudrillard, J. (1996), *The Perfect Crime*, Turner, C. (tr.), London, Verso.

Benjamin, W. (1973), *Illuminations*, Zohn, H. (tr.), London, Fontana.

Borges, J. L. (1973), 'The Creation and P.H. Gosse', in *Other Inquisitions 1937–1952*, Simms, R. L. C. (tr.), London, Souvenir Press, pp. 22–5.

Bowie, M. (1993), *Psychoanalysis and the Future of Theory*, Oxford, Blackwell.

Brande, D. (1996), 'The business of cyberpunk: symbolic economy and ideology in William Gibson', in Markley, R. (ed.), *Virtual Realities and Their Discontents*, Baltimore and London, Johns Hopkins University Press, pp. 79–106.

Brennan, T. (1993), *History After Lacan*, London and New York, Routledge.

Bronfen, E. (1992), *Over Her Dead Body*, Manchester, Manchester University Press.

Bronfen, E. (1994), 'Death: the navel of the image', Bal, M. and Boer, I. (eds), *The Point of Theory*, Amsterdam, Amsterdam University Press, pp. 79–90.

Browne, Sir T. (1964), *The Works of Sir Thomas Browne*, 3 vols, Keynes, G. (ed.), London, Faber and Faber.

Bukatman, S. (1991), 'Postcards from the posthuman solar system', *Science Fiction Studies*, 55, 343–57.

Bukatman, S. (1993), 'Gibson's typewriter', *South Atlantic Quarterly*, 92: 4, 627–45.

Carter, A. (1982), *The Infernal Desire Machines of Dr Hoffman*, London, Penguin.

Chapman, G. (1993), 'Taming the computer', *South Atlantic Quarterly*, 92: 4, 827–49.

Cixous, H. (1976), 'Fiction and its phantoms: a reading of Freud's *Das Unheimliche* (The "uncanny")', *New Literary History*, 7, 525–48.

Copjec, J. (1994), *Read My Desire: Lacan Against the Historicists*, Cambridge, Mass., and London, MIT Press.

Csicsery-Ronay, I. Jr (1991), 'Cyberpunk and neuromanticism', in McCaffrey, L. (ed.), *Storming the Reality Studio*, Durham and London, Duke University Press, pp. 182–93.

Davis, E. (1993), 'Techgnosis, magic and memory, and the angels of information', *South Atlantic Quarterly*, 92: 4, 585–616.

Deleuze, G. (1990), *Logic of Sense*, Lester, M. (tr.), London, Athlone.

Deleuze, G. and Guattari, F. (1983), *Anti-Oedipus: Capitalism and Schizophrenia*, Hurley, R., Seem, M. and Lane, H. R. (trs), Minneapolis, University of Minnesota Press.

Derrida, J. (1976), *Of Grammatology*, Spivak, G. C. (tr.), Baltimore and London, Johns Hopkins University Press.

Derrida, J. (1978), 'Structure, sign and play in the discourse of the human sciences', in *Writing and Difference*, Bass, A. (tr.), London and Henley, Routledge and Kegan Paul, pp. 278–93.

Derrida, J. (1982), 'Ousia and gramme: note on a note from *Being and Time*', in *Margins of Philosophy*, Bass. A. (tr.), New York and London, Harvester Press, pp. 29–67.

Derrida, J. (1984), 'No apocalypse, not now', *Diacritics*, 14, 20–31.

Derrida, J. (1985), *The Ear of the Other: Otobiography, Transference, Translation*, Kamuf, P. (tr.), Lincoln and London, University of Nebraska Press.

Derrida, J. (1987), *The Post Card: From Socrates to Freud and Beyond*, Bass, A. (tr.), Chicago and London, University of Chicago Press.

Dolar, M. (1994), 'La Femme-machine', *New Formations*, 23, 43–54.

Eagleton, T. (1990), *The Ideology of the Aesthetic*, Oxford, Blackwell.

Bibliography |

Ehrmann, J. (1971), 'The death of literature', *New Literary History*, 3, 31–47.

Felman, S. (1985), 'Postal survival, or the question of the navel', *Yale French Studies*, 69, 49–72.

Felman, S. (1987), *Jacques Lacan and the Adventure of Insight*, Cambridge, Mass., and London, Harvard University Press.

Felman, S. (1993), *What Does a Woman Want?: Reading and Sexual Difference*, Baltimore and London, Johns Hopkins University Press.

Fiske, J. (1989), *Reading the Popular*, London and New York, Routledge.

Foucault, M. (1970), *The Order of Things*, London, Tavistock.

Foucault, M. (1979), *Discipline and Punish: The Birth of the Prison*, Sheridan, A. (tr.), Harmondsworth, Penguin.

Foucault, M. (1981), *The History of Sexuality: Vol. I An Introduction*, Hurley, R. (tr.), Harmondsworth, Penguin.

Foucault, M. (1987), *The Use of Pleasure*, Hurley, R. (tr.), London, Penguin.

Foucault, Michel, (1988), 'The concern for truth', in *Michel Foucault: Politics, Philosophy, Culture*, Kritzman, L. D. (ed.), London, Routledge, pp. 255–67.

Foucault, M. and Deleuze, G. (1977), 'Intellectuals and power', *Language, Counter-Memory, Practice*, Bouchard, D. F. and Simon, S. (trs), Ithaca, New York, Cornell University Press, pp. 205–17.

Freud, S. (1955), 'The "uncanny"', *The Standard Edition of the Complete Psychological Works*, vol. 17, Strachey, J. (tr.), London, Hogarth, Press, pp. 218–52.

Freud, S. (1976a), *The Interpretation of Dreams*, Strachey, J. (tr.), Harmondsworth, Penguin.

Freud, S. (1976b), *Jokes and their Relation to the Unconscious*, Strachey, J. (tr.), London, Penguin.

Fukuyama, F. (1992), *The End of History and the Last Man*, London, Penguin.

Gallop, J. (1985), *Reading Lacan*, Ithaca and London, Cornell University Press.

Gallop, J. (1992), *Around 1981: Academic Feminist Literary Theory*, New York and London, Routledge.

Gibson, W. (1984), *Neuromancer*, London, HarperCollins.

Gibson, W. (1996), *Idoru*, London, Penguin.

Gibson, W. and Sterling, B. (1991), *The Difference Engine*, London, VGSF.

Gosse, P. H. (1857), *Omphalos: An Attempt to Untie the Geological Knot*, London, John Van Voorst.

Gould, S. J. (1995), *Adam's Navel and Other Essays*, London, Penguin.

Goux, J.-J. (1990a), *Symbolic Economies: After Marx and Freud*, Gage, J. C. (tr.), Ithaca and London, Cornell University Press.

Goux, J.-J. (1990b), 'General economics and postmodern capitalism', *Yale French Studies*, 78, 206–24.

Gray, C. H. (1994), '"There Will Be War!": future war fantasies and militaristic science fiction in the 1980s', *Science Fiction Studies*, 21: 3, 315–36.

Gray, C.H. and Mentor S. (1995), 'The cyborg body politic: version 1.2', in Gray, C. H. (ed.), *The Cyborg Handbook*, London, Routledge, pp. 453–67.

Haraway, D. (1990), 'A manifesto for cyborgs: science, technology and socialist feminism in the 1980s', in Nicholson, L. J. (ed.), *Feminism/Postmodernism*, New York and London, Routledge, pp. 190–233.

Huston, N. (1995), 'Novels and navels', *Critical Inquiry*, 21, 708–21.

Hutcheon, L. (1986–87), 'The politics of postmodernism: parody and history', *Cultural Critique*, 5, 179–207.

Hutcheon, L. (1994), 'The post always rings twice: the postmodern and the postcolonial', *Textual Practice*, 8, 205–38.

Huyssen, A. (1981–82), 'The vamp and the machine: technology and sexuality in Fritz Lang's *Metropolis*', *New German Critique*, 24/25, 221–37.

Jameson, F. (1984), 'Postmodernism, or, the cultural logic of late capitalism', *New Left Review*, 146, 53–92.

Jardine, A. (1985), *Gynesis*, Ithaca and London, Cornell University Press.

Kuhn, A. (ed.) (1990), *Alien Zone: Cultural Theory and Contemporary Science Fiction Cinema*, London and New York, Verso.

Lacan, J. (1953), 'Some reflections on the ego', *International Journal of Psycho-Analysis*, 34, 11–17.

Lacan, J. (1975), *Encore*, Paris, Éditions du Seuil.

Lacan, J. (1977a), *Écrits*, Sheridan, A. (tr.), London, Tavistock.

Lacan, J. (1977b), *The Four Fundamental Concepts of Psychoanalysis*, Sheridan, A. (tr.), Harmondsworth, Penguin.

Lacan, J. (1977c), 'Desire and the interpretation of desire in *Hamlet*', *Yale French Studies*, 55/56, 11–52.

Lacan, J. (1982), *Feminine Sexuality: Jacques Lacan and the école freudienne*', Mitchell, J. and Rose, J. (eds), Basingstoke and London, Macmillan.

Lacan, J. (1988a), *The Seminar of Jacques Lacan Book I: Freud's Papers on Technique 1953–1954*, Forrester, J. (tr.), Cambridge, Cambridge University Press.

Lacan, J. (1988b), *The Seminar of Jacques Lacan Book II: The Ego in Freud's Theory and in the Technique of Psychoanalysis 1954–1955*, Tomaselli, S. (tr.), Cambridge, Cambridge University Press.

Lacan, J. (1992), *The Ethics of Psychoanalysis 1959–60*, Porter, D. (tr.), London, Routledge.

Lacan, J. (1993), *The Psychoses: The Seminar of Jacques Lacan Book III 1955–56*, Grigg, R. (tr.), London: Routledge.

Lajoie, M. (1996), 'Psychoanalysis and cyberspace', in Shields, R. (ed.), *Cultures of the Internet. Virtual Spaces, Real Histories, Living Bodies*, London, Sage, pp. 153–69.

Land, N. (1993a), 'Circuitries', *PLI: The Warwick journal of philosophy*, 217–35.

Land, N. (1993b), 'Machinic desire', *Textual Practice*, 7:3, 471–82.

Landsberg, A. (1995), 'Prosthetic memory: *Total Recall* and *Blade Runner*', in Featherstone, M. and Burrows, R. (eds), *Cyberspace/Cyberbodies/Cyberpunk: Cultures of Technological Embodiment*, London, Sage, pp. 175–89.

Laplanche, J. and Pontalis, J.-B. (1986), 'Fantasy and the origins of sexuality', in Burgin, V., Donald, J. and Kaplan C. (eds), *Formations of Fantasy*, London, Methuen, pp. 5–28.

Lauretis, T. de (1987), *Technologies of Gender: Essays on Theory, Film, and Fiction*, Basingstoke and London, Macmillan.

Lichtenberg-Ettinger, B. (1992), 'Matrix and metamorphoses', *differences*, 4:3, 176–208.

Lichtenberg-Ettinger, B., (1994), 'The becoming threshold of matrixial borderlines', in Robertson, G. *et al.* (eds), *Travellers' Tales: Narratives of Home and Displacement*, London and New York, Routledge, pp. 38–62.

Lyotard, J.-F, (1983), 'Fiscourse digure: the utopia behind the scenes of the phantasy', *Theatre Journal*, October, 333–57.

Lyotard, J.-F. (1984a), *The Postmodern Condition*, Bennington, G. and Massumi, B. (trs), Manchester, Manchester University Press.

Lyotard, J.-F. (1984b), *Tombeau de l'intellectual et autres papiers*, Paris, Galilée.

Lyotard, J.-F. (1988), *The Differend*, Van den Abeele, G. (tr.), Manchester, Manchester University Press.

McCaffrey, L. (1991), 'An interview with William Gibson', in McCaffrey, L. (ed.), *Storming the Reality Studio*, Durham and London, Duke University Press, pp. 263–85.

McCarron, K. (1995), 'Corpses, animals, machines and mannequins: the body in cyberpunk', in Featherstone, M. and Burrows, R. (eds), *Cyberspace/Cyberbodies/Cyberpunk: Cultures of Technological Embodiment*, London, Sage, pp. 261–73.

McGrath, P. (1989), 'The Angel', in *The Angel and Other Stories*, London, Penguin, pp. 1–18.

Markley, R. (1996), 'Boundaries: mathematics, alienation and the metaphysics of cyberspace', in Markley, R. (ed.), *Virtual Realities and Their Discontents*, Baltimore and London, Johns Hopkins University Press, pp. 55–77.

Mehlman, J. (1975), 'How to read Freud on jokes: the critic as *Schadchen*', *New Literary History*, 6: 2, 439–61.

Mehlman, J. (1981), 'TRIMETHYLAMIN: notes on Freud's specimen dream', in Young, R. (ed.), *Untying the Text*, Boston, London and Henley, Routledge and Kegan Paul, pp. 177–88.

Melville, H. (1994), *Moby Dick*, London, Penguin.

Miller, J.-A. (1988), 'Extimité', *Prose Studies*, 11: 3, 121–31.

Nichols, B. (1988), 'The work of culture in the age of cybernetic systems', *Screen*, 29: 1, 22–46.

Olsen, L. (1991), 'The shadow of the spirit in William Gibson's matrix trilogy', *Extrapolation*, 32, 278–89.

Plant, S. (1995), 'The future looms: weaving women and cybernetics', in Featherstone, M. and Burrows, R. (eds), *Cyberspace/Cyberbodies/Cyberpunk: Cultures of Technological Embodiment*, London, Sage, pp. 45–64.

Plant, S. (1996), 'On the matrix: cyberfeminist simulations', in Shields, R. (ed.), *Cultures of the Internet. Virtual Spaces, Real Histories, Living Bodies*, London: Sage, pp. 170–183.

Platt, C. (1995), 'Superhumanism: interview with Hans Moravec', *Wired*, 1.06, 62–67.

Penley, C. (1986), 'Time travel, primal scene, and the critical dystopia', *Camera Obscura*, 15, 67–84.

Pynchon, T. (1975), *V*, London, Pan.

Ragland, E. (1995), *Essays on the Pleasures of Death*, New York and London, Routledge.

Ragland-Sullivan, E. (1988), 'The limits of discourse structure: the hysteric and the analyst', *Prose Studies*, 11: 3, 61–83.

Ragland-Sullivan, E. (1989), 'Dora and the Name-of-the-Father: the structure of hysteria', in Barr, M. S. and Feldstein, R. (eds), *Discontented Discourses: Feminism/Textual Intervention/Psychoanalysis*, Urbana and Chicago, University of Illinois Press, pp. 208–40.

Rosenthal, P. (1991), 'Jacked in: fordism, cyberpunk, Marxism', *Socialist Review*, Spring, 79–103.

Roudinesco, E. (1990), *Jacques Lacan & Co.*, Mehlman, J. (tr.), London, Free Association Books.

Rougemont, D. de (1993), *Love in the Western World*, Belgion, M. (tr.), Princeton, Princeton University Press.

Rucker, R. (1994), *Wetware*, in *Live Robots*, New York, Avon Books, pp. 169–357.

Rushkoff, D. (1994), *Cyberia: Life in the Trenches of Cyberspace*, London, HarperCollins.

Samuels, R. (1993), *Between Philosophy and Psychoanalysis: Lacan's Reconstruction of Freud*, New York and London, Routledge.

Sartillot, C.(1993), *Herbarium Variorum: The Discourse of Flowers*, Lincoln and London, University of Nebraska Press.

Schad, J. (1992), 'The end of the end of history: Graham Swift's *Waterland*', *Modern Fiction Studies*, 38: 4, 911–25.

SHaH, (1997), 'Incorporating the impossible: a general economy of the future present', *Cultural Values*, 1:2, 178–204.

Seltzer, M. (1992), *Bodies and Machines*, New York and London, Routledge.

Serres, M. (1993), *Angels: A Modern Myth*, Cowper, F. (tr.), Paris, Flammarion.

Sophia, Z. (1992), 'Virtual corporeality: a feminist view', *Australian Feminist Studies*, 15, 11–24.

Springer, C. (1991), 'The pleasure of the interface', *Screen*, 32:2, 303–23.

Springer, C. (1993), 'Sex, memories, and angry women', *South Atlantic Quarterly*, 92: 4, 713–33.

Stone, A. R. (1992), 'Virtual Systems', in Crary, J. and Kwinter, S. (eds), *Incorporations*, New York, Zone Books, pp. 609–21.

Swift, G. (1984), *Waterland*, London, Pan.

Virilio, P. (1991a), *Lost Dimension*, Moshenberg, D. (tr.), New York, Semiotext(e).

Virilio, P. (1991b), *The Aesthetics of Disappearance*, Beitchman, P. (tr.), New York Semiotext(e).

Virilio, P. (1994), *The Vision Machine*, Rose, J. (tr.), Bloomington, Indiana University Press.

Virilio, P. (1995a), *The Art of the Motor*, Rose, J. (tr.), Minneapolis, University of Minnesota Press.

Virilio, P. (1995b), 'Speed and information: cyberspace alarm!', *CTHEORY*, http://www.aec.at/ctheory/a30-cyberspace_alarm.html.

Voller, J. (1993), 'Neuromanticism: cyberspace and the sublime', *Extrapolation*, 34: 1, 18–29.

Wiener, N. (1954), *The Human Use of Human Beings: Cybernetics and Society*, London, Eyre and Spottiswoode.

Wilson, L. (1994), 'Cyberwar, God and television. Interview with Paul Virilio', *CTHEORY*, http://www.aec.at/ctheory/a-cyberwar_god.html.

Wilson, S. (1995), *Cultural Materialism*, Oxford, Blackwell.

Young, R. (1984), 'Psychoanalytic criticism: has it got beyond a joke?', *Paragraph*, 4, 87–114.

Žižek, S. (1989), *The Sublime Object of Ideology*, London and New York, Verso.

Žižek, S. (1991a), *For They Know Not What They Do*, London and New York, Verso.

Žižek, S. (1991b), *Looking Awry*, Cambridge, Mass., and London, MIT Press.

Žižek, S. (1992), *Enjoy Your Symptom*, London and New York, Routledge.

Žižek, S. (1993), *Tarrying with the Negative*, Durham, Duke University Press.

Žižek, S. (1994), *The Metastases of Enjoyment*, New York and London, Verso.

Žižek, S. (1996), *The Indivisible Remainder*, New York and London, Verso.

✧ Index

Note: 'n' after a page reference indicates a note on that page.

2001 169
Adam 3–4, 104
Alien 169
Alpen, E. van 140n.1
Althusser, L. 94, 167
Apollo 4, 34, 190
Appignanesi, L. and Forrester, J. 61n.1
Arnold, M. 141
Asimov, I.
  law of robotics 142
Attenborough, D. 75

Babbage, C. 141
  and Lovelace, A. 208n.1
Bal, M. 6, 174
Balsamo, A. 13, 18n.1
Barlow, J. 168, 174
Barnes, J. 71, 73–80
Barthes, R. 121, 148–9, 175, 226
  Camera Lucida 191–4
Bataille, G. 140, 177
Bataille, L. 18n.5
Baudrillard, J. 4, 9, 72–3, 82–3, 87–9,
    93, 144, 151, 196–7
Benjamin, W. 97, 130
Blade Runner 9, 150–1, 162, 186–91,
    208, 218, 222–3
body 13–14, 141–209

Booth, W. 72
Borges, J-L. 4
Bowie, M. 60
Brande, D. 208n.3
Brennan, T. 140n.2
Bronfen, E. 4, 6, 34, 190
Browne, (Sir) T. 3–4, 18n.3
Bukatman, S. 12, 166
Burroughs, W. 195
Butler, J. 15

Cadigan, P. 18n.1
capitalism 93–5, 127–8, 144, 151, 165,
    167, 208n.3
Carter, A. 165–6
Chapman, G. 209n.6
Cixous, H. 220
Clancy, T. 12
cloning 2, 197
Conrad, J.
  Heart of Darkness 75
Copjec, J. 15, 121, 128–9
Crane, S. 18n.4
creationism 4, 108, 112–14, 130, 140
Csicsery-Ronay, I. 12, 208n.3, 209n.6
cybernetics 16, 145, 151, 198–9, 206,
    225
cyberpunk 8–9, 17, 146

cyberspace 8, 167, 170–2, 204
    see also matrix
cyborg 1, 144, 146, 158, 172, 174, 178

Darwin, C. 4, 74, 105
Davis, E. 208n.3
de Man, P. 32–4
Deleuze, G. 91, 95, 96n.2,
Deleuze, G. and Guattari, F. 225–6
Derrida, J. 6, 11, 99, 125, 174–7
Descartes, R. 61, 169
Dolar, M. 221
Dolly 2

Eagleton, T. 87, 90–4
Ehrmann, J. 212
evolution 4, 107–8, 141, 156, 160, 164

Felman S. 13, 21, 31–4, 47, 64
Fiske J. 10
Foucault M. 14, 91, 95, 98–9
Freud, S. 15, 61, 99, 116, 170, 228
    Beyond the Pleasure Principle 48, 138
    Interpretation of Dreams 6, 16, 19–
        31, 35
    Jokes and their Relation to the
        Unconscious 64–6
    Oedipus 103, 114–15, 185
    Thanatos 146, 181
    Totem and Taboo 47, 150
    'The Uncanny' 220–3
Fukuyama F. 127–8, 132–3
future present 11–12, 147

Gaia 4, 34, 190
Gallop, J. 47
Gibson, W. 12, 204
    Idoru 9, 211–18, 223–4, 226–9
    Neuromancer 166–8, 179–85,
        208n.3, 218, 229
Gibson, W. and Sterling B.
    The Difference Engine 141

God 155–7, 160–2, 178
Gosse, P. H. 4, 105–8, 128, 142
Gould, S. J. 4, 105–7, 128
Goux, J-J. 116–7, 128–9, 178–9, 184
Gray, C. H. 12
Gray, C. H. and Mentor, S. 146
Grossman D. 4–5

Habermas, J. 87
Haldeman, J. 12
Haraway, D. 147, 172, 174, 178
Hegel, G. W. F. 61, 116, 140, 142–3,
        145, 180
Hirsch, M. 172
history 17, 82, 97–140, 141–53, 178,
        192–3, 196
    end of 127, 129, 146
    Natural History 104–8
Hoffman, E. T. A. 220
Huston, N. 4–5
Hutcheon, L. 71–3
Huyssen, A. 221

Internet 207–8
Irigaray, L. 173
irony 71–3, 79

Jacobson, R. 56
Jameson, F. 82, 87, 93–6, 147, 208n.3
Jardine, A. 83

Kant, I. 61, 145
Kerouac, J. 154
Kojeve, A. 127, 143
Kuhn, A. 150

Lacan, J. 6, 13–14, 35–61, 94, 99, 103,
        107, 117, 134, 137, 185, 219–20
    death drive 48, 130, 138–40, 181–
        6, 224
    desire 48–9, 84, 115–16
    ego 40–4

ethics 14–15, 118, 139, 184
fantasy 84, 157–8, 186, 204, 216–18, 222, 224
four discourses 136, 138
gaze 20
hysteria 123–8, 130
imaginary 40–3, 50–4, 57, 85, 190, 203
jokes, 57, 62–3, 66–8
jouissance 54–5, 116–18, 158, 161, 170, 173, 204, 210, 223–4
love 154–7
machines 199–202, 206–7
metonymy 48, 57, 98
mourning 74, 83, 85–7
Name-of-the-Father *see below* paternal metaphor
objet petit a 20, 34, 38, 49–54, 58, 74, 84, 186, 201, 203–4, 207, 224
Other 42, 44–6, 49–50, 59, 62–3, 186
paternal metaphor 38, 55–6, 60, 67–8, 75, 85–96, 113–15, 205
phallus *see above* paternal metaphor
pleasure principle 115
psychosis 59, 74, 79, 83, 85–9, 204–6
Prisoner's Dilemma 205–6
quilting point 56
real 35–7, 50–3, 55, 74, 83–5, 88–9, 96, 109, 132, 139, 203
return to Freud 16, 21, 45–8
signifier 55–8
subject 48, 50–4, 140
symbolic 37–45, 50–4, 85, 130, 181–2, 199–202, 204–6
symptom 51
Thing (*das Ding*) 20, 48 53–4, 69, 111–15, 118, 130, 139, 163, 210
transference 50, 136
unconscious 42, 45, 51–2, 69, 228

Lajoie, M. 170, 203
Land, N. 145–6, 165, 172, 181, 186
Landsberg, A. 148
Lang, F.
   Metropolis 221
Lauretis T. de 14
Levi-Strauss C. 125
liberal democracy 128–9
Lichtenberg-Ettinger B. 170–1
Lyell, C. 4
Lyotard, J-F. 14, 62–3, 95, 96n.4, 127, 133, 224–5

McGrath P. 7–8
Madonna 10
Mandel, E. 95
Markley, R. 209n.4
Marx, K. 61
marxism 95, 116
materialism 178–9
matrix 54, 61, 141–209
McCaffrey, L. 12
McCarron, K. 209n.4
McKenna, T. 168, 174
Mehlman, J. 30–1, 96n.1
Melville, H.
   Moby Dick 5–6
Miller, J-A. 49, 163
Moravec, H. 141–3, 146
   Mind Children 208n.2
Morrison, T. 4–5

Nichols, B. 143–4, 147, 203
Nietzsche, F. 6, 175–6, 198

Olsen, L. 209n.5

Penley, C. 149
photography 6, 148, 189–96
Plant, S. 147, 172–3, 177–8, 208n.1
Poe, E. A. 154
postmodernism 12, 17, 62–96, 194

Pynchon, T.
  V 18n.4, 80–2

Quayle, D. 12

Ragland, E. 96n.2
Ragland-Sullivan, E. 123–4, 128, 136
Reagan, R. 128
Rembrandt 6
revolution 130–9
romance 210–29
Rosenthal, P. 12
Roudinesco, E. 46
Rougemont, D. de 210, 218
Rousseau, J-J. 177
Rucker, R.
  Software 160
  Wetware 9, 151–66, 183, 218

Samuels, R. 206–7
Sartillot, C. 7
Saussure, F. de 55
Schad, J. 140n.1
Seltzer, M. 18n.4
Serres, M. 8, 225

SHaH 149, 210
Silverthorne, J. 6
Sofia, Z. 12, 169
Springer, C. 14, 145–6, 169–70, 203,
  208n.2, 209n.5
Star Trek 2
steampunk 141
Stone, R. 169, 174
Swift, G. 97–140

teletubbies 4
Terminator 149–50
Total Recall 190

Virilio, P. 144–5, 149, 180–1, 194–8,
  202, 206, 216, 226–7
Voller, J. 184

Wiener, N. 198–9
Wilson, S. 97, 136

Young, R. 63

Žižek, S. 83–4, 87, 107, 124, 129–30,
  139, 204–5, 208, 219